遠く過ぎ去ったと思っていた私の青春を
もう一度 思い出させてくれた 心の友 ジャネットへ。

地球のこちら側にも、一つの生活様式があり、
そして 一つの人間社会がある。

そして、あなたは その社会にも 常に招かれていることを
おぼえて いて ほしい。

東洋で生まれ、西洋に学び、そして 今、東洋に生きている
あなたの友、隆より。

昭和56年 5月24日 東京にて。

To Janet, my friend in the heart who made me
recall my youth in the past.

There is one life pattern and one human
society even on this side of the globe.

And, ... Please remember that you are always
invited to that society, too.

From Takashi, your friend who was born in the
Orient, studied in the West and now is living
in the Orient.

May 24th, 1981, Tokyo.

JAPAN
Patterns of Continuity

JAPAN

Patterns of Continuity

by FOSCO MARAINI

Published by
KODANSHA INTERNATIONAL LTD.
TOKYO, NEW YORK and SAN FRANCISCO

Design and Layout: MAEDA DESIGN ASSOCIATION

Published by Kodansha International Ltd., 2–12–21, Otowa, Bunkyo-ku, Tokyo 112 and Kodansha International/USA Ltd., 10 East 53rd Street, New York, New York 10022 and 44 Montgomery Street, San Francisco, California 94104. Copyright © 1971 by Kodansha International Ltd. All rights reserved. Printed in Japan.
    LCC 76–107610
    ISBN 0–87011–106–x
    JBC 0325–781321–0070
First edition, 1971
Fifth printing, 1976

CONTENTS

PREFACE

A FIRST GLANCE at contemporary Japan leads one to conclude that the country lives in a state of bewilderment, of schizoid tension, jumpily divided between the extremes of jet-age modernity and the remnants of an archaic past.

Japanese cities of today (which James Kirkup sees as flourishing "under some evil enchantment"[1]) can be interpreted as living symbols of chaos. The first things one notices from one's hotel window are tall buildings of steel and glass, often topped by pinnacles of strange shapes and extraordinary dimensions, with cryptic cascades of ideograms, overlooking shacks of wood and plaster. A closer inspection will probably reveal shops selling utensils for the tea ceremony, or samurai swords, or accessories for kimono, standing next to gaudy shop windows with displays of the latest electronic gadgets, or next to *pachinko* pin-ball halls; a small Shinto shrine, with a *torii* gate and two stone foxes like sharp-eyed sentinels, smiling at passers-by, may appear nearly crushed by gigantic office blocks flaunting the names of prestigious international companies on their windows. Streets are like torrents filled with a roaring avalanche of trucks, buses, taxis, cars. Never-ending crowds flow along the sidewalks, including in their midst beatific little grannies in kimono—they make one wonder if a precious ivory *netsuke* carving had suddenly come to life—who rub elbows with the long-haired, wide-trousered, indefinable beings of undecided sex. These are the images of a world that is astonishing, amusing, and full of vitality, but impossible to call harmonious.

The Japanese themselves, it often seems, encourage visitors to regard their country with perplexity. Our culture as it is today, says one author, "forms a hopeless jumble of ancient and modern."[2] One of Japan's most gifted writers, Mishima, after surveying the landscape for years with a disgusted eye, left the scene banging the door. Tanizaki has many passages in his novels in which he laments the confused nature of life around him. Foreign observers are instinctively attracted by what one might call "the contrast theme," in which ancient, traditional, praiseworthy Japan is seen in fatal juxtaposition to a modern, aggressive, detestable junior of the family. On the jacket of a recent book for instance, one reads, "The ancient kimono worn on occasions and in homes and the 'lily walk' lope that goes with them, the samurai swagger of many men, the primitive, native music still alive in homes on all TV and radio, the tatami way-of-hierarchy give a noticeable clue to this throwback existing in the people in whom up-to-date ideas of materialism coexist with pre-feudal primitivism and feudal customs and thought."[3] Similar views, usually

[1] J. Kirkup, *Japan Behind the Fan* (London: Dent, 1970).
[2] Shunkichi Akimoto, *Exploring the Japanese Ways of Life* (Tokyo: Tokyo News Service, 1961), P. 9.
[3] Helen Heick, *Vittles and Sentiments: A Guide to a Frame of Mind in the Japanese* (Osaka: Illume Press, 1967).

less explicitly stated, can be found in most writings on Japan, from the papers of economists to the articles of foreign correspondents or the books of missionaries.

The author feels inclined towards different conclusions. Thirty years of loving acquaintance with Japan, its people, its language and culture, have been a progressive discovery of unity and continuity underlying all superficial confusion and change. Of course it would be childish not to acknowledge the outward chaos, the mad samsara of appearances confronting the eye. This sight is sometimes prodigious, sometimes frightening, because of the evident inner stresses that seem to reach breaking point, the hidden faults (in a geological sense), the sudden rises in blood pressure. But deep down one detects a monolithic something that functions like a structural frame holding all parts of the complicated machinery together. Shocks, blows, bumps are absorbed and eventually converted into stimulants to further progress.

What is this inner bastion? Can it be perceived with Western eyes? If so, can it be translated into Western terms? This book is essentially about such matters; about the unity and continuity of Japan beneath a surface of change.

Alas, this book about unity and continuity is fragmentary and desultory! Some motifs are elaborated upon, others barely touched, many completely forgotten. The author's main hope is that pranks and paradoxes, tangents and flashes in words and in images may put the reader in a consenting frame of mind and act like an invitation to him to make further discoveries of his own.

The author considers a typewriter and a camera the twin tools of his job, both useful to get beyond the face of things and reach the secret little wheels behind. A few of the photographs in this book were made with the purpose of illustrating a point, but most have been chosen from some twelve thousand taken over many years throughout Japan, at all seasons, at all hours of day and night. In a carefully planned campaign, the survey would have been more systematic, but among pictures taken as the occasion arose, suddenly and unexpectedly, there was a much greater chance of finding some grains of that ultimate gold: reality in the living present.

Tokyo
March, 1971

NOTE: Except in the footnotes, the names of Japanese are in their customary order, that is, with the family name preceding the given name. The readings of *kanji* in lower case italics are the *kun*, or Japanese pronunciations; those in upper case italics are the *on*, or Chinese pronunciations.

1

NATURE and ART

ONE MORNING, the French writer and philospher Paul Valéry wanted to speak about Leonardo da Vinci. We shall postulate, he said, the existence of a mind conterminous in its depth and scope with the intellectual limits of man. Let us endow the owner of this mind with a sensitivity of the highest imaginable level and give him eyes and hands capable of creating works of unsurpassed beauty. If we wish to give a name to this unique imaginary being, we can only call him Leonardo da Vinci.[1]

Let us—the reader and myself—now imagine a country formed by a small group of islands, remote from the main centers of human development, lacking all but a bare minimum of natural resources, often visited by natural disasters, overcrowded with people. It is a country that, in the brief space of one hundred years, leaps from a zero level of international presence to one of the foremost places among the rich, powerful, industrialized, civilized nations of the world. Let us further imagine that this astonishing career is built upon historical and spiritual foundations that are entirely at variance with those required, by common consent, for such impressive performances. If we wish to give a name to this most improbable entity, we can only call it Japan.

Everybody knows that countries aiming at positions with the highest prestige are expected to follow a rigorous, prescribed course. This "Approved Course for Great Civilized Nations" starts with a solid foundation in Greece and Rome, or at least in Hellenism and the Byzantine tradition; it requires a long and possibly tormented training in some form of Christianity; it includes extramural studies in the institutes for Renaissances, Reformations and Counter-Reformations, Enlightenments, Romanticism, and Bourgeois Liberalism. Generally a brief and energetic bout at the French Revolution and Napoleonic training center is also a prerequisite, though Great Britain and the United States managed to stay out and make good all the same. Marxism, of course, is up-to-date and very important, though authorities disagree on this point.

This is the well-trodden path to civilization, the way that guarantees distinction and eminence if followed assiduously. It is also the way that opens the doors of the best clubs and bestows the

11

[1] Paul Valéry, *Introduction à la Méthode de Leonardo da Vinci* (1895)

proper social credit. Anything else is deviation, heresy; some people might even consider it immoral. In short, it is not done.

Recently, however, an unimpressive newcomer has appeared on the world scene, proudly brandishing a most implausible list of credits: a thorough grounding in Shinto fundamentals, total immersion in Confucianism, a varied and fairly tormented series of exercises in many schools of Buddhism, some brief visits to provincial Taoist institutes, a number of protracted personal contacts with highly gifted but slightly mad Zen masters, a rigorous apprenticeship in the Tokugawa military acadamy followed by a postgraduate Meiji refresher course.

A background of this sort is unorthodox, atypical, aberrant. The best one can say is that it may lead to a cultural hotchpotch in which the remains of a feudal, agrarian, "Hydraulic," mythological, Asiatic past are mixed in with a technocratic, electronic, computerized, industrial, international present. One could possibly close one's eyes to Greece or Rome, to the Renaissance, the Enlightenment and all that, but when it comes to Christianity—well, too much is too much. A country both pagan and civilized is a contradiction in terms, as one used to say. Leaving this prejudice aside, when we find that this pagan entity is not only civilized but advanced, prosperous, disciplined, industrious, and progressive, then the situation becomes absurd, ludicrous, blasphemous. Things in General are blatantly ridiculed.

Japan is the country that disturbs Things in General.

On the other hand, to disturb, reconsider, revise Things in General is a most important, salutary seminal cure. All views of life, history, man—the world of Things in General—tend to become complacent and stale with time.

The presence of Japan in the modern world takes us back to the absolute foundations of things, human and divine, sublunary and celestial, individual and collective. Japan is a great electric shock. It makes us realize that modern civilization, the one that we so fondly and naturally imagine to be civilization *tout-court*, can have different versions, alternative patterns. The Western model of modern civilization, as it prevails under different political dispensations in Europe, America, Russia, and in other parts of the world, turns out one of a series of possibilities. Japan opens our mental horizons, just as the invention of non-Euclidean principles by Minkowsky and Lobachevsky opened new worlds of space and geometry prior to the surge of modern physics. Japan makes possible a non-Euclidean sociology, a non-Euclidean economy, a non-Euclidean culture. Japan is both a lesson in historical humility and a powerful radar focused on the inner workings of man and his civilizations. By looking carefully at Japan we learn not only about an unfamiliar part of the world or culture but about ourselves. Comparison gives wings to eyes; it takes us up into space and permits us to look at the planet Earth from a new distance, from a point where backgrounds and positions can be seen in lights of revealing wavelengths. If Japan did not exist, Japan would have to be urgently invented.

～

The picture in front of us is highly complex. The best way to deal with it is through symbols; the most appropriate and natural symbol is a mandala.

What is a mandala? The word is Sanskrit, the object mainly Buddhist. Mandala originally meant a circle, a disk, a halo; it also meant a district, a territory. The word soon became more specialized and was used when referring to a magic circle. Finally it referred to a cosmic map, a symbol of the universe, a "geometric projection of the world reduced to an essential pattern."[2]

Mandalas as they are usually seen in temples, museums, private collections, or in the illustrations of books dealing with Buddhist art, philosophy, or ritual, may be described as multicolored pictures with geometrical patterns, with squares, circles, triangles, fitting harmoniously into one another. In Japan they often look like stylized flowers. Normally Buddhas appear seated, or standing, or dancing, or even (in Tibet) ritually copulating with their female energies (*shakti*) in the company of other divine beings, holy men, protecting genii looking like demons, in various key positions of the design; or they may be replaced by "seed characters," stylized Sanskrit letters implying deeper levels of understanding.

Mandalas can also be composed of sculptures, or they may be embodied in the design of buildings. Stupas, and their descendants the pagodas, reveal subtle connections with the mandala design in plan and elevation. Java's famous Borobudur shrine is a mountainlike mandala, just as the Kum-Bum pagoda at Gyantse in Tibet and similar ones in Mongolia are palacelike mandalas. Even a city such as Angkor Thom in Cambodia, built by order of the Buddhist king Jayavarman VII, can be interpreted as a monumental mandala. On the other hand, mandalas may be traced lightly in the sand or designed on the floor with colored rice, pebbles, or other small objects. Finally they may be quite invisible, mentally conceived during meditation. Indeed, the well-known Buddhist scholar Tajima Ryūjun reminds us again and again that "*le véritable mandala se fait dans le fond du coeur*" ("the true mandala is created in the depths of one's heart").[3]

That is why a mandala is not something static—except for us late and disenchanted observers from the frozen level of "culture" and "museums." In the warm reality of living religion, mandalas have a dynamic function. Probably they were invented in remote and thaumaturgical times. "The first step of a magician who wishes to conjure up a magical power," says Edward Conze, "has always been to mark off from its profane surroundings a Charmed Circle, in which the power can manifest itself." In the purer and more subtle atmosphere of Hinduism and Buddhism, mandalas became diagrams showing "deities in their spiritual or cosmic connections," and they were used "as a basis for winning insight into the spiritual law thus represented."[4] A mandala, in other words, is a launching platform for man's inner forces, a propellant toward inward understanding and illumination.

The mandala concept is so vast and comprehensive that it can be applied to phenomena beyond the limits of Asian religion and art. Many Orthodox icons have the qualities and appearance of a mandala. Dante's *Divine Comedy* has the structure of a sublime and intricate mandala in verse. When translated into painting it suggests forms and designs very similar to Buddhist mandalas. The concentric circles representing the celestial spheres, each with its presiding spirit, the central terrestrial orb, the mountain of Purgatory, the pit of Hell—everything has its proper place in a chart of the universe as seen through the eyes of medieval Western theology and philosophy.

And what about our sober, scientific times? Do we have a legitimate mandala of our own?

[2] Giuseppe Tucci, *The Theory and Practice of Mandala* (London: Rider & Co., 1969), p. 20.
[3] Ryūjun Tajima, *Les Deux Grands Mandalas et la Doctrine de l'Esoterisme Shingon* (Tokyo: Maison Franco-Japonaise, 1959), p. 43.
[4] E. Conze, *Buddhism: its essence and development* (New York: Harper Torchbooks, 1959), p. 187.

The answer is that we do, and it can be found in Mendeleev's periodic table of elements. All the essential requisites are there: the universality of the claim, the mysterious rhythm expressing cosmic interrelations, the esoteric symbols, the awe-inspiring names (Lanthanium, Praseodymium, Yttrium, instead of, say, Acalanatha, Yamantaka, Trailokyavijaya), the final graphic pattern when presented on a chart in a chemistry or physics laboratory (the temple of our day). An irreverent mind might be tempted to exclaim that we too have our "mandalaev" —but here we are descending into the netherworld of puns, and we shall leave it at that.

———

At the very heart of Japan's mandala will be found a symbol for nature. Nature is the Piccadilly Circus, the Times Square, the Nihonbashi bridge, the Place de la Concorde—a point from which all avenues of thought depart, and to which they finally return.

The relations between man and nature in Japan are vastly different from those traditionally operative in the West. Let us look at things from a point of total non-involvement, somewhere in outer space; from there we shall be able to observe two models of ultimate reality, both perfectly legitimate and fruitful. The Western model of the universe has its principal motor separate from the main body of nature; the Japanese model has its motor embedded in nature. In the Western model, relations between man and the Absolute generally go over and beyond nature to a third supreme center of power called God. The Japanese model takes nature to be a direct embodiment of the Absolute.[5]

From this apparently simple difference in structural design, consequences start flowing in all directions, finally reaching the level of everyday life, the conduct of business, of family affairs, the choice of pleasures, the cooking of food, the addressing of letters, the most insignificant details of our ways of thinking, our tastes, and our behavior. In this sense every civilization is a mandala, as deeply and carefully structured as a crystal.

The Western model produces a triangular arrangement in which man, nature, and God variously interact. As a result, an impressive array of dualisms takes shape (man–God, man–nature, body–soul, spirit–matter, good–evil, subject–object, natural–supernatural, individual–society, and so on) governing thought, speech, and much of our action. The Japanese model functions on a binary system of man–nature; the third pole of the Western model (God) is diluted into, and fused with, nature. Therefore in Japan all spiritual activity tends to avoid dualisms and clear distinctions, and subjects merge into objects; emotion and thought exist in intimate contact with each other.

In the Western model, nature, lying outside the supreme dynamics of the Absolute, is finally considered something passive and brutally material, something opposed to spirituality, possibly a source of evil. In the Japanese model, nature is permeated through and through by divinity and appears as an organic living whole, essentially good. The Western model prompts man to dominate, subdue, and exploit nature as a legitimate colony; the Japanese (and Far Eastern) model invites man to achieve a state of harmony with nature, to develop all the potential richness of relations implied in an essential brotherhood with the sky, the sea, mountains, trees, flowers, animals, the wind.

[5] Hajime Nakamura, *Ways of Thinking of Eastern Peoples: India—China—Tibet—Japan* (English translation edited by P. P. Wiener) (Honolulu: East-West Center Press, 1964). See especially chapter 34, p. 350.

The Japanese people first appear in history with a culture already highly sensitive to nature. The *Kojiki* and *Nihongi*, the Norito rituals and the *Manyōshū* anthology are permeated with reverence and love for nature. When Ōtomo no Yakamochi visits Etchū and sees a splendid mountain, he sings:

> Mount Futagami, round which flow
> The waters of Imizu,
> When I come out and gaze upon it
> In the rich and blossomed spring,
> Or in the glorious leaf of autumn—
> How sublime it soars
> Because of its divinity,
> And how beautiful it stands,
> With its shapely peaks![6]

And here is what may have been a folk song, recorded both in the *Kojiki* (II: 86) and in the *Nihongi*:

> Direct across
> From WOPARI
> On the cape of WOTU you stand
> O lone pine
>   —O my brother!—
> O lone pine
> Were you a man,
> I would give you a sword to wear,
> I would dress you with clothes,
> O lone pine
>   —O my brother![7]

But let us approach nature in its simple, everyday usage: let us take it to mean just landscape, mountains, rivers, wild coasts, trees and forests, clouds, storms and stars—all those objects that exist independently of man and contrast with man-made things, most dramatically with the city.

***

The extraordinary attachment the Japanese have always felt for their native islands is due, I think, to two characteristics: fragmentation and variety. This does not mean that unity and uniformity are necessarily ugly: North African deserts, Siberian forests, Tibetan uplands testify to the contrary, although they inspire men in a different way.

In Japan, the thrill is discovery, an unending chain of discoveries. What lies beyond that cape? Where does that narrow valley lead? Is there a waterfall hidden over there, among those rocks and trees? What happens on the other side of those hills? Peninsulas seem to generate islands; bays or bights turn unexpectedly into lakes, as happens in Wakasa. Nature in Japan may rarely

[6] *The Manyōshū*, translated by the Nippon Gakujutsu Shinkōkai (New York: Columbia University Press, 1965), p. 144.

[7] Donald L. Philippi, trans., *Kojiki* (Tokyo: Tokyo University Press, 1967), p. 247.

be grand or sublime, but it is never monotonous or uninteresting. Geologists tell us that Japan, though made of old rock, was molded late in the planet's history into its present shape: Japan is geologically young. The islands are shredded fragments of continents in motion, further contorted by the disruptive activities of volcanoes. Land and sea are interwoven as warp and woof in a tapestry. Most of the country is sculpted, sometimes tortured, by the hands of an invisible artist. Hills are small, steep, and crop up suddenly from the narrow plains; valleys are infinitely winding and complicated. Seen from the air, most of Japan is pure geographical embroidery. That is why, at least to my mind, the most typically Japanese natural features are not mountains, though some are great, bold, and rugged in detail, nor even volcanoes, though one is of surpassing beauty, but coasts and gorges.

Where mountains and sea meet, the unending fury of waves and wind carves high cliffs into isolated pinnacles and contorted natural arches; deep clefts are cut, sudden walls and palisades are smashed into heaps of rocks the size of houses. The Rikuchū Kaigan up in the north, the Izu peninsula, some portions of Shikoku and Kyushu, the Iwami coast near Tottori, the bays and capes of Wakasa, the dented coasts of smaller islands like Oki, Yaku, or Hekura (*41*), are among the finest—and least known—natural beauties of Japan. Local people often see familiar Hotoke (a strange word, perhaps from the Mongol *Hutuktu*, meaning "Buddha"), or cherished *kami* ("gods") in the chance shapes of the great bastions; one cliff may be Kannon Iwa ("the rock of the Bodhisattva Avalokiteshvara"); another, Ebisu no Miya ("the palace of the god Ebisu"); but the subtle enchantment felt by a modern visitor from far away has something to do with the abstract beauty of the sight: why not think of ideograms here, with their bony joints, their catapulted dots, their cusped, converging lines?

Speaking of nature in Japan, one must always keep in mind that the country today is sorely devastated. When men moved over the land in much smaller numbers and with much deeper respect, tremendous forests covered the greater part of hills and mountains. Those who have seen some of the few remaining areas of the country where stands of *sugi* ("Japanese cedar"), *hinoki* ("Japanese cypress"), or other great trees still remain intact may have an idea of what majesty, wonder, and richness has been lost. A valley or gorge when covered with ancient trees seems deep, mysterious, and vast; echoes from the trunks (in Japanese echo is *kodama*, "the spirit of the trees") populate the place with myriad presences. Look at the same place when everything has been cleared away; it has suddenly become small, commonplace, and flat. A fragment of prehistoric Japan still survives on the hills behind the Kasuga shrine in Nara, thanks to special protection for religious reasons: a walk up to Mikasa-yama or to Wakakusa-yama will lead the visitor into a setting for myths (*7, 61, 87*).

Fortunately the trees perched on the inhospitable portions of Japan's coastline are generally too contorted to be useful and are left there to grow in peace (*47, 68*). Pine trees in such places seem to be perched on their stony pedestals like dragons gripping jewels in their five-clawed feet. Branches caress the rock, then bounce off at just the right point and angle. Some trees seem to be dancing, or welcoming the wind. Others make gestures with their gnarled arms, as if they were trying to say something, hopelessly, to someone, somewhere.

Hiroshige and Hokusai come to mind here, and Sesshū too, and behind him Wang Wei or Ma Yüan. This is exactly as it should be. Great artists discover and capture a type of beauty; they colonize nature for us, and we look at the world with eyes enriched by their discernment. Art imitates nature, nature imitates art; a cycle of causes and effects is produced in which we are entangled. This is civilization, a mandalalike unity of man, nature, art, and belief, where echoes of each are repeated at different levels of existence and consciousness.

Gorges are even more Japanese than coasts, if that were possible. They are also one of the least known natural features of Japan. Dozens of gorges exist; some are very well known—Sōunkyō in Hokkaido, Kurobe in the Japan Alps, Ōboke in Shikoku; others are less striking or not so famous, or simply difficult to get at, such as the Sugidani gorge in the Kii peninsula. A gorge is something like two rugged, savage coasts facing each other, running parallel to each other, often only a few feet apart. Gorges wind their contorted ways from mountain to valley, hemmed in by towering cliffs crowned with pine trees or (as in the Oirase valley, near Lake Towada; *12, 37*) with vigorous old beeches. Water flows abundantly in most Japanese gorges, and waterfalls are met in rapid succession. Japanese alpinists have developed a special branch of their sport—*sawanobori*, "gorge-climbing," which offers thrills and aesthetic enjoyment of a very particular kind.

Completely different from coasts and gorges, and also from most normal mountains, are volcanoes. Fuji (*1, 2, 44*) speaks for them all. Coasts and gorges are rock, water, trees, in the hands of an artist who delights in precision and intricacy, who carves *netsuke* ("toggles") of granite or limestone, paints *inrō* ("medicine case") miniatures in branches and waterfalls. But Fuji is vast and simple; detail has no place in its immense and elemental shape. Other volcanoes have something of its grace—Ezo Fuji (*3*) in Hokkaido, Kaimon in Kyushu—but none has its power and boldness. One wonders how it must have appeared to the eyes of ancient travelers when it was active, crowned with smoke and possibly lit at night by the glow of molten rock inside its crater. Since 1707 the giant has been asleep. But one should not forget that when Vesuvius exploded in A.D. 79 and buried Pompeii, it had been dormant for so long that all local memory of its volcanic nature had been lost.

Natural beauty in Japan is due not only to its variety but also to the marked seasonal changes of temperature, skies, winds, and precipitation.

Winter is richer in differences than summer, when a certain uniformity prevails. In winter, from warm hills looking south, covered with orange groves and inundated with sun, you can travel in one day over mountains that are increasingly rust-colored and wind-swept, and then snowy, more snowy, heavily snowy, finally reaching the desolate coasts of northern Hokkaido, where the sea of Okhotsk freezes deeply for months on end around the lonely cliffs of Cape Shiretoko (*49, 58*).

Japanese snow is particularly fine. One may object that all snow is the same, beautiful or hateful according to one's point of view. This is not correct: a knowing and loving eye detects many differences. Japanese snow is rich, frothy, often sumptuous (*52*). It is the result of great moisture and great cold combined. The trees on Mount Hakkōda or on Mount Zaō become completely enveloped in snow: they are no longer trees but ghosts. Someone started calling them "monsters," but this seems to me a very ugly name for such a beautiful thing. Zaō in February is one of the choicest Japanese sights, and should be enjoyed even by those who do no skiing (*96*). The flower-like fungi of ice forming near the craters of volcanoes such as Tokachi in Hokkaido, or Asama and Chausu in Honshu, are again something rare outside New Zealand or the Andes. Some portions of Japan boast a climate that is quite unique. Along the Hokuriku coastal ranges overlooking the Japan Sea, one finds a combination of winters with excessively heavy snowfalls (up to thirty feet) and hot summers. Here, however, the quality of snow is generally not very good, owing to the relatively high temperatures.

Spring is a gamble. Personally I would call it less enjoyable than the same season in Europe. It comes later, and is often broken by storms, cold waves, rains, and lingering snow. The sudden blossoming of cherry trees all over the land may give it an incomparably festive look, but such a wonder only lasts a few days, in some cases only a few hours. Probably this is the reason why poets in Japan, when mentioning *sakura* ("cherry blossom") (*234*), often feel in it an intimation of sadness—the passing of love, of youth, of life, the samurai's destiny with its sudden call to supreme renunciation. Later on the azaleas and peonies will be in flower, and many gardens then have a truly exceptional touch of color (*60*). Finally the rhododendrons usher in the rainy season.

The months of June and July, in which rain prevails, may well be considered a fifth season, which is the most Japanese of all in some ways and which reveals to its lovers subtle and ethereal natural beauty. When mists get entangled in a mountain forest, one can stand for hours just looking at the way trees appear and disappear in utter silence against a background of grey void. Suddenly the sun may vaguely be felt on one's skin as a wave of heat, and by one's eyes as a glow of promising light, only to vanish again, hidden by drifting billows of vapor. All color then disappears; suddenly one thinks that color is vulgar (*18, 19*).

The rainy season displays its wonders magnificently in forests and mountains, gorges and coasts, but it displays them on a more humble scale too. The flooded paddy fields, for instance, become mirrors, reflecting the houses, trees, and people around; or perhaps a temple entrance with people passing, their umbrellas open—alas, rarely now the graceful *janome-gasa* of paper and bamboo. At night in the city, the headlights of cars, the neon signs and advertisements speak a fairy language, uttering strange things in color and splendor, painting sudden and ephemeral pictures on the shiny, black asphalt. There are also marvels of a minute, nearly microscopic variety—the pearl-like drops of water on the broad, waxy leaves of *satoimo*, the edible lotus plant, or a spider's web hung between two trees and covered with dew. During the rainy season frogs sing gaily in the fields at night. Fireflies used to be seen everywhere, but now chemicals have indiscriminately killed innocent insects together with harmful pests, and nights are dark and lonely.

Summer again, like spring, is often a disappointment in Japan. If one has the summer of Mediterranean lands in mind, then it is sheer hell! Skies are overcast much too often, and rain falls insistently, drearily; and when the sun does appear, the air is hot and sultry. Fortunately not all of Japan is as bad as the lowlands along the Pacific coast where the major cities are lined up. Some parts of the Inland Sea are much drier and sunnier, and so are the coasts of the Japan Sea, together with the high valleys in the center—Matsumoto, Nagano, and the district around Mount

Asama. Hokkaido, which lies at the extreme northern margin of the monsoon area, is often at its very best when the rest of Japan is at its very worst.

Autumn comes to close the Japanese year in full glory. Winds from the south, which bring with them typhoons and rains, no longer blow; crisp, clear skies prevail again. While spring is less enjoyable in Japan than it is in Europe, autumn is far pleasanter. Warmth lingers in the air; there are more fine days; there is less rain and far less gloom.

Maple trees (*momiji*) turn red, and their delicate and fiery colors light up valleys, fields, temple gardens, mountain forests, waterfalls, and gorges. *Momiji* rarely turn red all in one wave: emerald green leaves can be seen next to yellow and orange ones, slowly building up temperature and intensity towards a final explosion of crimson-tipped branches. Each tree is an embroidery of impalpable precision and elegance (*8, 11, 71*).

The Japanese love and reverence for nature has been such a signal spiritual experience since the beginning of time that the very core of religious belief took shape under its guidance. The ensuing faith, a braid of many different strands—nature worship, fertility cults, ancestor worship, shamanism—shows interesting, though little-known, points in common with folk religion in other areas of East Asia as far apart as Korea, Taiwan, mainland China, Thailand, Burma, and Indonesia. Just as Tibetans have no special name for Buddhism—it is simply *chö*, religion *par excellence*—the ancient Japanese found no need to give a name to their ancestral system of beliefs and ritual. A verbal discrimination became necessary when, in the sixth century A.D., Buddhism was introduced from the mainland. Then people started speaking of *Kami no Michi* (the "Way of the Gods"), as opposed to *Hotoke no Michi* (the "Way of the Buddhas"); when the ideograms with which this expression was written were given a Chinese reading adapted to local pronounciation, the name of the indigenous religion became Shinto.

The word *kami*, which denotes a central conception in Shinto, is often taken to mean God. If this term is used with a small g, and better still in the plural number, the mark is not missed too badly; but a large G and the singular number impose upon the concept a complex heritage of monotheistic and ultimately biblical connotations that are entirely foreign to its nature. It is true that nowadays *kami* and God have become interchangeable in many cases, but this is a very recent development, an interesting example of Westernization to which we will return. *Kami* has also been translated as "spirits," which is not at all unsatisfactory. In fact *kami* belongs to that class of fundamental concepts that lies at the very core of a civilization and that is, strictly speaking, impossible to translate exactly. "Of all the words for which it is hard to find a suitable English equivalent," says B.H. Chamberlain in the introduction to his translation of the *Kojiki*, "*kami* is the hardest. Indeed there is no English word which renders it with any near approach to exactness."[8]

Shinto has a long and complicated history, much of it barely explored. At its base lies a warm-hearted, positive cult of life. This world, the here and now, is not seen as a pale image of a more substantial reality, as a land of exile for souls in transmigration (Buddhism) or awaiting

19

[8] B. H. Chamberlain, *Kojiki or The Records of Ancient Matters* (Yokohama: Lane Crawford, 1883).

judgement (Christianity and Islam) but as a living organism sanctified by its very nature, by its *"kami*-ness." Now it can be seen why the concept of *kami* is only partially rendered by such words as god or spirit, expressions that are too personalized and too much imbued with transcendence to be truly fitting. A *kami* may be a divine being, a mythological hero, a great sage or sovereign, a famous ancestor, but it may also be thunder, an echo in the forest, a fox, a tiger, a dragon—or a mere insect, as Motoori Norinaga reminds us in a poem.

> All who are called Kami,
> You may think,
> Are one and the same.
> There are some which are birds,
> And some, too, which are bugs![9]

Perhaps we may imagine the universe animated by an all-pervading radiation: wherever this current attains a particular intensity, a higher temperature or voltage, revealing itself as beauty, power, wonder, there the ultimate becomes apparent: there is *kami*. This interpretation may seem unsatisfactory. The bonds of Western languages compel us to treat a noun in certain definite ways. Does it refer to an individual, to a class, to something concrete or abstract? Is it to be singular or plural? Are we going to relate it to pronouns, and how? Are we going to speak of a he, a she, a they—or an it? Thoughts are driven along familiar alleys by ancestral habits of classifying experience. But in Japanese and in the ideographic script, *kami* is just a signpost of the most general significance. It channels thoughts and emotions in a certain direction, that is all. Details concerning the objective event, the moment, place, mood, inspiration are left entirely undefined. Grammar does not project the grid of its secret lines on the throbbing substance of life. That is why a *kami* can even be a bug!

The Japanese religious attitude toward this world as the ultimate reality contains the seed of two different lines of belief and worship: one directed toward nature as the mysterious fountainhead of all life and as the generous provider of man's bounty; and the other addressed to the host of ancestors, whose presence continues to be felt in this material world. Death, which in Shinto is supremely unclean and polluting, is overcome by the collective immortality of ancestors. Yanagida Kunio has pointed out that the "solidarity between the dead and the living, and the possibility of dialogue between them, are the central themes of the indigenous folk belief among the Japanese"; he has also stressed the fact that this faith antedated the influence of Buddhism. In fact Buddhism, Yanagida continues, with its idea of an afterlife, in which the soul "migrated far away," was strange and foreign to most Japanese.[10]

The host of ancestors repeated, on an invisible plane, the realities of Japanese society as it existed on earth. With the growth and consolidation of the Yamato line of sovereigns in Japan, it was inevitable that the imperial ancestors should acquire a place of particular importance in the pantheon of higher, personalized *kami*. Professor Ienaga is perfectly right when he considers that the *Kojiki* and the *Nihongi*, the first literary monuments of the Japanese language, were essentially great dynastic apologies. At some time or other the line of imperial ancestors found a meeting

---

[9] Quoted in Tsunetsugu Muraoka, *Studies in Shinto Thought*, translated by D. Brown and J. Araki (Tokyo: Government Printing Bureau, 1964), p. 151.

[10] Kazuko Tsurumi, *Social Change and the Individual: Japan before and after defeat in World War II* (Princeton: Princeton University Press, 1970), p. 167.

point with the nature gods of Shinto, the gods presiding over the life of an agricultural people, and the highest nature divinity, the sun goddess Amaterasu ("Heavenly Radiance") was identified as the first and most illustrious imperial ancestress.

Thus Shinto gradually came to have two noticeably different aspects. On the one side was the simpler faith of the people, centered around robust cults of fertility, abundance, physical well-being, wealth, and a reverence for a host of ancestors; on the other was the more sophisticated cult of national imperial ancestors and of the sovereign himself.

This last cult reached a very high, and lethal, degree of sophistication during the nineteenth century when the ancient myths and the person of the sovereign himself were skillfully unified into the emperor system. This latter form of Shinto is the one more generally known because it lay at the very roots of Japanese militarism, and was implicated in the origins and conduct of World War II a generation ago. The two aspects of Shinto, however, are not necessarily bound to one another, any more than the pope and Catholicism are bound to Christianity. It is quite possible to conceive of Christianity without a pope, and it is quite possible to conceive of Shinto without an emperor.

Here, however, I simply wish to stress the fundamental importance of Shinto in all aspects of Japanese life and culture. I fear that not many people will agree with me, especially among my Japanese friends. Most of them—rightly in a way, as we have seen—connect the very name of Shinto with militarism, with disasters, Hiroshima, repression, reaction, the worst irrationality, the most hateful obscurantism. Others may laugh it off as a set of mildly amusing antics, kept alive to please the lovers of folklore—*matsuri* ("festivals") and all that. It is true that most Japanese get married according to Shinto ritual, but, they will answer, it is only a question of tradition (and not a very old one at that), something like crackers at Christmas, Mardi Gras, or christening ships.

When I first took an interest in Japan, many years ago, I was told that Buddhism is by far the most important spiritual influence, that all higher, nobler culture starts and ends with Buddhism, that nothing can be understood without reference to Buddhism.

After a war, an Olympiad, a world Expo, and thirty years of loving study and familiarity with Japan, I have come to a different conclusion: Buddhism is less important than one generally thinks. Of course, its influence has been both deep and splendid, and in some fields it has been quite exclusive: Buddhism has nurtured philosophy and literature; it has inspired artists and poets; it is the soul of Nō plays; it has caused the land to be covered with temples and gardens of memorable beauty and significance; but other spiritual forces must be reckoned with if one wishes to understand *Yamato-damashii*, "the soul of Japan."

Though Confucianism seems now quite dead and though it no longer has any place in formal education, its subtle influence permeates society and determines society's values and hence behavior, from the closed family circle to the wider horizons of learning, business, and politics. It seems to me, however, that it is Shinto that holds the ultimate key. Shinto, often unrecognizable, is all

21

around us, an invisible fluid running throughout Japanese society, from the amenities and habits of the home to the essence of artistic taste, from the ways of thinking as expressed in language to the basic attitudes towards the predicament of man on the planet Earth.

Muraoka Tsunetsugu, writing before World War II,[11] distinguished three main characteristics in Shinto: imperial patriotism (*kōkoku shugi*), realism (*genjitsu shugi*), and a cult of purity (*meijō shugi*). Of these three, realism, I think, should be considered the most important by far. If imperial patriotism had been fundamental, losing the war would have been an experience of traumatic magnitude, sufficient to disintegrate the country beyond all hope. No such thing happened. Realism offered a solid spiritual basis for a new start. Facts were faced (the war is lost; the allies are stronger; MacArthur is the blue-eyed shogun), and the entire outlook on life and the world, the very national identity and image, were instinctively revised. The old imperial patriotism was rejected—a rigorous proof of its secondary importance—and a hard, uphill trek was started, with little joy perhaps, but certainly with much determination.

Realism in Western languages is a term that conveys only partially the richness and depth of the corresponding Japanese value. Realism is a rather cold philosophical term; it makes one think of Aristotle as opposed to Plato and idealism, of St. Thomas Aquinas as opposed to St. Augustine and the medieval mystics. Philosophers use it to qualify two very different trends of thought: one attributes to material objects an existence independent of any perceiver; the other postulates the objective existence of general ideas. In common speech, it carries a down-to-earth, no-nonsense connotation (political realism, *Realpolitik*); in literature, it refers to the description of things as they are, with an emphasis on their brutal and unpleasant aspects. Finally, social realism in art corresponds to a sort of sugary or titanic idealism.

Genjitsu shugi, the realism of Shinto, has entirely different roots. It is a mystical and poetic realism based on the extremely ancient belief we have already mentioned: this world is not an image, a shadow, a reflection of something more perfect or more significant, but rather it represents the ultimate and final reality. This doctrine was not expressed in theories, or decalogues, or summae, but was experienced in life itself. *Kami* were felt to be everywhere: "There is no place in which a god does not reside."[12] Their presence gave a particular flavor to work and achievement. Shinto is permeated with a deep reverence for the forces of life, for the sun, for fertility, youth, production; its vocabulary is rich with expressions such as *musubi* (both "creation" and "union"), *seisei* ("generation"), *hatten* ("development"), *sōzō* ("creation"). The basic attitude towards life is optimistic. The cosmos is fundamentally harmonious; man is fundamentally good; people should flourish; life is viable. Inauspicious *kami*, like the "bending" *kami* (*magatsubi no kami*), who hindered growth and brought evil to man and beast, were recognized, but the "auspicious *kami* of birth and growth were dominant." Hence, "Liveliness, brightness, and gaiety were common to all forms of Shinto."[13] These details may be entirely forgotten nowadays, and the ancient beliefs may be laughed at, but such ways of thinking and such attitudes have vigorously survived and, it seems to me, constitute the very backbone of Japan's resilience and one of the main reasons for its phenomenal success in the modern world.

If we look around Japan today, what do we see? A hundred million people passionately com-

---

[11] Muraoka, *Shinto Thought*, p. 11 ff.
[12] Quoted in Nakamura, *Ways of Thinking of Eastern Peoples*, p. 350.
[13] Muraoka, *Shinto Thought*, p. 29.

mitted to life, enthusiastically doing things, making things, producing things, accumulating things, rushing after success and power in a mood that, at its best, is something akin to lyrical pragmatism, and, at its worst, may foster the aggressiveness of an "economic animal." The Japanese, both in work and relaxation, enjoy the mere fact of living to the hilt. They work, like myriads of buzzing bees, with a dedication that can only stem from an undivided and terribly healthy soul. No doubts, caused by the memory of some original sin in the backyards of the collective subconscious, trouble their sleep. No need for psychiatrists and couches. The world is good; man is a *kami* (*Ningen kami de ari*, "man is a *kami*"—Motoori Norinaga; "Man is the *kami* stuff of the world"— Kitabatake Chikafusa); work is good; wealth is good; fruits are good; sex is good; and even war is good, provided you win it. All this is entirely consonant with the spirit of Shinto, which seeks for the Absolute in the phenomenal world, but it has precious little in common with the spirit of traditional, historical Buddhism.

Buddhism and Christianity may reach some degree of accommodation with the world, the latter especially in its Catholic and Orthodox versions, but they do not accept it unconditionally or consider it a substantially good investment for man's love and attention. There are always greater, loftier, hidden realities beyond—Nirvana, dharma, Buddha, paradise, logos, God—to belittle achievement on this planet. Spirituality is set on a high pedestal and opposed to things, matter, the body, the world of samsara.

> I know that all these creatures
> Have failed in previous lives,
> Are firmly attached to base desires
> And, infatuated, are in trouble.[14]

Buddha Shakyamuni is supposed to have said this in his last great discourse on Vulture Peak, according to the *Lotus Sutra* (*Hoke-kyō*). Vimalakirti, Buddha's lay disciple, may live as a householder and achieve saintliness at the same time, but the *Vimalakirti Sutra* (*Yuima-kyō*), in which his biography is celebrated, appears extremely apologetic about the whole matter. "Though he is but a simple layman . . . though living at home . . . though possessing wife and children . . . though using the jeweled ornaments of the world. . . . though eating and drinking . . . though having a profound knowledge of worldly learning . . ." he somehow attains salvation. Every worldly achievement weighs on Vimalakirti's shoulders with a great "though," which implicitly contrasts these qualifications of a solid, healthy citizen with other, more worthy requisites for spiritual excellence: the monastic life, celibacy, poverty, abstention, religious learning. This is certainly not a philosophy of commitment to life, nor one endorsing worldly success.

The normal Japanese attitude to work, the production of goods, to wealth, power, achievement, is on the contrary supremely positive. I will always remember a trivial but significant experience I once had. I was showing a Japanese friend the famous sculptures by Iacopo della Quercia on a frieze around the main entrance of the cathedral in the Italian city of Bologna. The sculptures represent stories from Genesis.

"That is Adam," I pointed out, "and there is Eve in the Garden of Eden. Further on you can

23

---

[14] "The Lotus of the Wonderful Law," translated by W. E. Soothill, as quoted in R. Tsunoda et al., *Sources of Japanese Tradition* (New York: Columbia University Press, 1958), p. 123.

see them eating the forbidden fruit, an act that God considered a most heinous offense. In the next panel the miserable couple is being chased out of Eden into the cold, wide world. Eve has been condemned to give birth to children with pain, and Adam to work by the sweat of his brow."

"What?" exclaimed my Japanese friend. "Is work considered a punishment over here?"

This attitude, rarely crystallized or put into words, seems to me very similar to the one that has prevailed for a long and important period of history among the Protestant peoples of northern Europe. Weber, Troeltsch, Tawney, and many others have studied the manifold connections between "The Protestant Ethic and the Spirit of Capitalism," to quote the title of a famous paper by Max Weber. The medieval gulf that separated religion from business was somehow bridged in the seventeenth century by the Puritan conception of a "calling." Man should work for God's glory and should have faith (spiritual calling), but he should also fulfill his obligations to society (secular calling). A conscientious businessman was therefore putting into practice "the loftiest of religious and moral virtues."[15]

Japanese realism and vitalism, derived from ancient Shinto beliefs, seem to me singularly near the Jewish philosophy of life, according to which wealth and success are proofs of God's favor (Psalms 112 and 113). Shinto and Judaism have also in common a joyful acceptance of all the bountiful things that *kami* and God can offer to man on this uncertain planet of ours, from sex to food, from honors to wealth. Ascetism runs contrary to the main currents of both Shinto and Judaism, though in both religions and both cultures there are exceptions.[16]

Instinct prods the Japanese to build small, and sometimes large, Shinto shrines wherever people are doing, making, or exchanging things, wherever there is activity, wherever people gather together; you find them on the roofs of department stores, in shipyards and factories, near airports and railway stations, in fields and near fishing grounds, on boats and in shops. There is a traditional sanctity in work. A Buddhist chapel or image would be considered incongruous in such places, except in cases of special personal or corporate devotion. A Buddhist "economic animal" sounds like a monstrosity; a Shinto "economic animal" is just someone who overdoes things a little.

Shinto is also essentially a communal religion (*28, 32*); a "village religion" Yanagida Kunio has called it. Buddhism and Christianity are fundamentally religions that foster individualism. In Christianity you are finally left alone with your bag of sins to face judgement; in Buddhism you are finally left alone with your load of karma to face reincarnation. Neither religion is comfortably at home in the modern world, where collective operations overwhelm the individual. Christianity is now suffering one of the most dramatic crises in its two thousand years; Buddhism is groping for a new adaptation. The communal spirit of Shinto, on the other hand, works in close harmony with the times.

It is well known that the Japanese have little place for individualism in their social structure. Responsibility, whenever possible, is diluted into the complex working of groups, just as many shoulders of young men carry, anonymously, the tremendous weight of a *mikoshi* palanquin in festivals (*32, 149*). The Japanese lack of individuality, which was a liability in the bourgeois world

[15] R. H. Tawney, *Religion and the Rise of Capitalism* (London: Penguin Books, 1966), chapter 4.
[16] A recently published book by Isaiah Ben Dasan, *Nihonjin to Yudayajin* (Tokyo: Yamamoto Shoten, 1970), has been a great success among the Japanese.

of the nineteenth century, is becoming an increasing asset in the socialized world of the twentieth. Here again I see Shinto as the ultimate fountainhead of traditions that have become so deeply ingrained in the social fabric as to be unnoticed by those who live them, and difficult to isolate for an outside observer.

Further, I see the breath of Shinto in the unanimous Japanese veneration for science. Buddhism leads to meditation and to philosophy, to humanism and to charity; it may encourage medicine as the art of healing and relieving suffering, but pure science, as understood from Galileo and Newton onwards, is extraneous to it. Science in the sense of a study of the worthless world of illusion, the world of empty appearances, is strictly absurd from a Buddhist point of view. This is not so if you observe it with the attitudes peculiar to Shinto tradition. The same eyes that formerly, in a climate of myth, looked at nature with numinous reverence or superstitious awe, now observe it, dissect it, analyze it, in a climate of dispassionate rationality. Ritual has been replaced by technique, liturgy by electronics, the *nusa* (purification wand) and the *gohei* (symbolic offerings) by the microscope and the computer. The approach may be entirely different but the attitude of reverence for nature, buried deep in the collective subconscious, not only survives but is turned into a precious asset.

Another important characteristic of Shinto, as Muraoka pointed out, is the love of purity and brightness, and the cult it inspires (*meijō shugi*). There are highly irrational, strangely emotive aspects in this cult: why should salt purify, for instance? Why should fish be an acceptable offering to the gods but not meat? These details, however, have little importance. What matters is the principle of purity itself, which has been one of the principal inner forces of Japanese civilization.

Purity is a very comprehensive notion. Originally, in Shinto cults, it was mainly physical in sense, and it meant something akin to cleanliness and brightness. Good (*yoshi*) and bad (*ashi*) were seen in simple and artless perspective. Good was everything "fortunate, exalted, delightful or excellent"; bad was the opposite. Contact with evil—death, birth, dirt, corruption, illness, menstruation—caused contamination (*kegare*). To remove contamination it was necessary to undergo purification (*harai*). As contact with ills and evil were inevitably frequent, purification became a sort of obsession. The effects of this obsession have outlasted the fading of Shinto as active worship and have influenced Japanese life and culture most beneficially.

One may start from the humblest level—the home.

That most celebrated Japanese trait, a love of cleanliness, especially noticeable where the body is concerned, has its origin in the ancient rituals of *yuami* and *misogi*, which consisted of frequent and meticulous ablutions. The ubiquitous *ofuro*—the comfortable, relaxing, joyful, often communal bath in home, hotel, temple, or *onsen* ("hot spring")—is a gift of Shinto; a gift not only to Japan but, let us hope, in the future to the world.

Another gift is Japanese cuisine, so utterly different from its Chinese counterpart. Purity, in a faith that holds nature to be sacred, means a certain respect for the natural consistency and appearance of food. Only the best fruits of land and sea were deemed worthy of being offered on the altars of the *kami*—fish that was still shiny, just out of the water, turgid fruit, clear saké wine, rice as white as snow; elaboration would have been, to say the least, in bad taste. Who could presume to improve upon nature? Such attitudes have passed from the shrine to the home. Japanese cuisine manifests a delicate and poetic respect for the gifts of field, mountain, and water, as they are presented to man by nature; elaborate concoctions and sophisticated sauces in ancient times might have been akin to sacrilege, but now they would simply be offensive to the refinements of style. While a Chinese meal is a communion with man's art (How is that extraordinary sauce obtained? What were those strange blobs—originally?), while a Western meal is a communion with man's power (The quantity! The solidity! Those instruments of war—knives, forks! The shining metal cutting red flesh!), a Japanese meal is a communion with nature (a root is a root; a leaf is a leaf; a fish is a fish; and quantity is measured to avoid satiety and hence a possible feeling of disgust); this is pure Shinto on the table (*196*).

Leaving the home and taking a broader view, the pervasive influence of Shinto's cult of purity can be noticed in every field of Japanese art. It forms the essence of that *je ne sais quoi*—difficult to describe and analyze, but quite unmistakable—which is called Japanese taste. Respect for nature required that all objects of the Shinto cult, everything pertaining to shrine and ritual, should be simple and pure, should show the original grain and texture; beauty was sought in shape and design rather than in ornamentation. The shrine itself was often a building of unpainted wood, paper, and straw, as one can still see at Ise. The costumes of men and women officiating in shrines were simple in cut and generally of pure, uniform colors (*23, 26*).

The salutary influence of this cult of purity is recognizable throughout fifteen and more centuries of history, from Yayoi pottery and the protohistoric tombs in Kyushu to the folk, and even the commercial, art of the present day, and of course to the works of many major modern artists. Beauty of function and line, and beauty of actual material texture (be it enamel on a pot, iron of a kettle, bamboo, paper, reinforced concrete in a building, or gold in jewelry), as opposed to the idea of ornamentation being something added afterwards to a purely utilitarian and functional skeleton, are two universal characteristics of Japanese taste, both of them solidly rooted in Shinto traditions and in the Shinto belief that nature is divine and sacred.

In due time, purity came to be considered not only as a physical and quasi-magical quality, as an emotional and aesthetic value, but also as a moral virtue. The ethical expression of purity was conceived as sincerity (*makoto*), which has been a cardinal virtue in Japan down the centuries and which is still highly admired today. Sincerity can be defined as the outward manifestation of an inner purity. Sincerity is the antithesis of duplicity and cunning. Its symbol is the mirror, which "harbors nothing within itself. As it reflects all phenomena without a selfish heart, there is never an instant when the forms of right and wrong, of good and evil, fail to show up."[17] Sincerity brings us the full circle back to art, since artistic beauty consists in being sincere to the essential nature and purpose of an object, whether it is a skyscraper, a teapot, a comb, or a kimono.

Finally, a most important legacy of Shinto is the matter-of-fact Japanese attitude to the human body, to nudity, to all bodily functions, and to sex. If man is fundamentally good and if he is essentially a *kami*, what reason is there to be ashamed of his physical frame? Anybody who has

[17] Kitabatake Chikafusa, as quoted in Muraoka, *Shinto Thought*, p. 39.

26

been even for a short time in a Japanese hospital will have certainly noticed both a total lack of privacy and a perfectly natural, wholesome attitude to bodily functions like urination and defecation. As for sex, it may be proper or improper according to the time, place, occasion, age, and position in the social scale of the participants, but there is nothing sinful or hateful in sex as such. Fertility cults were an important aspect of ancient Shinto and innumerable survivals exist today, some very explicit in the shape of resounding, hearty festivals, others barely discernible in half-symbolic garb. Traces of fertility cult are even found in the greatest of all Shinto ceremonies, the *Daijō-sai*, which is the consecration of a sovereign on his succession.

The imprint of Confucianism is much more important than one might imagine at first. The complete lack of any surviving cult for Master Kung and the nearly complete ignorance of the younger generations about this whole subject do not mean very much. The Confucian spirit, in many of its good aspects and in some of its bad ones too, runs all through Japanese society.

Two characteristic traits—the respect for state and authority as something independent from the ethnocentric emperor cult fostered by latter-day Shinto, and the firm belief that learning makes people better, that learning is the royal avenue to success, power, and wealth[18]—may have existed before Confucianism played any part in Japanese society, but they have certainly been strengthened by its prolonged influence. The modern phenomenon that may be called "*daigaku*-ism," that is, the ferocious race and competition for the best places at the best universities, is simply the ancient Chinese system of state examinations to accede to the class of *jugakusha* ("literati") in a modern context. Today one may gloss Karl Marx instead of Mencius, or write an essay on spherical trigonometry instead of defining filial piety, but the terms, rules, and outcome of the game have changed very little.

Powerful Confucian influences are at work wherever the Japanese gather for the production or exchange of anything, and they are recognizable both in management and in labor, both among businessmen and among customers. It has been said that the company is really the feudal clan adapted to the new technological and democratic era; that the *kaisha* ("company") is the *han* ("clan") in a dark flannel *sebiro* ("suit"). This does not seem to me to be a paradox or a heresy, as many critics argue, but rather a very natural aspect of continuity in a vital culture. In fact, one may also validly maintain that the power of the *kaisha* as an institution and as a unit in the economic competition of the modern world is due to its roots being firmly fixed in age-long tradition. The Japanese *kaisha*, it has been aptly put, hires "the whole man," not merely "a hand," and assures him continuous employment, taking him into a sort of new family and paying him with more than a simple check at the end of the month. In return the employee gives the company his undivided loyalty.[19] All such relationships, together with the subtleties of *oyabun-kobun* (boss and his henchman) ethics and casuistry, and with certain traits of behavior prevalent in academic circles or in the world of politics, are governed much more by the *Rongo* ("Analects") of Confucius than by later works of the human mind, such as *Das Kapital*, or *The Theory of Employment, Interest, and Money*.

[18] See the outstanding work of E. P. Dore, *Education in Tokugawa Japan* (London: Routledge and Kegan Paul, 1965).

[19] See T. F. M. Adams, N. Kobayashi, *The World of Japanese Business* (Tokyo: Kodansha International, 1969), p. 105.

Confucianism may be responsible for the high saving rate of the Japanese public.[20]   Undoubtedly it has something to do with the entrenched power of elderly men, against which, repeatedly and apparently uselessly, younger waves of recruits are waging battle.   Confucianism lurks in every police station in ancient patterns of behavior crystallized around the enforcement of law, enacted and expected on both sides of the fence.   In Japan, a frequent sight is a patrol car drawn up next to a private vehicle.   The driver, probably culpable of excessive speed, is sitting inside the patrol car not only paying his fine but being paternally lectured about his unethical behavior.   There the spirit of Master Kung may be hovering in glee, for the very essence of his teachings—the perfectability of human nature—is being acted upon!   A portrait of Confucius should be hung in the premises, real or imaginary, of all the "old school tie" groups (dōsō), the wires of which connect the inner transistors and neuralgic spots of nearly all important Japanese power structures. Confucius, of course, looms tall and invisible behind most family arrangements, adoptions, marriage contracts and intrigues, the elaborate code of behavior regulating entertainment, the giving and receiving of gifts, the exchange of letters and namecards, and all the bowing, throat-scraping, and hissing (Pierre Loti called these last "sifflements de vipère").   Finally, it may have something to do with the exquisite art of wrapping things, from five eggs[21] to the betrothal yuinō. Why has Christmas been accepted so enthusiastically by the Japanese?   Not only because of its commercial advantages, not only because it is the thing to do if one wishes to keep up with the trans-Pacific Joneses, but because it is such a splendid Confucian occasion in all its ceremonial as-pects: "rites and music," gifts, exchanges of letters and cards, well-wishing, visits, children and grannies, the family's joy and the state's prosperity.   It also happens that the paternal and avun-cular figure of Santa Claus, with his reassuring smile and his bag full of good things, fits admirably into the company of other smiling, gift-bestowing, benevolent mythological worthies of the Japa-nese pantheon and of Japanese folk religion.

During the Middle Ages a subtle theory was developed to justify the claim that Shinto gods were the manifestation (suijaku) of the great celestial Buddhas, conceived as universal essences (honji).   The honji-suijaku theory, as it is known, may now be elegantly and legitimately applied to this new English-speaking god of goodwill and (inevitably) of trade.

If Hotei, the pot-bellied "Laughing Buddha" of many European and American parlors and mantlepieces; if Fukurokuju (god of wisdom), with his strange skull disproportionately high; if Jurōjin (god of happiness and longevity), accompanied by a stag; if Ebisu (god of fishermen, traders, and work in general), with a large fish in his arms; if Daikoku (god of prosperity), with his strange peaked cap, with his heavy bag full of gifts, with the bulging bales of rice on which he stands—if all are for a moment considered genuine honji, then Santa Claus will inevitably appear as their latest and most successful suijaku.   He may be a suijaku who has just arrived by jumbo jet, with a plastic container full of chronometric, electronic, space-age, transistorized gadgets, the most sophisticated avatar in a long line of magicians of happiness dating back to man's remote past.

The gods mentioned above—together with Bishamon, another bestower of riches and also a martial protector of the Buddhist faith, accoutered as a warrior, holding a small pagoda in his hand, together with Benten, goddess of love, music, the arts, and eloquence—are often seen gaily

---

[20] Ibid., p. 200.
[21] Hideyuki Oka, *How to Wrap Five Eggs: Design in Japanese Packing* (Tokyo: Weatherhill, 1967).

passing by on a boat under full sail, loaded with riches. This is the *Shichi-Fukujin* family ("the Seven Gods of Good Luck") on their *takara-bune* ("treasure ship"), a favourite subject of Japanese artists since a Kanō master conceived this ornamental device to delight Tokugawa Ieyasu, the first shogun, over three hundred years ago. If one more passenger is added to the ship—Santa Claus in his red coat trimmed with fur standing valiantly near the bowsprit—we shall have a new version of the treasure ship and one that is particularly fitted to navigate the international waters of the future. Magic and industry, religion and commerce, mythology and finance may develop and prosper under the symbolic sign of *WA* (和), "peace, harmony, compromise, addition, inclusion."

Confucius should also be honored by all students of the Japanese language whenever they notice its extreme sensitivity to gradations and shades of social status. Germs of refinement existed in the original Yamato speech, before contacts were established with the mainland and its highly complex civilization. Here again we see a native trait vigorously reinforced by foreign influences working in the same direction. Indo-European languages possess an objective logic: they set great store by variations of being, by number and (often) gender, by who does what to whom, and when. The Japanese language could not care less. *Ikimasu* can mean a dozen different things: I go, but also I come; he, she, it goes or comes, or they go or come; it is going; I will go; I shall go, and so on. Objective qualifications are left royally vague. But degrees of respect, friend-ship, condescension, and haughtiness are calibrated with the nicest attention, to be used in specific circumstances. *Ikimasu* may be highly improper if *mairimasu* ("humbly going") or *irasshaimasu* ("honorably going") is required. And further hardening or softening of expression may be obtained by a score of different grammatical or lexical devices. The ceremonial logic of human intercourse is much more important than the four-dimensional logic of objective existence.

Buddhism has deeply influenced the higher levels of Japanese spiritual life and Japanese culture. An understanding of Buddhism is essential when considering Japanese philosophy from Shōtoku Taishi to Nishida Kitarō, literature from Murasaki Shikibu to Mishima Yukio, the arts from the Asuka Daibutsu to Munakata Shikō, the theatre (and cinema) from Zeami to Kurosawa. It can also be useful to understand shades of Japanese feeling, from the expression *mono no aware* ("the sadness of things")[22] to the idea that love in this life may be caused by a chance meeting of souls somehow related in previous existences. Generally speaking, however, it helps one only in a limited way to understand behavior, especially contemporary behavior.

In former times a reluctance to eat meat was widespread. I have heard more than once of strict grandmothers of the Meiji period who required the home to be purified by priests after the visit of a foreigner to whom, as a most reproachable concession, a dinner with meat had been offered. Now I think little of such an attitude survives: *sukiyaki*, *teppanyaki*, steaks of all sizes (and prices) seem to be devoured by young and old without any signs of a bad conscience. I have heard Tibet-ans murmur a prayer for the soul of a recently deceased yak, whose limbs had been eaten with satisfaction on the mountain pass a few moments before, and I have been to a Japanese *kuyō* ("service") in a Buddhist temple, performed for the souls of animals sacrificed during scientific

[22] See many acute observations on *mono no aware* in J. J. Spae, *Japanese Religiosity* (Tokyo: Oriens, 1971), pp. 122, 181.

experiments at the Medical College of the Imperial University of Hokkaido. But that was thirty years ago, and it all seems lost in a vague, legendary mist.

The Japanese characteristic of extraordinary patience—the capacity to remain motionless and silent for hours, a stoic endurance of painful or miserable conditions—most probably has its roots in Buddhist teaching, in the practice of ascetic exercises (*zazen*), in resigning oneself to the slow grinding of the karma wheel. Unfortunately one also notices the influence of Buddhism in certain negative twists of its exalted message. Animals, for instance, are often treated abominably. I noticed the same many years ago in Tibet, then a lamaist country. A lingering superstitious fear of taking life remains in the air. The kitten is "thrown away" (*suteru*), rather than being mercifully suppressed, and its miserable whine can be heard far away among the fields. Perhaps, also, the Buddhist idea that animals, though possessing a soul, are expiating evil, somehow encourages people, by a perverse turn of logic, to make the poor beast's expiation harder and thus more effective. This same line of thought probably applies to the traditional treatment of the *eta*, the outcast population of Japan, members of which in Tokugawa days disposed of animal carcasses, tanned skins, and executed criminals. Now, in theory, all discrimination is against the law, but in practice much remains to be done. The problem is not marginal as it concerns over a million people.[23]

Just as Christmas owes at least part of its success to a felicitous concordance with the Confucian spirit, with Confucian attitudes, with ancient indigenous mythology, *pachinko* (the pin-ball game) owes much of its phenomenal diffusion during the last twenty-five years to some stray remnants of Buddhist practices. Look at a *pachinko* hall, with its rows and rows of men, and women too, lost in the repetition of a gesture. There is little hope of winning much more than some cakes, magazines, toys, or cans of food, worth at the most two or three thousand yen. It is not the goal that matters but the process. The game quite clearly acts as a drug, a soporific; it is a mild substitute for LSD, marijuana, opium—a flight from reality. It is well known that one of the basic Buddhist techniques for obtaining illumination consists in freeing the mind from all contingent thoughts through the endless repetition of a brief phrase, a name, a mantra, a *dharani*, until consciousness is annihilated. Similar processes are also encountered in shamanistic ritual (for instance, the beating of drums) that was widely diffused in ancient Japan. This, I think, is the hidden collective subconscious ground that has nourished the colossal success of this game. Most probably not one of the thousands who play it has ever performed Buddhist spiritual exercises of any type, and they would probably laugh at the explanation and might even resent it.

Buddhism, on the whole, agrees very poorly with the original spirit, ways of thinking, and moods of the Japanese people, which are on the other hand expressed in the traditions that center around Shinto. When Buddhism reached Japan in the sixth century A.D., it attracted the aristocracy because men and women of education and refinement felt that they were suddenly confronted with something splendid, highly civilized, profound, and perhaps potently magic. Entire new worlds of thought, fantasy, and beauty were opened to their eyes, and the ultimate secrets of existence seemed somehow within reach. But how much of the essence was really grasped in the difficult, abstruse Indian terminology, translated into Chinese and adapted to Chinese mental habits and outlook? Recent scholars have taken a very critical view of the whole subject. Wata-

[23] See G. de Vos, H. Wagatsuma, *Japan's Invisible Race* (Berkley: University of California Press, 1966).

nabe Shokō is very disheartening when he remarks that the "Japanese learned Sanskrit from Europe after Meiji,"[24] that is, twenty-six centuries after Shakyamuni Buddha.

From the sixth century onwards, the work of adapting Buddhism to Japanese ways of thought and tastes was undertaken. Professor Nakamura has shown with great intellectual nicety how the major Japanese Buddhist masters subtly, imperceptibly, perhaps involuntarily, transformed the original teachings to suit the Japanese faithful and their mental habits. Metaphysical and universalistic Indian Buddhism was irresistibly changed into a religion centered upon this world. Thus, it is probably more correct to say that Buddhism has been Japanized than the reverse. This is certainly true in the case of the Amidist schools, and in the case of Nichiren and his followers down to the latest descendants (Sōka Gakkai) who occupy such a showy place in the social and political scene of present-day Japan. On the other hand, sects that were rather uncompromising, like Hossō and Sanron, have now practically disappeared.

The case of Zen is a very special one. Undoubtedly its influence on Japanese art, taste, criticism, attitudes, and language has been profound, but all this has been possible because Zen has worked with the main tendencies of Japanese civilization and not against them. Zen reached Japan already combined with the naturalistic philosophy of Taoism.[25] Taoism itself has many points and possibly much ancestral ground in common with Shinto. Even Motoori Norinaga, with all his enthusiastic admiration for ancient "pure Shinto," admitted this. The influence of Zen on the masters of garden design, of tea ceremony, flower arrangement, poetry, pottery, archery, on the authors of Nō plays, on architects, painters, and sculptors has been so powerful and effective just because Zen took up the very themes dearest to the heart of the Japanese people: a love of nature; an appreciation of intuition and action; a direct instinctive approach to things, coupled with a lack of interest in theory and metaphysics; and a cult of essentiality and purity. It is enough to have a brief look at Ise and its shrines to understand how Zen was bound to succeed in a country and among a people that cherished such ideals of beauty. One may well say that Zen has transformed the primitive and often brute material furnished by Shinto into an exquisite spiritual flower. If Zen had gone against the grain, where would it be nowadays? Possibly a mere footnote to history, together with most of the six Buddhist sects of the Nara period.

There is one aspect of Japanese society which Buddhism dominates without competition—death. This is easy to understand since Shinto is a religion of life and of this world, and it has always considered death the supreme pollution. On the other hand, death, in Buddhist belief, is an ever-recurring event, an episode in the cycle of births and rebirths regulated by karma, and it is a deeply significant and possibly redeeming event. Buddhists have always been specialists in death. The Tibetan language has a whole literature about it; the *Bardö Tödöl* is just one famous classic on the subject.

The fact that Shinto is so emphatically a religion of creation, whereas Buddhism is a religion that projects men into a spectacular cosmic destiny beyond this transitory world, has probably been an important element in allowing these faiths, which are tangential, to coexist peacefully together. There has been a sort of gentleman's agreement to divide the destiny of man evenly between two different ministrations, two spheres of spiritual adhesion, two jurisdictions.

[24] Shokō Watanabe, *Japanese Buddhism: a critical appraisal* (Tokyo: Kokusai Bunka Shinkōkai, 1964), p. 24.

[25] Heinrich Dumoulin, S. J., *A History of Zen Buddhism*, translated by Paul Peachey (New York: Pantheon Books, 1963), p. 264.

It has thus become normal for most Japanese to present their children at a Shinto shrine (*omiya mairi*), to get married with Shinto ritual, but to bid a last farewell to this planet with Buddhist rites. Buddhism also introduced to Japan the ancient Indian custom of cremation as the normal way of disposing of the body. The posthumous name is also Buddhist. The rare Shinto cemeteries are easy to recognize since the memorial monuments bear actual names: Tanaka so and so, Suzuki so and so.

As for the case of another great world religion, Christianity, it has halted at the entrance to Japan, though all the doors were opened a long time ago. Not even the moment of defeat in war and the need for new spiritual nourishment had any effect on the obstinate refusal to show interest in this faith. If Japan were really a Buddhist country, Christianity would probably have some chance for the two faiths possess many points in common. Christ can easily be seen as a bodhisattva; *jihi* and *charitas* resemble one another; ritual is often strikingly similar, especially in the case of Shingon and Catholicism. But Japan is essentially a Shinto country: "'that which is Shinto' should probably be considered as forming the most important part, if not the whole, of that which is Japanese."[26] Shinto and Christianity, however, clash in a confrontation of absolute incompatibility, not so much because of doctrine—the differences could be overcome, and nearly were in the mind of Hirata Atsutane (1776–1843) with his Creator Kami—but in the general attitudes to the world and life. Christianity is monotheistic in theology and dualistic in philosophy; Shinto is polytheistic in theology and monistic in philosophy; Christianity is strongly other-worldly, Shinto is strongly this-worldly; Christianity stresses universality, Shinto is traditionally ethnocentric; Christianity takes an ambiguous posture towards achievement in this world, Shinto is enthusiastically optimistic; Christianity is tendentiously ascetic and anti-sex, Shinto is mostly against asceticism and definitely pro-sex. The list of contrasts could be continued. They all epitomize a polar opposition and explain, I think, the reason why Christianity will never succeed in Japan unless it decides to compromise with the essence of Shinto spirit—or unless the Japanese people change beyond all recognition.

Most lines of Japanese spiritual development start from nature. We can easily understand, therefore, why the Japanese have been, and still are, such great designers and builders of gardens.

Man may have first conceived gardens as a convenient enclosure in which to grow vegetables and fruits. A parallel and less utilitarian development may have occurred when princes and nobles started to plan gardens as status symbols for pleasure and display. But in its later and maturer stages of evolution, the garden tends to express in a revealing way the fundamental attitudes of a civilization towards life and the world.

Could any two things be more different than a garden of Renaissance Italy and a garden of Muromachi Japan? Let us compare briefly the Villa Medici at Castello, near Florence, with the Golden Pavilion (Kinkaku-ji) at the foot of Kinugasa-yama, in Kyoto. Let me say at once that I am not trying to assert that one has finer qualities, nor to criticize either of them. They are both enchanting; they must have been an utter delight for the fortunate mortals who enjoyed them as

[26] Muraoka, *Shinto Thought*, p. 47.

32

private adjuncts to their residences, and they are an utter delight for us mere visitors, passing for a brief moment through them, centuries later. But they are profoundly different.

In the Florentine garden, one finds a composition of paths, hedges, flower beds, fountains, trees, statues, all organized into a harmonious geometrical design, which is gently but firmly imposed upon nature. Shrubs, flowers, trees, creepers, bushes, stones do not exist as individual elements, but as anonymous examples of a class; there are so many cubic feet of box, a blue patch here, so many square feet of lilies, a green border there. The beauty is Euclidean and intellectual. Such a garden closely approaches architecture. It forms a special type of architectural space, where hedges, trees, and flower beds are mere variations of walls, columns, and marble pavements. Stepping out of doors brings no fundamental change since you do not pass from man-made surroundings to nature. It is all one man-made surrounding and real nature is kept carefully and safely at a distance. The visitor feels at once confronted by the consummate product of a civilization that sets man at the very center of a paradise created for his domination and satisfaction.

The first thing that strikes the visitor to the Kinkaku-ji garden in Kyoto is the irregular composition. It looks like a rare and fortunate corner of nature, where all manner of pleasing details have spontaneously grown together (35). Geometry and symmetry are carefully avoided. The mind and the hands of man have definitely been at work here, actually creating it out of nothing, but they have left few visible traces. The immediate feeling is one of complete harmony between man and nature. This is the exquisite flower of a civilization that sees man and nature on the same plane, not as master and servant. Shrubs, trees, water, and stones have been invited to take their place in carefully selected spots, to set their minds at ease and exist according to their inclinations, as if they were honored guests from the green family of plants and from the silver-grey family of rocks, different from man because they are without speech and movement, but not belonging to another and totally alien world, not expendable in a web of geometry.

In the Florentine garden there is immense respect for the dignity of man; here there is infinite respect for the dignity of things. A Western garden may be a convenient place to sit and meditate in simply because it is quiet and beautiful, but it hardly invites thoughts to wander beyond the limits of humanity. It is clear here that we belong to a civilization that has solved all its mysteries through God, delegating to Him the responsibility for everything obscure and problematic. An Eastern garden, on the contrary, is in itself a subject of, and a starting point for, meditation. The trees growing as if on a mountainside, the flowers that look as if they have blossomed of their own accord in the wilds, the water falling among the rocks as it would in a remote mountain gorge —all these invoke something of the mystery of autonomy and spontaneity. What are birth, life, death, the changing of the seasons? And what is it to be a stone?

A Western garden is mainly conceived as a splendid background for the ceremonies and pleasures of man. Everything is there in hierarchical order; it is a syllogism in stone and leaf. Statues repeat the human form and reassert his presence with marble or bronze. The Eastern garden is not a background, but a living event in which the visitor can slowly become involved. Hierarchy is most subtly but skillfully discouraged. Here language, too, should be reformed: this is a place for leaf-man to flower-kiss in sun-joy, to let water-thoughts flow in stone-quiet silence-clouds.

33

A garden such as the one of the Kinkaku-ji can be considered the product of a long evolution, of a deepening reflection united with an ever-greater technical virtuosity. Since its dawn, Japanese civilization had manifested a deep-felt reverence for every natural thing and for nature in its totality. A similar taste prevailed in China and Korea, and from there the first garden designs were borrowed during the Asuka and Hakuhō periods (sixth and seventh centuries A.D.).

Early gardens must have been much larger and more open than the ones developed during the Muromachi period under the influence of Zen masters. Early gardens contained, as their most important feature, a comparatively large lake, on which guests used to move about in small boats, playing music, composing poems, making courtly love, or viewing the moon (80). The nearby princely residence was generally built so that part of it projected over the lake, supported by tall piles. Usually there was also an island. Originally, in the classic Chinese models, this was intended to suggest the Mystic Isles P'eng Lai, where the Immortals dwelt, somewhere in the Eastern Ocean. In Japan it was known as Hōrai. Some such lakes still exist, like the Ōsawa Ike near Kyoto, though the gardens surrounding them and the palaces have long since disappeared.

The introduction of Buddhism opened up unfathomed universes of thought. The primeval and naive love of nature developed a counterpoint of stimulating intuitions, upon which the Zen masters based their spiritual achievements. Gardens became increasingly imbued with messages and suggestions. Every stone had its innuendo; every blade of grass could touch off a vortex of reflections. A garden became *une machine à satori*, a possible gate to illumination and delivery from the bondage of illusion and the chains of reincarnation.

With time, a number of styles emerged. On the one hand were the gardens of the rich and powerful, such as that of the *Taikō* Hideyoshi or those of some of the Tokugawa shoguns, and these contained a lavish display of rare stones, as one can see in the Sambō-in garden at Daigo, near Kyoto. Here abundance takes the place of refinement, and a roar is used to convey the message of a whisper. Other garden designers favored daring abstractions, excluding from their works flowers, trees, shrubs, grass, and water. Finally only stones and sand survived the drastic pruning, and the Ryōan-ji garden (45, 62) was born, the prototype of a vigorous line of *kare sansui* ("dry landscape") gardens, much favored by monks of the Zen religion and now eagerly taken up again by many modern landscape architects.

———————

Japan has benefited immensely from encounters that have been both chance and felicitous. One, already mentioned, has been the confluence of such a great and giddy philosophy as Zen with the very essence of indigenous thought, attitudes, and taste, thus adding power to power and producing results of astonishing depth and originality. Another coincidence of great import, working out its effects under our own eyes, is the one that has enabled modern science and technology to converge with a native set of values working exactly and powerfully in the same general directions. But more about this further on.

A third happy coincidence: China is a world in itself, a subcontinent with immensely varied natural features. It so happens, however, that those regions of the country with large cities are not particularly exciting (Hankow is an exception).   Artists and poets in China have always been taken by their dreams to those distant and somewhat visionary lands of the southwest, to the mountains of Lu-shan or Hua-shan, to the precipitous crags of Kiang-hsi, which appear mysteriously draped with forests among hanging monsoon vapors.   Trees must fight the laws of gravity to secure a precarious foothold on narrow ledges of rock, and they develop contorted roots and trunks in a lifelong battle against wind, rain, and snow.   This is the world towards which T'ang and Sung painters returned repeatedly and always with a fresh delight.

Those same natural features that in China are exceptional and usually difficult to reach, in Japan are commonplace and easily accessible.   The Japanese may not have gone to study their subjects on the spot and may have imitated great classics from beyond the sea while sitting in their studios or temples, and yet something of that real natural landscape, which they certainly saw often, passed into their work.   One need not imagine Sesshū or the Kanō masters trekking up the Kurobe gorge or taking brisk walks, like avatars of the Reverend Walter Weston, round Mount Hodaka or at the foot of Yari Peak; in those days, reaching such places would have meant organizing a considerable expedition.   But it certainly was, and is, enough to visit Mino-o Gorge in Settsu, Iwaya Fudō or Kurama just north of Kyoto, Shōsenkyō in Kai, the Nishiki-ga-ura cliffs of Izu, the pine-clad islands of Matsushima in Rikuzen, the steep hillsides of Itsukushima in Suwō, the savage coasts of Wakasa or Tajima, to behold Chinese idealized landscape in splendid, living reality.

This same natural landscape has been the constant inspiration of garden designers.   A pond in the wild woods of Kamikōchi (33) is nearly indistinguishable from the smaller and more refined ones in the gardens of Kinkaku-ji and of Saihō-ji in Kyoto (35, 34).   A sea full of islands can be admired from many places along the coast of Japan (22, 39, 63, 64).   There is something Greek in such views.   René Grousset once said that the Japanese archipelago reminded him of the Aegean Sea.   Such Eastern Sporades and Cyclades are living models of many a garden.   In some cases actual water surrounds the carefully chosen rocks (34, 35, 38), in others it is symbolic sand, as one finds in the Ryōan-ji garden and in other *kare sansui* displays.

Lonely cliffs of Shikoku, or monoliths rising from the frozen seas of Ezo (though, in fact, they could be anywhere along Japan's three thousand miles of coast) live again as art in the miniature garden of Daisen-in, in Kyoto (47–50).   Mountains, such as Mizugaki (46) on the border of Kai and Shinano, or Nokogiri in Kazusa (54), can be taken as prototypes both of a great classical garden (Ryōan-ji: 45), and of a bold modern one (53).   Japanese nature acts continuously as a dynamic, inspiring force.   A chance heap of surplus sand near Ginkaku-ji in Kyoto, not part of the original plan nor foreseen as an element in the composition, has been shaped by local gardeners almost automatically into the form of Mount Fuji (43).   Trees in nature and trees in a garden are bound to resemble each other, but it is surprising and amusing to see the unity of Japanese nature and gardens brought to one's attention by the similarities of ice floating on the sea of Okhotsk, north of Hokkaido (58), and floating water lilies in the pond of the Jōruri-ji, north of Nara (57).

Painting and gardens comprise only one fraction of Japanese art that has been inspired by nature. A systematic review tracing the influence of nature would take us the length and breadth of many centuries, from *Manyōshū* poetry to Kurosawa films, from *haniwa* (ancient earthenware statues) to *tsuba* ("sword guards"), and from *kimono* motifs to porcelain. The inquiry would take us also to Japanese customs, such as the offering of flowers to the moon in September (O-tsuki-mi) (*230*), and to Japanese folklore and the inexhaustible field of *matsuri* ("festivals"); from the offering, at the Izakawa shrine in Nara, of the first lilies from the woods of divine Mount Miwa to the *ta-ue* ("rice-planting") festivals held in June and July practically all over Japan (*114*).

If inspiration moved only in one direction, from nature to art, a survey would contain an immense quantity of material, but substantially it would be simple. Instead, all sorts of fertilizations occur, binding nature with art, with echoes returning to nature and thence back to art again.

Loraine Kuck, in her fine study on Japanese gardens, notices how Sesshū's superb brushwork as a painter of rocks actually suggested in some cases the choice of particular stones for a garden. "Thus the interrelationship of the gardens to the painted landscape pictures—of stonework and brushwork—came to a full cycle when the strokes of the painters were used to recreate the essentials of natural rocks, and actual rocks were used in gardens to suggest the brushstrokes of painters."[27]

This, however, is only one among the many possible cycles. Others take shape: nature–painting–architecture (*78–80*); gardens–paintings–rocks (*35–37*); full-grown trees–miniature trees (*bonsai*)–paintings (*82–84*); nature–painting–calligraphy (*92–94*); and on and on, in ever-expanding waves and ripples, resounding through the entire structure of Japanese culture.

This is not something unique to Japan. Any civilization that has had a long time in which to flourish and mature becomes a vast mandala in which all parts respond and reverberate in subtle relationships with each other. In Japan, the interweaving is particularly tight due to the slow and steady development that has taken place over many centuries and for the greatest part in isolation. It is also particularly rich due to the superlative talent and skill of its artists and artisans.

As a sort of supreme symbol and signpost at the crossroads of everything—nature, thought, painting, semantics, gardening, poetry, language, dance, philosophy, and abstract art—the ideogram stands in all its glory.

Any discourse on ideograms must perforce lead us back to the genius of China, the land where these cryptic instruments of communication were first invented and then brought to sublime perfection. But the Japanese have been gifted and reverent borrowers in this field. The ideographic script has become so intimately connected with their language, so interwoven with their thought processes that very few people indeed would entertain the idea of changing such an elegant, impractical, esoteric, wonderful, maddening script for the demotic and much less fascinating alphabet.

Some ideograms, though not many, are directly traceable to nature and its features: a mountain shows the three peaks of the original conception (山); a horse has its four legs (馬) and a forest has many trees (森); the sun (日), though now square, is recognizable, and so is rain with its drops (雨).[28] But there are subtler echoes resounding to and fro between ideograms and nature. Shapes of things and strokes of the brush; natural objects, snow-clad branches, strange phenomena, calligraphic styles—all become interwoven through the operations of the eye and of the hand (*92, 93*).

The world of ideograms has produced a new nature, parallel to the primeval one: a Tao of Tao.

[27] Loraine Kuck, *The World of the Japanese Garden* (Tokyo: Weatherhill, 1968), p. 153.
[28] For a detailed examination of ideograms and their origins, see L. Wieger, *Chinese Characters*, (New York: Dover Publications, 1965).

▲ 1

▼ 2

Just as Venice and its gondolas, or the Bay of Naples with Mount Vesuvius, or the Coliseum in Rome may seem unbearably trite to many Italians, so the sacred tourist triad of cherry blossoms, geisha, and Fuji appears irritating to many harassed Japanese. Enough of Fuji! Down with Fuji! Forget Fuji! are expressions commonly heard among young people nowadays. If one somehow manages to get away from the worn-out rhetoric enveloping the mountain, and if one actually confronts the giant from a lonely, silent, wind-swept pass on a winter's morning, its beauty has something magical and overwhelming. Then one feels inclined to understand the loving obsession of certain artists, such as the photographer Okada Kōyō, who have devoted their entire lives to this one subject: Mount Fuji observed in all imaginable seasons, lights, moods.

4 ▼ ▼ 5

JAPAN

Lumbermen drive horse-drawn sledges loaded with wood through an open, snowy valley towards the small railway station of Hirafu, in Hokkaido. Above them Yōtei-zan (6210 feet) rises in the golden light of the afternoon (3). The resemblance of this volcano to its famous brother further south (1, 2) is such that people often call it Ezo Fuji, Ezo being the ancient name of Hokkaido.

In Honshu, the main island of Japan, mountains composed of sedimentary rocks rise to considerable heights (4). There are no glaciers, but the generally rugged appearance of the mountains led the first Westerner to explore them, the British climber William Gowland, to speak instinctively of the "Japan Alps." The name was made famous by the books of Walter Weston and is now universally accepted.

Rocky ridges and savage ravines covered with vegetation are typical Japanese mountain scenery. Mizugaki Peak (7316 feet) in Yamanashi Prefecture is noted for its massive granite bastions (5); the Omogo gorge in the island of Shikoku (6), hemmed in by towering cliffs to which pine trees cling precariously, reminds one of natural scenery as it was cherished by Chinese painters.

NATURE AND ART

7 ▲

◄ 8

Japanese forests must have been fabulously beautiful until comparatively recent times. However, they suffered great destruction during World War II and, more recently, after modern logging machinery was introduced. Some remnants of this former natural wealth can be discovered in remote areas, such as the Shiretoko peninsula of Hokkaido (10), the island of Yaku, some districts in the prefectures of Gifu, Nagano, Toyama, and Fukui, or on the slopes of sacred mountains near famous Shinto shrines, such as Wakakusa-yama behind Kasuga-jinja in Nara (7), where a religious respect for nature has effectively resisted commercial exploitation. Originally, Japanese forests were mostly mixed, with conifers and deciduous trees growing next to one another.

▲ 9

▲ 10

11 ▶

Forests of bamboo (*9*) are, in fact, very carefully tended. The wood is employed in many ingenious ways by artisans of consummate ability; the young shoots are considered a delicacy by Japanese gourmets. Many such groves can be seen near Kyoto, especially to the west of the city.

In autumn, *momiji* ("maple") trees turn red and paint the landscape with sudden flames of color. In Hokkaido, *momiji* start turning early in September; then the crimson wave moves slowly southwards, reaching the furthest capes and islands in December. *Momiji* trees may grow wild (*8*), but they are more often seen in the gardens of temples and shrines (*71*) or near villages (*11*).

▲ 12

14 ▲

◄ 13

When seen from the air, Japan is a lacework of brooks, torrents, gorges (*13*), rivers, like the veins and arteries on a limb in an anatomy textbook. Water often meets sudden faults in the land and turns into a furious white foam as it falls. The ideogram for waterfall combines the elements of "water" and "dragon," perhaps suggesting that in such places water becomes dragonish. The highest waterfall in Japan, at Nachi in the Kii peninsula (*14*), is considered so beautiful that it is identified with a Shinto god. Another waterfall in the Oirase valley is created by such a regular cut in the rocks that it looks artificial (*12*).

Waters often gush from the earth at very high temperatures (*17*), testifying again—if that were necessary—to the youthful and unsettled nature of Japanese geology. Beppu, in the island of Kyushu, is famous for its pools of boiling water, some an emerald green (*15*), others a disturbing red (*16*). Ferns and plants from other, more tropical climates grow here.

▲ 15

16 ▼   ▼ 17

NATURE AND ART

18 ▲

◄ 19

The four seasons of the Japanese year could easily be
increased to five if the rainy months of early summer
were counted as one. During this period, the sky is
mostly overcast, but wandering vapors and delicate
tones of green and gray create a world of unexpected
beauty. Woods on a hill appear as vague shadows
(*18, 19*); manes of mist get caught among the branches
of trees; distances convey a feeling of submarine depths.
Rains are particularly heavy, and mists especially rich

and deceitful among the hills of Kii Peninsula, and in the southernmost parts of Shikoku or Kyushu.

Straight, flat, sandy coasts exist in Japan, but normally land meets sea in a tormented tracery of water and stone. Rocky crags break into a hail of isolated boulders; garlands of small islands rise from the waves (20–22). Pine trees ride astride the tops of cliffs with the pleasure of children clinging to the back of some vast, sleeping beast.

23 ▲

24 ▼

▲ 25

▲ 26

27 ▶

Shinto, the native religion of the Japanese people, is a compound of many different elements: ancestor worship, shamanism, fertility cults, a (probably later) emperor worship, and a basic reverence for the spirituality underlying the world, a cult of nature and its mysterious forces of endless renewal.

Shinto shrines are generally very simple and unassuming—huts for the gods rather than impressive palaces; the real shrine is the natural setting itself, especially the great stands of *sugi* ("Japanese cedar") that can be seen at Ise, where the sun goddess and the goddess of farms, crops, food, and sericulture are enshrined.

The New Year is greeted in the uncertain, bluish light of dawn by lines of priests clad in garments of druidic simplicity (*23–25*). Offerings to the gods are presented by female attendants called *miko* (*26*); a white horse is paraded as a symbolic conveyance for the gods (*27*).

NATURE AND ART

JAPAN

30 ▲ ▲ 31

32 ▲

Shinto rituals and festivals are amazing in the variety of their forms. The more exclusively religious rites are sober and solemn: offerings are made to the gods; prayers (*norito*) are entoned in a modulated voice; hieratic dances are performed. In some rituals, men parade wearing the costumes of ancient courtiers (May 15, Aoi Matsuri, Kyoto; *31*). On other occasions the congregation may be regaled with sacred wine (*miki*) poured out of silver vases by young shrine attendants (April 18, Hanashizume Matsuri, Miwa, Nara; *30*).

Later in the day, the actual festival will take place—a boisterous, youthful, prevalently male gathering. Great drums may be beaten (July 25, Tenjin Matsuri, Osaka; *28*), or there may be dances (September, Kujira-odori, Aki Matsuri, Kushimoto, Wakayama; *29*). At all events, there will certainly be a procession of young men carrying a heavy, guilded palanquin around the god's territory in village, town, or city ward, chanting as they go "*Wasshoi, wasshoi, wasshoi!*" (*32*).

NATURE AND ART

JAPAN

▲ *36*

37 ▶

Nature, admired in that state of spiritual exaltation usually associated with religious experiences, is the prime inspiration of art: secret links between man and nature survive long after the more explicit elements of belief have been lost or forgotten.

A small lake at the foot of Hodaka Peak in the mountains of Nagano (*33*) shows us which aspects of nature may have been considered ideal by the designers of some highly sophisticated gardens of Kyoto. Its resemblance to a pond in the moss garden of Saihō-ji (*34*) or to the larger one in the garden at Kinkaku-ji (*35*) is striking.

The author of a famous screen painting in the Myō-shin temple in Kyoto (*36*) may have found his inspiration anywhere in the mountains of Japan, for instance among the rocks, trees, shrubs, flowers, and waters of the Oirase gorge, and the torrents flowing out of Lake Towada, away in the north of Honshu (*37*).

NATURE AND ART

JAPAN

▲ 41

42 ▶

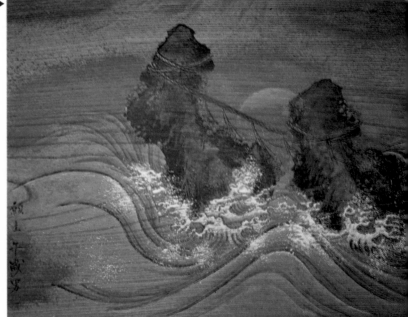

The round, mossy stone "island" seen in a small garden of a temple on Mount Kōya (*38*) is a visual transposition of elemental motifs in the Japanese landscape—the domelike island covered with wild shrubs, so often seen in the Inland Sea (*39*), or the rounded cliff with a tuft of pine trees stunted by brine and wind, like this one (*40*) near the coast of Izumo.

The two crags emerging from the sea at Futami-ga-ura, near Ise, are called *meoto-iwa* ("husband and wife rocks") and they are popularly likened to Izanagi and Izanami, the mythical creators of the Japanese islands. The heavy straw rope joining them is replaced with great ceremony every year on January 5. The *meoto-iwa* (*42*) are sometimes the subject of folk art votive images (*ema*). Such powerful natural monuments, suggestive of a legendary hero's stature and strength, are common along the coasts of Japan. For example, this splendid obelisk of black volcanic rock (*41*) rises among the Seven Islands (Shichi-tō), north of Noto.

43 ▲

◄ 44

The thoughts of Japanese artisans turn readily to Mount Fuji. It is said that a heap of white sand in the garden of the Silver Pavilion (Ginkaku-ji) in Kyoto was fashioned into a likeness of the great volcano by unknown laborers who were cleaning up the garden. Its final form appears exactly like Mount Fuji when seen above the wild forest of Jukai ("the Sea of Trees") that lies at its foot on the northern side (43, 44).

Innumerable crags may have inspired Sōami (if it really was him) when planning the Ryōan-ji garden in Kyoto in the late fifteenth century. There a naked expanse of white sand acts as a setting for stones that appear like jewels in their purest, primordial beauty (45). The geological veracity of the garden is immediately apparent if we compare one of the stones with a real mountain—for instance, the cliffs of Mizugaki Peak (7316 feet) on the northern borders of Yamanashi Prefecture (46).

▲ 45

46 ▶

47 ▲

◄ 48

JAPAN

49 ▲

50 ▶

No gardens in the world may seem more abstract and more esoterically symbolic than those inspired by the masters of Zen philosophy. Yet Zen aims at ultimate realities. Exhortations to distrust the written word and the representational plane hovering above the essence of things (*furyū-monji*; 不立文字) is a fundamental teaching. The power of Zen to say the most with the least strikes us when our eyes return from art to nature. In the Daisen-in courts of the Daitoku temple in Kyoto, a stone with a diminutive flower (*48*) may suggest the upright stance of pine trees on a crag by the Pacific Ocean (*47*); or a bare shape and a bare wall (*50*) may suggest the bleak loneliness of cliffs rising from the frozen sea of Okhotsk, along Hokkaido's Shiretoko Peninsula (*49*).

▲ 51
◀ 52

53 ▶
54 ▶

Snow, the great equalizer, creates secret relationships between a stone lantern (*ishi-dōrō*) on a wintry day in the precincts of Zenkō-ji, in the city of Nagano (*51*), and a mountain brook in the wilds of Hokkaido (*52*). But this is pure chance—fun in images! A much more significant relationship binds architect Tange's conception of a modern stone garden, designed for the prefectural building at Takamatsu, in the island of Shikoku (*53*), and the clean-cut precipices of Mount Nokogiri in the Bōsō peninsula, east of Tokyo (*54*). The modern master has caught the brutal mineral beauty of cleft rock with the same eye for essentials and the same capacity to become a part of nature himself that his ancestors revealed when painting trees on crags tortured by winds (*69*) or a majestic old trunk bursting forth with flowers in the ever-fresh miracle of spring (*73*).

▲ 55

56 ▶

Again chance, fun in images; and yet at the same time sudden intimations of Japanese visual unity. A carefully tended bush in the garden of the Imperial Katsura Villa near Kyoto (55) is not unlike a small tree in the wilds of Hakone (56), through the branches of which one can just make out the bay of Suruga and the distant hills of Izu Peninsula.

One can easily imagine the studious care with which floriculturists of the Imperial Garden Service, using neat little instruments, must have pruned every branch, every single twig of the Katsura bush, finally shaping it to surge like a green flame from the stem of a small stone lantern. The result turns out to be—as it should—a homage to nature itself.

57 ▲

◄ 58

Leaves of a water lily, leisurely floating in the soft glow of a late summer afternoon on the pond of Jōruri-ji, near Nara (57), seem to repeat (in totally different keys of color, temperature, and light) the pattern of ice slowly flowing by on the sea that separates Hokkaido from Sakhalin (58).

▲ 59

▲ 60

▲ 61

Japan, as Barthes observed, is an "Empire of Signs." The word "sign" has many meanings, but here it leads us straight to that elemental visual device, central to all Far Eastern aesthetics—the ideogram. In such signs, art and nature are connected by a web of relationships acting on many levels. There is the basic one of primeval pictographs, the point in history where painting and writing have a common source. At this point we find those amusing signs so often referred to in elementary texts on the subject: man with his two legs (人), the moon as a crescent (月), a horse with its hoofs and mane (馬), rain with its drops (雨), competition depicted as two diminutive beings abreast (競), and so on. On this level, connections between nature and the art of writing are direct and simple. Nature flows into calligraphy barely stylized, mostly with elegance, often with humor: three women (姦; *kashimashii*) carries the idea of "boisterous," and the sign for prison shows

man's most precious possession, the word, hemmed in cruelly by a beast and a dog (獄; *GOKU*). But there are much subtler levels where signs, no longer small pictures, become pure, graphic devices, awakening thoughts and working on the emotions in ways that in the West pertain rather to music or to abstract art. The splendid sign for light (光; *hikari*) may or may not have something to do with a man carrying a torch as L. Wieger suggests. What matters is its powerful, elegant, reverberating lines that gush forth from an imaginary center. Suddenly all sorts of secret relationships with nature—not etymological but still substantial—become evident. On this level, light and its sign may have something to do with fountains and water (59), with grass and flowers (60), with the branches of a vigorous *sugi* ("Japanese cedar") (61). Signs, like the sea and the mountains are one of the quintessences that go to make up the bones and blood of Japan.

63 ▼ ▼ 64

▲ 62

The sea may take us back to that great symbol, that supremely abstract monument, the *kare sansui*, the "dry landscape" garden of Ryōan-ji, in Kyoto (62). Designed in the late fifteenth century for a powerful lord, Hosokawa Katsumoto, possibly by the Zen master Sōami, it offers multiple levels of interpretation. In this, it acts exactly like many important ideograms. *Michi* (道) may simply mean a "path" in the country, a "road," a "lane," a "street," but it may also mean "duty," "morality," "teaching," a "system of teachings"; ultimately it may signify Tao—the Absolute behind all appearances. *Fuji* (不二) may simply mean "not two," i.e., peerless, and it may be used as one of the possible writings for

Mount Fuji, but it may also subtly suggest the abolition of all distinctions between subject and object in a monistic view of reality. Visitors can "read" all sorts of messages, at all sorts of level, into the Ryōan-ji garden: it may appear to catch the essence of the sea with its islands (63, 64), of lofty crags (46), of peaks towering above the clouds (4). There are literal levels (a tigress wading through a river with her cubs) and symbolic tangents thereof (the animals are crossing the seas of illusion toward the shore of *satori*, "illumination"). Like all great works of art, the Ryōan-ji garden is a point of departure, new for each visitor, for every generation.

NATURE AND ART

▲ 65   66 ▼ ▼ 67

JAPAN

▲ 68   ▼ 69

The first buds on plum trees are the cherished symbols of spring's return.

After we, dear friends, have drunk together,
Setting plum-blossoms afloat in our wine-cups,
I care not if those on the tree be gone.
(Lady Ōtomo of Sakanoue—*Manyōshū*, Nara period; eighth century)

Modern painters have often treated the ancient theme of plum blossoms with dignity and renewed originality (*67*).

Fifteenth-century Zen masters had sterner tastes than Nara courtiers and fixed their eyes on broken cliffs with angular, spiky trees battered by the wind—expressions of discipline and abnegation—as seen in this painting in Tenkyū-in, in Kyoto (*69*). The inspiration may have been Chinese, but Japan offered inexhaustible subjects for observation, for a return to the genuine sources in the open-air world of living nature (*68*).

70 ▲

71 ▶

The link between man and nature in Japan is manifest in the detailed, ritual, sometimes obsessive, attention to the seasons.   Each of them was, and still often is, celebrated in literature and art, and each had its specific attributes of flowers, animals, plants, natural phenomena, and human moods.   "The first question the average Japanese will unconsciously ask himself when appraising anything... is most probably this: 'to which season does it belong?'" [1]   Spring brings us plum and cherry blossoms; summer, lilies and lotuses; autumn, the glory of maples turning red (71); winter, the magic of snow (92).   Artists of the Momoyama (1573–1603) and early Edo periods used themes from nature to decorate vast spaces on sliding doors or screens.   The plum trees and birds in the Myōshin temple of Kyoto have been traditionally attributed to Kanō Sanraku (1559–1635) (70, 73).

[1] Shunkichi Akimoto, *Exploring the Japanese Ways of Life* (Tokyo News Service, 1961).

▼ 72

73 ▼

NATURE AND ART

74 ▲

◀ 75

The Tokugawa dynasty of shoguns (1600–1868) brought a long period of peace to Japan, but the lack of stimulation caused a certain loss of creative power. Nature was thoroughly and sensitively explored for themes, but the results, though usually impressive for their technical skill, are most often limited to a decorative value. Pine trees, as seen by the painter of sliding doors (*fusuma*) now in the Nishi Hongan-ji in Kyoto (74), have become an elegant exercise in color, composition, design. Birds, nets drying in the sun, fanciful rocks, golden powder representing mists in the somewhat dubious taste of rich tycoons, have detracted from the original simplicity and vigor of actual pine trees on a mountain slope (75).

Flowers were studied with passionate delight by artists of the long Edo period. The unspoken belief of these men in the essentially divine nature of life lends

▲ 76

77 ▶

their work depth and nobility—qualities that break through the themes fashionable at the time. There was also a growing interest in what may now be called a scientific vision of nature. The school of Maruyama Ōkyo (1733–95) was influential in bringing artists back to real life and in discouraging them from merely copying classical (mostly Chinese) models. Ceilings decorated with flowers were in vogue for a long time, and many examples can still be found all over Japan. Generally one biological species forms a medallion; many hundreds of these units cover the ceilings of a temple or a mansion. Here a detail from a chapel in Nishi Hongan-ji of Kyoto, depicting a bunch of camellias (76), is matched with a wild flower of the same species (77), growing in a rare spontaneous thicket near Cape Ashizuri, at the southernmost point of Shikoku Island.

NATURE AND ART

JAPAN

81 ▶

Sometimes it is difficult to establish the direction taken by inspiration. Which was the prototype? Did the sliding door (78) from the Shōden temple near Kyoto, provide a possible model for the shrine at the foot of Mount Daisen (79)? Or was it the other way around? Most probably no direct relation exists between the two; both are descended from long, parallel lines of ancestors that merge perhaps somewhere in Sung or T'ang China, or even further, even earlier, just as in the West parallel lines of ancestry may come together in Rome, Attica, Jerusalem, or Babylon.

Were the trees in a row along the shores of the lake of Hiraizumi in north Japan (80) planted as shown in a painting on sliding doors of the Shōren temple in Kyoto (81)? Or did the painter of the Kyoto panels portray some similar row of the present trees' ancestors? Things, patterns, lines, ideas, forms circulate incessantly in the cultural space of a civilization, moving from nature to eyes to hands in a vast counterpoint.

NATURE AND ART

▲ 82

▼ 83

▼ 84

◀ 86

Places, things, rooms are often evaluated in Japanese taste by what may be called an arboreal scale: they are not A, B, or C, but rather *shō-chiku-bai* (松竹梅), "pine-bamboo-plum." The pine tree is admired as supreme: it is vigorous, evergreen, living long enough to become the patriarch of a wood or forest. Its presence is felt to be auspicious at all times. In Japanese gardens, it holds the preeminent position. A small, but exquisitely elegant pine tree greets the visitor entering the garden of Katsura Villa, in Kyoto (*82*). Potted dwarf pine trees (*83*), some centuries old, have an honored place in many Japanese homes. On the other hand, gigantic pine trees painted by the brushes of masters cover sliding doors of famous temples, castles, palaces. A pine tree is the only ornament of a Nō stage. The pine tree under snow, boldly delineated (*84*), belongs to the Kongōbu temple on Mount Kōya. Pine tree motifs, ingeniously simplified, are often used as family crests (*see opposite*).

The relationship between a water lily (*85*) and bowls (*86*) is not direct, but the clean, crystalline quality of both expresses something fundamental in Japanese taste.

NATURE AND ART

▲ 90

91 ▶

Often nature appears not so much as an inspiration but as a more direct participant.   The great tree in the forest (*87*) may become the central post in a traditional Japanese cottage (*88*) or the pillar of a temple (*89*), and it maintains intact the beauty of its grain, possibly enhanced and mellowed by age and weathering.   The central post of a Japanese cottage is called *Daikoku-bashira* ("the pillar of the god Daikoku") and is treated with great respect.   In days past, only the householder would dare touch it.   The *Daikoku-bashira* is the subject of a rich lore that is now perhaps being forgotten. Daikoku is a Shinto god who is said to combine in his mythical person the ancient Japanese hero Ōkuninushi no Mikoto ("Sovereign Holder of the Land") and the Indian god of wealth and treasure, Kuvera, a guardian spirit of celestial Buddhas.

The rampart of Osaka Castle (*91*) has the same soaring outline as mountains, for instance the steep hill above Miyajima Shrine, not far from Hiroshima, on the Inland Sea (*90*).

NATURE AND ART

▲ 92

May we return for a moment to the theme of snow? An ancient snow-covered willow tree, on which some cranes are perched rather miserably, spreads across a room of the Kongōbu temple, on Mount Kōya (94). The painting is attributed to Kanō Kaikei. Comparing this work with a real frozen branch from the forests of Mount Yokote (92), we can notice how successfully the artist has caught the essence of Japanese snow, so rich, so velvety and frothy, which clings immediately to trees and rocks in the icy air that is full of maritime moisture, transforming them into fairylike creatures from outer space.

The snow writing of branches on the blue sky leads us inevitably to brush writing on paper, in this case to a large screen standing at the entrance to the Sambō temple at Daigo, near Kyoto (93). The ideogram, traced in bold, vigorous strokes, stands for Hōō, the mythical phoenix.

Nature–painting–calligraphy: another chord among many in the counterpoint of Japanese cultural unity.

NATURE AND ART

95 ▲

◄ 96

There are times when nature seems to be searching desperately for a satisfactory imitation of man.

The mysterious frozen trees on the wind-swept plateau of Mount Zaō, high on the border between Miyagi and Yamagata in north Japan (*96*), silently mock a procession of priests clad in silk, solemnly playing flutes and *shō*, seen during a festival at the shrine of Kurama, among the hills near Kyoto (*95*).

2

ART
and
PEOPLE

How OFTEN faces of apostles, saints, ancient kings, carved by medieval masons on the walls of Gothic cathedrals, appear suddenly as Bavarian, Austrian, Swiss, or Flemish farmers, with their curly, blond beards, their furrowed cheeks! How many Roman emperors walk up and down the Via Veneto in Rome as modern *commendatori* or sit leisurely in a café, sipping *Campari soda*? Paintings and sculptures of the Renaissance masters pass along the streets of Florence, perhaps disguised as a girl delightfully and precariously sitting on the pillion of her boyfriend's motorbike (Botticelli), as a young man lifting stones to build a wall (Michelangelo), or as a child just singing (Donatello). Shah Jahan and Akbar are nowadays seen more often in the lounge of Bombay's Taj Mahal Hotel, discussing the demotion of maharajas, the antics of the Naxalites, or the subtleties of Congress politics, than in their proper places among deodars and lions in the miniatures of a Mogul artist. Ming sages deal in antiques all the way from Seoul to Taipei, and an Aztec god may serve a dish of *paella* in a restaurant of Mexico City.

Every lover of art can find his living museum among the human beings of his day and age. Originally art may be said to reflect physical racial characteristics and the social data of costume, posture, work, ceremony, and play. But, at the same time, a reverse current is taking place. "Life imitates art," as Oscar Wilde observed. Art itself becomes an unending source of inspiration to all people in all roles of a society, from children jumping to lovers kissing, from dance to coronation, from deference to fury, from young gallant to old sage.

The more ancient and creative and exclusive a civilization has been, the more thoroughly all its elements become welded together into a substantial and formal unity. Currents both clear and invisible run in all directions. Men, gods, nature, law, music, sex, language, writing, cuisine, fashion—everything vibrates with uninterrupted echoes, just like voices in a deep and stately forest. Nothing is finally individual and private; every thought of ours is an echo of the civilization that has nourished us. Could anything be more secret and protected and, in a way, absolute than the orgasm of love? And yet perhaps one day someone will ascertain that Western girls at the culmi-

83

nation of pleasure tend to look like Santa Teresa in her divine ecstasy, as sculpted by Bernini on a baroque altar in Saint Peter's, while a Japanese girl may look more like the Buddhist god Aizen Myōō in the fury of his/her esoteric fire.

A tangible continuity is naturally to be expected where the human form is concerned. If we now look at the photographs, some striking examples become apparent. A *chigo* ("page boy") passes near an image of the Bodhisattva Jizō (*100, 101*) and makes us wonder if the sculpture is the portrait of the boy, or the boy a parthogenetic son of the statue.

Both *chigo* and Jizō are quintessentially Japanese. The word *chigo* originally meant a child, a baby, or a very young boy. The *chigo* of the picture is solemnly walking in a procession at a Shugen festival near Kyoto. Shugendō is a very special religious sect, founded in the seventh century by En no Gyōja, which combines Shinto, Taoist, and Buddhist elements in its esoteric teachings. Shugendō devotees are called *yamabushi* ("those who sleep on the mountains," i.e., hermits). Now the whole institution has become very much a Boy Scout club for earnest shopkeepers or minor officials, but in former times *yamabushi* were strange, frightening, prodigious magicians and shamans who practiced strenuous austerities in savage fastnesses among the mountains of Kii or Uzen. Some *yamabushi* went so far in their weird austerities as to die of slow starvation and become mummified, a condition that they imagined would turn them into Buddhas in the flesh. Some of these mummies are still objects of devotion in certain mountain villages of north Japan.[1]

A *chigo* may be said to represent the ceremonial and temporary survival of two different traditions. One is plainly secular; here the *chigo* is a page, a pretty young thing to have around the palace, an object of tender passion in a pansexual climate. Long ago, *chigo* were the favorites of abbots or senior monks, and later the amorous stories of the Genroku period often gave a prominent place to *chigo* in their plots. A whole class of medieval romances, very popular during the Muromachi period (fourteenth to sixteenth centuries), goes under the name of *Chigo Monogatari*.

A second traditional line of thought sees the *chigo* in an entirely different light. The Japanese "believe that children have purer spirits than adults and that as companions of Kami they have divine powers."[2] This leads us somewhere near those female shamans, who in a state of trance act as links between men and gods—the *itako* of north Japan, the *noro* of Okinawa, the *reibai* of Shinto tradition. For this reason most probably, *chigo* appear in a great number of festivals all over Japan, mainly in those of Shinto, but sometimes in ceremonies of a more significantly Buddhist character. There are cases in which children actually represent a *kami* and are temporarily honored as such. A well-known instance is the little girl who impersonates a goddess during the *Sanzoro Matsuri* in the month of November in a village of Aichi.

I have said that the two traditions are different, but they are not entirely so. It is fitting here to remember an important Shinto idea that is rarely explicit but that is clearly noted by Yanagida Kunio in his writings: *kami* enjoy the same things as men. A *chigo*, by his presence at religious rituals, serves the magic purpose of assuring protection and communication between

[1] Ichirō Hori, "Self-mummified Buddhas in Japan," *History of Religion*, vol. 1, no. 2 (Chicago: University of Chicago, 1962).

[2] Hideo Haga, *Japanese Folk Festivals Illustrated*, translated by F. H. Mayer (Tokyo: Miura, 1970), p. 13.

84

men and gods because of a special spiritual grace inherent in his childhood, but in addition he decorates and enriches the display of beautiful and pleasant things prepared for the descent of the invisible beings among the faithful, together with fruits, flowers, wine, dances, music, colored banners, drama, and—why not?—fireworks.

The Bodhisattva Jizō started his career in India as Kshitigarbha Bodhisattva, and became popular only much later and further north, in Central Asia and China, and finally in Japan. Jizō is supposed to take loving care of all sentient beings, particularly of children and sinners, during the aeons of time between Shakyamuni Buddha's entry into Nirvana and the descent of Maitreya in a future cosmic cycle. Jizō, under different names and appearances, wanders all over the six realms of existence (the worlds of gods, men, giants, beasts, famished ghosts, and the damned) to enlighten and save. It was perfectly logical that Jizō should assume a place of extraordinary importance in Japan, a country where, since the very beginning, Buddhism has been accepted mainly as a religion of salvation: salvation obtained by every conceivable means—esoteric, magic, or devotional.

In the sculptures of the Nara period, Jizō is often barely recognizable. He sits cross-legged, without any special attributes, and can be distinguished from other celestial beings in the Buddhist pantheon only by his *mudra*—the ritual positions of his hands and fingers. Later he appears standing. His final iconographic form was established during the Tokugawa period (1600–1867), when he became immensely popular. In such later figures Jizō is represented as a young monk in the garb of a pilgrim and holding a jewel in his left palm.

Jizō helps the souls of dead children with their painful task of filling the river of Hades (Sai no Kawara) with pebbles and stones so that they can cross the waters and thus gain the other shore and a happy rebirth. This is why the statues of Jizō often have small heaps of pebbles near their feet, laid there by the faithful as a symbolic gesture of help for the souls of departed children. Jizō is also known to grant women an easy childbirth. On top of it all, he is a lenient and understanding protector of those shady figures whom other gods or bodhisattvas might consider too low, or too wayward, for serious help.

> The Jizō of Takane
>   is of lax character:
> for sex and gambling
>   he's the one to pray to![3]

In that incredible confusion of supernatural beings that Japanese folk religion became through the fusion of Shinto with Buddhism, with local cults, and with stray echoes of Taoism, Jizō finally became the patron of victorious generals (Shogun Jizō). In this capacity he was intimately connected with the Shinto god of Mount Atago, west of Kyoto. Occasionally one meets this defiant Jizō in art, represented as a Chinese general in full armor, on horseback, with a staff in his hand that looks like a spear. Only a large aureole behind his body identifies him as a reincarnation of Jizō. Alicia Matsunaga, in her fascinating book on the encounter of Shinto and Buddhism, gives a list of twenty-five different Shinto gods supposed at one time or another to have been manifestations of Jizō.[4]

---

[3] Oliver Statler, *Shimoda Story* (Tokyo: Tuttle, 1969), p. 261.
[4] A. Matsunaga, *The Buddhist Philosophy of Assimilation* (Tokyo: Sophia University, 1969), p. 237.

A subtle brotherhood between flesh and wood, skin and patina, is easy to detect when comparing a rough image of the god Fudō, protector of the Buddhist faith, with a young *kannushi*, taking part in a Shinto ceremony early on a fine winter morning (*102, 103*).

The wooden portrait of Fudō strikes one at first sight as very modern, as the work of some contemporary artist who has looked with a keen eye to the cubists and is also possibly an admirer of Brancusi. The statue, however, was certainly carved before 1695, the year in which the artist Enkū died. Nobody knows exactly when Enkū ("Perfect Void") was born. His life was exceedingly humble; perhaps he was not even a professed monk. He loved to wander about the country, and he carved powerful, primitive statues of religious subjects in return for a night's shelter and a few bowls of rice gruel. His patrons were abbots, and farmers or merchants. He was extremely prolific, very inventive, often totally inaccurate from the point of view of accepted Buddhist iconography, and sometimes splendidly inspired.

Enkū's works survive in the strangest places, from Hokkaido to Shikoku, but they are mostly found in the vicinity of Nagoya, or among the hills of Gifu, in small, remote temples. He loved carving the wood of *sugi* ("Japanese cedar") because it is a soft material with an even grain; he often cut a trunk vertically into four tall pieces, which he promptly and boldly carved, seemingly in a state of frenzy. In this he may have been similar to a great contemporary wood-block printer, Munakata Shikō. Both artists express in their works a primeval, aggressive vitality; both achieve their ends with simple, virile strokes; both are steeped in tradition, especially Buddhist tradition. For both these masters, work seems a muscular liberation of energies, sport and creation combined, an elemental confrontation of man and matter. And both realize something playful and irreverent (though truly religious) in their bizarre improvisations.

Fudō ("The Unshaken") has a long history. Ultimately he may be the Indian god Shiva. Buddhism accepted him as an active, terrifying defender of the faith under the name of Acala (of which the Japanese name is an exact translation). He was considered to be an emanation of the supreme Buddha Vairocana (in Japanese, Dainichi Nyorai) and he appears "seated in a fire-producing *samādhi* (meditation)."[5] In China he was never very popular, but in Japan he has been one of the favorite subjects of Buddhist art from the Heian period until our own day. Possible reasons for the favor will be given presently. Fudō is believed "to burn out all human defilements and obstructions." He protects from disease, poison, fire, the violence of enemies, the guiles of tempters, and, of course, he ensures wealth to his devotees.

Wondrous repositories of Japanese portraits are to be found in the sculpted likenesses of the five hundred *rakan*. A number of such series exist here and there in Japan, in the precincts of remote Buddhist temples or in mountain fastnesses. One of the finest, however, is quite near Tokyo, in the garden of Kita-in at Kawagoe (*105, 106*). This temple was founded in A.D. 830 by the famous monk Ennin ("Perfect Benevolence"; 794–864), whose diary has been translated and commentated at length by E. Reischauer.[6] The *rakan* of Kita-in date from much later, and they may possibly belong to the early or even the middle Tokugawa period.

[5] Ibid., p. 249.
[6] Edwin O. Reischauer, *Ennin's Travels in T'ang China* (New York: Ronald, 1955).

86

The *rakan* concept is extremely ancient, going back to the very beginning of Buddhism. The Sanskrit expression was *arhat* ("worthy of adoration") and was employed long before the times of Buddha. An *arhat* was a human being who had reached the highest degree of spiritual perfection, was at his last reincarnation and was thus ready to enter Nirvana. E. Conze says that the scriptures of the Hinayana School describe an *arhat* with a standard formula: "An Arhat is a person *in whom the 'outflows'* (i.e. sense desire, becoming, ignorance, wrong views) *have dried up, who has greatly lived, who has done what had to be done, who has shed the burden, who has won his aim, who is no longer bound to 'becoming,' who is set free, having rightly come to know.*"[7] In the Old Wisdom School (Hinayana, Theravada), the *arhat* conception has remained very important up to the present time. In the New Wisdom School (Mahayana), it has been partially superseded by the bodhisattva concept. An *arhat* reaches Nirvana and accepts it; a bodhisattva is equally entitled to the supreme reward but renounces final bliss to remain immersed in the world of illusion so as to help all sentient beings on their way to deliverance.

Rakan are generally presented in series of sixteen, eighteen, or five hundred, which include some immediate disciples of Buddha together with worthies of later ages and, especially in the large series, some guests of an entirely foreign origin. In art, *rakan* are distinguishable from Buddhas and bodhisattvas because they are conceived in a more humanistic spirit and their features are treated with much greater realism. An *arhat*, after all, though worthy of Nirvana, is still a mortal being. Paintings and sculptures of *arhat* (Chinese: *lohan*) enjoyed much popularity in the Middle Kingdom from the late T'ang to the early Sung dynasties; in Japan during the Kamakura and Muromachi periods; in Tibet, up to our own time. In China, Taoist sages slipped into the select company, carrying with them an aura of magical power. Appearances often become grotesque. The combination of great self-assurance and deep spirituality, typical of beings approaching the ultimate freedom, is "frequently brought home by stark realism."[8]

Most series of *rakan* in Japan are the work of folk craftsmen. The "stark realism," mentioned by Seckel, is due to the simple fact that sculptors looked around in their town or village for inspiration and carved literal portraits of leathery peasants (*104*), shrewd artisans or shopkeepers, wanderers with an air of mysterious wisdom, old rascals and poets, crotchety boatmen at their ferry, austere and sometimes presumptuous abbots, slightly mad beggars, thoughtful fishermen, or inspired drunkards. Descendants of such models are alive around us all over Japan. Some are small shopkeepers or weather-beaten farmers, but others have made the grade and can be seen among the solid citizens who run things through committees or as chairmen of important boards. Sometimes, suddenly, a *rakan* appears as a company director at his desk or reclining in his long, black, shiny car on his way—to Nirvana?—no, to a head office in a paradise of steel and glass (*107*).

An important thread that runs through most of Japanese art—and secretly through Japanese life too—is an awareness that man's inner life moves between two poles: one of action, stress, violence —an outward explosion; and one of peace, serenity, meditation—an inward implosion. "Violence and beauty go hand in hand."[9] "To combine action and art is to combine the flower that wilts

[7] E. Conze, *Buddhism: its essence and development* (New York: Harper Torchbooks, 1959), p. 93.
[8] Dietrich Seckel, *The Art of Buddhism* (London: Methuen, 1964), p. 252.
[9] Takaaki Aikawa and Lynn Leavenworth, *The Mind of Japan: a Christian perspective* (Valley Forge, Pa.: Judson Press, 1967), p. 25.

and the flower that lasts forever," says Mishima in a somewhat different, but fundamentally related, trend of ideas.[10]

Since the most ancient times, this has been perceived as an important point. In Shinto thought, there is frequent mention of *ara-mitama*, "a rough, savage soul," as opposed to *nigi-mitama*, "a gentle soul." It may have been the very nature of the Japanese islands, with their sudden transition from volcanic eruption, typhoon, earthquake to calm and fruitful days of summer growth or autumn harvest that suggested this polarity as something fundamental.

With the advent of Buddhism, especially of esoteric (Mikkyō) Buddhism, some related ideas became prominent in Japan. Their most distant roots may be seen in Hinduism: Vishnu as creator, Shiva as destroyer. Late Tantric Buddhism, as it was expounded in the Mikkyō schools (principally Shingon), made great use of this polarity, though it was deeply transformed to suit the Buddhist outlook. Bodhisattvas came to be seen as belonging to two classes and as taking on two different aspects: the one calm, serene, and benevolent, and the other dynamic, passionate, and terrifying. In Tibetan art, such ideas were developed to the highest complexity and sophistication, and in Japan also they became popular and fruitful. Here again we have an example of Buddhist thought and attitudes working in the same direction as native intuitions and reinforcing them.

Anybody at all familiar with Japanese art will have noticed the contrasting appearances of serene Buddhas or bodhisattvas in deep meditation (*111*) or compassionately extending their hand towards the faithful, next to the ferociously grimacing Niō giants, standing at the entrances of temples (*108*), to the menacing Shitennō (*116*) (the "Guardian Kings of the Four Quarters"), or to Fudō Myōō with his aureole of flames. Artists have developed this polarity to an extraordinary refinement. In Tibet it is often expressed as a strange and baroque mixture of abstract symbolism and reckless sensuality; in Japan everything is more human. Artists have studied serenity as the expression of inner light, a glow that comes from the heart and mind. They have also studied fury, and the way it can move the whole body and transform every muscle of a face.

Echoes of this polarity are visible all over Japan, both in the theatre and in actual life. The theatre—that vast symbolic repository of roles and idealized behavior—alternates scenes of apparent calm, during which tensions accumulate and gain momentum, with sudden explosions and frightening dénouements. Something of the kabuki rhythm was apparent in the early months of World War II. At that stage, events were in full ceremonial control. Acts of concerted and concentrated fury took place at calculated moments over the greater part of an ocean. As soon as the ritual rhythm was lost, the war was lost.

Normally, Japanese people manage to maintain their composure. Reactions and emotions are carefully hidden under layers of self-control. Centuries of meditation, *zazen*, and discipline regulate behavior through invisible channels. No public in the world can hold its breath with such utter self-annihilation as a full house at the theatre in Japan. But if a certain point, or mark, or temperature is passed, an explosion may occur. The *nigi-mitama* turns red to *ara-mitama*. There is a sudden jump from Jizō to Fudō, from the halo of calm, morning light to the menacing crown of darting flames. This may happen at work, at play, in sports, in love and sex—or in the lurid light of hatred and war.

[10] Yukio Mishima, *Sun and Steel* (Tokyo: Kodansha International, 1970), p. 50.

When something has its place in religion, then one can be sure that it belongs to the very essence of a civilization. Intrigue is as Latin as Chianti or Saint Emilion wines; and so is auricular confession—an intrigue with God. A *kibbutz* is as Jewish as kosher food; and so is the principle of *minyan*, which requires at least ten people to be present at a religious service if it is to be valid—the group, the group! Dance is as Japanese as *sashimi* ("raw fish") or *miso-shiru* ("soya bean soup"); and so are *kagura*, *bugaku*, *otome-mai*, *Yamato-mai*, *dengaku*, and all the sacred dances of Shintō, whether ceremonial and courtly, or folksy and popular.

Kagura claims a mythological origin. The sun goddess Amaterasu Ōmikami hid herself in a cave, offended by the pranks of her unruly brother, Susano-o, and the world was thus sunk in darkness. It became urgently necessary to bring the sun out again, with her light, warmth, and glory. Fortunately *kami* are very human (as humans are potentially *kami*), and the goddess could be depended upon to show female curiosity if something strange and exciting were to take place near the cave. A young female celestial being, Uzume no kami, was summoned and asked to dance. The sun goddess peeped out, was amused, opened the rocky door of her cave, and light came back to the world. Dance, therefore, is effective with gods and consequently essential to humans.

"The *kagura* handed down in the Imperial Court has an extremely ancient tradition: the words and music are of great classical value; and the ceremony is performed solemnly all night long."[11] But there are also local, rustic *kagura* that dramatize myths. Famous are the *yamabushi kagura* of north Japan, and the *kagura* of Izumo district *(273)*, all of them lovingly kept alive today by groups of hereditary farmer-actors and dancers. *Otome-mai* ("the maiden's dance"), *Yamato-mai*, *Azuma-mai*, and others are all ancient courtly forms of dance, while *dengaku* ("field dances") seems to have originated among the pranks and high-spirits that characterized the ubiquitous rice-planting ceremonies.

The dances accompanying the Bon Festival of the Dead (July 15) are typical and show a great variety of form. Buddhism, with its concern for departed souls, has taken over most of the rituals performed during this festival, which lasts three days, but its origins are native and much older. Long ago, something rather similar to the transformation of the pagan Bacchanalia into the Christian Christmas must have taken place when a festival intended to celebrate the rebirth of the sun after the winter solstice was adapted to a new faith. During the Bon Festival, the souls of the dead are welcomed home among living relatives and friends; fires are lit to show them the way; food and entertainment is prepared to make the visit pleasant and happy, and group dances of many types are a major feature of the festival.

Dances are prominent in the new religions of Japan. The Tenri-kyō cult, for instance, considers them absolutely essential. One very important sacred dance, the *Kanrodai-mai*, can only be performed at the Jiba (the center of the world and of the faith in the city of Ōtenri, south of Nara—"where man was created") at dawn, by five men and five women, who are masked. Among them must be the presiding leader of the faith, the so-called Shimbashira, representing the god Kunitokotachi no Mikoto, and his wife, representing the goddess Omotari no Mikoto. A less portentous and secluded event is the *Te-odori*, a dance that is performed by six faithful (three men

89

11 *Basic Terms of Shinto* (Tokyo: Kokugakuin University, 1958), p. 26.

and three women) at dawn in most Tenri chapels. "Through graceful movements of hands, arms, and manipulation of a fan, the dancers express various sentiments—pain and suffering, joy and ecstasy. There is an atmosphere of dynamism and religious zeal which can be fanned into frenzy by the rhythmic percussion."[12]

One of the new religions, founded after the war by an energetic widow with a magnetic personality, Kitamura Sayo, has made dance so central to its cult that it is generally known as Odorushūkyō, "the Dancing Faith." Mrs. Kitamura's experiences are typically shamanistic; she falls into a trance and is possessed by a god called Tenshō Kōtai Jingū, "Princely Sovereign Celestially Shining," who announces messages and oracles through her voice. It is entirely natural that a "dance of ecstasy" should have been given such a prominent place in the rituals of this new religion.

An all-pervading education in movement and rhythm subtly extends its influence throughout Japanese life. The tea ceremony, which after all in Japanese is only called *cha-no-yu*, "tea's hot water," might quite well be called the Tea Dance. It is not a dance of the body in the narrower sense of the word, but it is certainly a regulated, harmonious, elegant litany of gestures and positions—a dance of the hands. It somehow evokes Buddhist *mudra*, the hand and finger symbolism.

Dance pervades the theatre as *buyō*, and it is one of the foremost accomplishments of the geisha. Dance appears in sport as the supple elegance of a skier caressing his slope of snow in rapid turns, in the neat and sudden evolutions of a gymnast, in the flowing strokes of a swimmer. Even much sculpture is inspired by dance. A famous pagoda in Nara is called *kōreru ongaku*, "frozen music"; the *Jūni-shinshō*, "Twelve Divine Generals," of Murou-ji, attributed to Unkei, could well be called *kōreru odori*, "frozen dance." Menacing gods, defenders of the faith, bamboo-cutting monks in a strange ancient festival near Kyoto, dragon dancers, Hokkaido lumbermen at work—each of these finds its place in a mandala of gesture and movement, action and rhythm (*116–118*).

Finally there is that supreme, secret, silent dance of the hand leaving its trace on paper—the dance of writing, calligraphy. The sweeping downward stroke of *sakari* (盛), "climax, prime, bloom," has the same boldness as a sword in the hands of a Deva king in a temple near Nara, and the same earthy quality as the gestures of a man moving elemental things—blocks of stone, trunks of trees, the oars of a fisherman's boat.

Calligraphy, apart from the actual semantic meaning of its signs, can express, like dance, the entire universe of human feeling and moods. It can be delicate, mysterious, insinuating, like that page from the diary of a Heian court lady reproduced in a book by Roland Barthes and significantly captioned: "*Pluie, Semence, Dissémination, Trame, Tissue, Texte, Ecriture*" ("Rain, Seed, Diffusion, Thread, Texture, Text, Writing").[13] It can be brilliant and intuitive; it can be literal or limited; it can be monumental, Babylonian, absolutely final. However, an ideogram is essentially a trace, a graphic device, the record of a movement. A superior piece of writing records the faultless dance of the hand. We would never have known that it had existed unless we had this shadow to tell us about it.

[12] Harry Thomsen, *The New Religions of Japan* (Tokyo: Tuttle, 1963), p. 39.
[13] Roland Barthes, *L'Empire des Signes* (Geneva: Skira, 1970), p. 14.

Ideographic calligraphy is the traditional abstract art of the Far East as compared to its young Western counterpart. However, it is also something more. Each sign has also a precise place in the semantic order. Western abstract art is fundamentally vague; ideographic calligraphy is fundamentally precise, lexical, technological.

———

Westerners, understandably enough, are almost unanimous in their condemnation of the ideographic script as a means of communication, and even among people from Far Eastern cultures there have been some severe critics. Liang Ch'i-ch'ao, we are told by W. W. Lockwood, gave as the third of his five historical reasons for China's stagnation "the inefficiency of ideographic writing."[14] Mao and his government tried hard to adopt an alphabet, but it seems now they have found simplification of existing ideograms a better solution, perhaps because a thorough phonetic transcription of the language would divide China into a number of isolated blocks and make communication virtually impossible.

While detractors of the ideographic script have been legion, very few people indeed have paused to reflect on the advantages of it. It cannot be denied that the system is cumbersome and difficult to learn (though children pick it up very quickly); once it is learned, however, it has many points of superiority over an alphabet. An alphabet creates a much longer and more devious route for meanings to follow as they are transmitted from mind to mind. They must be coded into sounds and subsequently decoded. With the ideographic script there is a direct leap from eye to meaning, and the pause for sound is less imperative. Westerners also follow a similar process when numbers are used: 1970 can be read as one thousand nine hundred and seventy, but also as *mil neuf cent soixante-dix* or *millenovecento settanta*. The cipher has a universality and a directness that is entirely lost in seemingly interminable phonetic transcriptions. One might also remember signs put up along an expressway: a sign indicating a dangerous bend ahead and the stylized picture of a gasoline pump are immediately comprehended, even though one may be passing at a hundred miles an hour. If, however, the same ideas were to be displayed phonetically, the messages could not possibly be absorbed.

In addition there are subtler advantages—and here we return to the dance of the hand on the sheet of paper. A training in ideographic writing is a tremendous education for the hands and eyes. Space is perceived with supreme intensity; vagueness and nebulosity cannot possibly survive the daily challenge of minute precision. *"En n'importe quel endroit de ce pays, il se produit une organisation spéciale de l'espace"* ("Everywhere in this country there is a special organization of space").[15]

Eyes are used from childhood to distinguish in a split second the difference between 太 ("thick") and 犬 ("dog"), between 臼 ("mortar") and 白 ("white"), between 束 ("bunch" i.e. of flowers) and 棘 ("thorn"), between 愛 ("love") and 受 ("receive"), between 芋 ("potato") and 竿 ("bamboo pole"), and so on.

Eyes can pass with elegant ease from a text of a classic to an integrated circuit, from a page of *Genji Monogatari* to a page of Norbert Wiener. Eyes have been subjected to a rigorous training in

[14] W. W. Lockwood, "Japan's Response to the West: the contrast with China," *World Politics*, vol. IX, no. 1 (Oct. 1956).
[15] Barthes, *L'Empire des Signes*, p. 145.

labyrinths. A superb power of resolution has been built into the human mechanism. Ancestral software becomes a precious asset in dealing with the most advanced hardware.

Other invisible lines flow out of dance and meet the primordial Japanese taste for ceremony. Here we are driven straight back to Shinto fundamentals. If this world and this life are somehow divine, man must be accepted as he is. The idea of equality may be useful politically and important as a foundation of law, but it is an abstraction. Men, like plants, animals, and days (some with clouds, some with sun), are different. Inferiors should defer to superiors—it is the natural order. *Uyamau* ("to respect, to esteem") is a key concept in this area.[16] *Tsutsushimi* ("modesty," a respectful attitude before *kami*) appeared so important to Yamazaki Anzai (1618–1682) that he founded an entire school of Shinto thought, the Suika Shinto, upon this concept. Confucianism gave philosophical depth to these primitive intuitions and attitudes.

Inevitably, dance leads one to *matsuri* ("festivals")—that living, creative, and conservative nucleus of Japanese traditions. We have spoken of *matsuri* before; all lanes and lines of Japanese civilization seem to converge towards it and then depart from it.

Dance and ceremony are exquisitely united in what must have been, in days gone by, one of the major events in the social and spiritual life of rural Japan: the *ta-ue* ("rice-planting") festivities. This festival is still held today during June or July, depending on the place. Indeed it is even advertised, and buses loaded with tourists are driven to famous shrines, such as the Sumiyoshi-jinja in Osaka. At the Sumiyoshi shrine, rice seedlings are given by Shinto *kannushi* priests to two geisha, who are dressed in extraordinary costumes, with ripe cereal ears surrealistically represented over their headgear (*114, 232*). The seedlings are carried in procession to the shrine's field to be planted in the flooded soil, while well-known actors dance, sing, and pantomime legends and myths on a wooden platform.

Dance and ceremony may also lead us to roles. As in the West, art is a repository of role images: the saint, the king, the sage, the bewitching beauty, the young hero, the beggar, the captain, the merchant, the burgher, the martyr, the child, the barbarian. A Chinese sage-king goes forth under an umbrella held by a servant in a landscape of woods and golden clouds, accompanied by literati and greeted by peasants and artisans (*123*); a Shugendō dignitary passes by, protected from the sun by a wide umbrella held by an attendant (*124*) during the bamboo-cutting festival (*takekiri matsuri*), which takes place every year in June at Kurama, near Kyoto. A *bugaku* dancer lifts his wand in the golden sky of a painted screen (*120*); a lion dancer at Osaka's Tenjin Festival lifts his sword in the real bustle of a crowd (*117*). A Buddhist teacher, whose memory is celebrated by a portrait of Ashikaga times (sixteenth century) (*122*) may well have suddenly risen and started moving four hundred years later (*121*).

Roles can be followed in unsuspected quarters or directions. An elderly woman pilgrim, leisurely visiting the eighty-eight temples of Shikoku Island (*hachijū-hachi-kasho no junrei*), dresses as the occasion demands and as may have been suggested by the image of Kōbō Daishi (794–835), the founder of esoteric Shingon Buddhism, with his wide stone hat and his staff. Some thoughtful believer has also given him a red stole to protect him from evil influence and to keep him warm (*129, 130*).

[16] *Basic Terms of Shinto*, p. 77.

▲ 97

▲ 98

99 ▶

The colors of spring and autumn are interwoven in the gay kimono of the pretty visitor to a Shinto shrine at Obihiro, in Hokkaido. She is rinsing her mouth with pure water at the fountain near the entrance. It is *Shichi-go-san*, November 15, when little girls of seven and three, together with boys of five, visit their local shrine dressed in their best traditional clothes.

▲ 100

101 ▶

A page boy (*chigo*) in the procession at Kurama, near Kyoto (*100*), could well be the reincarnation of a stone Jizō standing by a path in Hiraizumi in north Japan (*101*). Or is it the other way around? Is the Jizō statue a portrait of the boy?

Originally, Jizō may have been the Indian goddess Prithivi, a personification of the earth, later adopted into Buddhism with a change of sex and the new name Kshitigarbha ("Earth Womb"), which implies that he is lord of the netherworld and protector of souls suffering in hell. Jizō is one of the most popular among Buddhist bodhisattvas—beings who are believed to have attained perfect illumination but who have also renounced their right to enter Nirvana so as to help humans and animals along the road to salvation. The Japanese name Jizō (地蔵; "Earth Storehouse") is a literal translation of the original Sanskrit. Jizō is considered the special protector of children, wayfarers, and criminals. He is generally represented as a young monk with a shaven head, wearing the sandals of a pilgrim and holding a staff in one hand and a jewel in the other.

103 ▲

◀ 102

Was the young Shinto priest, photographed one clear winter's morning during a ceremony at Ōmiya, near Tokyo (*103*), the model for the wooden sculpture (*102*)? In fact the statue was carved in the seventeenth century by the wandering monk Enkū (died 1695). The chance likeness to a man of our own day shows both how quick Enkū's eye was to catch characteristic features and how little Japanese looks have changed over the centuries. The monk Enkū carved thousands of Buddhist images in soft *sugi* wood with his bold and extremely personal style. His works strike us as powerfully modern—especially when considered in the context of the rather conventional sculpture produced during the early Edo period. The god represented here with a stern face and high crown of standing hair is Fudō, one of the Five Myōō (Vidyaraja, "Kings of Knowledge"). Originally Fudō may have been the Indian god Shiva in the aspect of Acala ("Immovable", "Impassive"). The name Fudō (不動) is the exact Japanese translation of the latter.

JAPAN

▲ 106

107 ▶

The saintly human disciples of Buddha were called *arhat* in India and in Japan they appear as *rakan* (羅漢). At an early date these men formed a popular subject of Buddhist art in China, Tibet, and Japan. Groups of sixteen, eighteen, or even five hundred are known. The purely human nature of the *rakan* is suggested in sculptures and paintings by a vivid, playful, sometimes grotesque, realism. Most probably artists looked for models among their relatives, friends, or neighbors, and they succeeded in carving astonishing galleries of contemporary portraits. A famous and very successful series of five hundred statues representing the *rakan* can be seen not far from Tokyo, in the precincts of Kita-in at Kawagoe (*105, 106*), on one of the trunk roads leading north. Descendants of the models chosen by the anonymous sculptors are alive all around us. Some may still be shopkeepers or leathery farmers (*104*), while others are now solid citizens who run things through committees or as chairmen of important boards (*107*).

ART AND PEOPLE

▲ 110

◄ 108

109 ▼

Since ancient times Northern Buddhist art has stressed two basic aspects in which spirits, both human and divine, may become manifest: one is calm and appropriate to meditation, the other fierce and appropriate to passionate commitment. The opposition is not between good and evil, between gods, Buddhas, and demons, but between peaceful detachment and burning passion. One of the two Niō (仁王) guardians at the entrance of the Ishite temple in Shikoku (108) is diametrically opposite the sublime and serene image of Amida Buddha, sculpted by Jōchō in the eleventh century for Byōdō-in, at Uji, south of Kyoto (111). Has the concept of these two aspects or "temperatures" of spiritual activity subtly pervaded Japanese life? On observing the manner in which the abbot of a monastery in Kyoto unconsciously adopts the posture of Amida (110), or how a lumberman in Hokkaido likewise unconsciously expresses the tension of a Niō's grimace as he works at a colossal tree (109), one feels inclined to answer in the affirmative.

111 ▶

◀ 113

112 ▲

Once a year, in the north of Honshu near the city of Haranomachi, the descendants of old samurai families gather for two days of competitions on horseback and religious ceremonies and parades (*sōma-oi noma-oi*). The event could justifiably be called one of the most colorful *matsuri* ("festivals") of Japan. Normally the suits of armor, swords, and banners are kept in the home as heirlooms. On the appointed day, farmers leave their tractors in the sheds, businessmen close their offices, clerks abandon their desks, and for a few hours old Japan comes alive again (*112*). For the Children's Festival on May 5, banners are hung up outside homes with sons, especially in Yamanashi Prefecture. Many of these banners show heroes of the sixteenth century— Toyotomi Hideyoshi, Katō Kiyomasa, Takeda Shingen (*113*). These idealized portraits on the banners and the living man in armor clearly belong to the same tradition.

JAPAN

▲ 114

115 ▶

Japanese girls may wear minis and maxis, they may have their eyes made rounder by an operation, or have their hair dyed red, they may love go-go dancing, but when the time comes for them to dress in kimono, the gestures, bearing, movements, gait, voice, the very choice of words, are altered. Every year in June a colorful *ta-ue* ("rice planting") festival is held at Osaka's Sumiyoshi Shrine, and propitiatory ceremonies are performed to ensure a plentiful harvest. At a certain moment, bunches of rice seedlings are ceremonially handed by Shinto priests to two *sa-otome* girls dressed in extraordinary costumes and wearing hats decorated with stylized ears of corn (*114*). These two then walk slowly to the shrine's field where the seedlings are finally given to a group of farmers for the first transplanting. A votive picture (*ema*) in the temple of Ichijō, not far from Himeji, shows the large umbrellalike hats (*kasa*) worn by women in feudal days when traveling (*115*).

▲ 116

One of the protector gods of the Four Quarters in the Jōruri temple near Nara (116), a lion dancer at Osaka's Tenjin Festival in July (117), a warrior-monk (sōhei), ready to cut bamboo in a competition held every year at Kurama (118), a gagaku dancer in Kyoto (119), the painting of a masked dancer impersonating Raryō the handsome Chinese prince who, in order to frighten his enemies, was forced to wear a terrifying mask to hide the radiance of his face (120)—all are somehow united in their gestures and movements by the imperious, elegant, downward slashing stroke of the brush in the ideogram 盛 (sakaru; "to flourish, prosper").

▲ 117

▲ 118

▲ 119

120 ▶

121 ▲ ▲ 122

Religion and its rituals are an obvious area in which to expect continuity. However, when resemblances in a chance encounter reach across the centuries, one always reacts with a surprised delight. The young abbot (121) of the Nichiren sect, proceeding solemnly at dawn towards the main hall of the Minobu temple for a morning service, belongs to Buddhist tradition that is entirely different from that represented by a Zen master whose statue has been sitting in the Ginkaku-ji ("Silver Pavilion") in Kyoto since the sixteenth century (122). Despite this, there are subtle links connecting the two, not only in their robes but also in the fixity of expression that seems to reveal similar habits of meditation and introspection.

123 ▲   ▲ 124

A Chinese sage-king goes among the people, setting an example of benevolent government. This painting (123) of the early Edo period, on sliding doors in the Nishi Hongan-ji in Kyoto, shows the sovereign advancing paternally toward some humble peasants, while an assistant holds a large umbrella over the august head. Centuries later a priest walks with dignity on his thick wooden clogs toward the main temple of Kurama for an important ceremony (124). Both sovereign and priest wear similar gowns, both have practically identical gestures. Even the slanting angle of the large umbrellas seems the same. Ancient Chinese models act subtly on Japanese habits and rites, as Cretan, Arcadian, and Byzantine examples recur in Western fashion and ritual.

ART AND PEOPLE

JAPAN

▲ 127

128 ▶

Boating on the river at Arashiyama near Kyoto, where a splendid, primeval forest grows down to the water, has been considered a refined pleasure since long ago. Girls may now leave their offices instead of wooden pavilions called "Wisteria Jar" or "Auspicious Cloud," students may break off reading Marx or Sartre instead of treatises on filial piety, but on a sunny spring afternoon boats and young people are there as faithfully as they have always been (125, 126).

An ox-cart was the uncomfortable but prestigious conveyance of princes and ladies in the peaceful days when Heian (now Kyoto) was founded, over a thousand years ago (128). Now it is only seen once a year, on May 15 in the Aoi Festival, first performed in the sixth century to placate the deities of the Kamo shrines who manifested their displeasure at neglect by causing disastrous storms. For the occasion an imperial messenger (*chokushi*) proceeds in colorful procession from the Gosho palace to the Kamo shrines (127).

129 ▲

◄ 130

JAPAN

▲ 131

132 ▶

Many pilgrims make the round of the eighty-eight temples connected with the Shingon sect that are scattered haphazardly over hills and valleys in the island of Shikoku. The most devout believers, such as the old lady in white (*129*), cover their heads with a wide straw hat and carry a begging bowl, a rosary, and a staff. That great Buddhist saint and innovator, Kōbō Daishi (弘法大師; 774–835), the founder of Shingon Buddhism in Japan, stands in stone on a pedestal above a fountain in the court of the Ishite temple near Matsuyama (*130*). A kindly soul has covered him with a red cloak as a protection against cold, rain, and evil. If the sun gets too hot, other pious hands will sprinkle water over his body—the wooden ladle lies ready at the feet of the statue.

As for the *kokeshi* dolls from north Japan (*131*), is it they who have captured the essence of childish innocence and trepidation? Or is it the children (*132*), in their light summer *yukata* donned for Kyoto's Gion Festival in July, who have been mesmerized into a *kokeshi*-like pensiveness?

Encounters can be strange and unexpected sometimes. The red-haired Shōjō (*133*), a character in a Nō play who is an auspicious, mythological being noted for his love of saké, may be linked by some subterranean ties with the disgusted red-haired hussy selling sugar dolls at a country fair (*134*). Both, probably and ultimately, related their colorful manes to the "red-haired barbarians"—the demon in parody, the hussy in homage.

A great *oni-gawara* ("devil tile") on the roof of Zōjō-ji in Tokyo was intended to frustrate the possible evil intentions of lightning (*136*). Emma-ō, the King of Hell, distributes horrendous torments to miserable souls at his feet (*137*). Then suddenly one may encounter a grinning *oni* who has felt the strain of a procession along the streets of Tokyo's *shita machi* ("lower quarters") on a sultry spring day, sitting happily on the bumper of an old car for a few moments of well-earned rest and recuperation (*135*).

135 ▲ ▲ 136

▲ *138*

139 ▲

Sometimes the five hundred *rakan* (pages 86–7) are a motley lot. It was usual for many different sculptors to work on them, with a resultant variety of styles, as we see in the grottoes of Mount Nokogiri in the Bōsō peninsula (*138*). Few people visit the place, but when someone steals a head to sell to foreign tourists, a well-meaning visitor replaces it with another picked up nearby. The final result is a pathetic congregation of saints, some humbly resigned, others looking sour and annoyed, all gossiping together in the humid silence of a mountain night. The same variety distinguishes a group of good but nervous provincial ladies after a long, and possibly rather tedious, lesson in tea ceremony under a severe and demanding tea master (*139*). A young *oku-san* ("wife") smiles, another speaks to a friend planning a trip away from Shizuoka and its humdrum routine, an old lady sits glumly thinking of her latest urine analysis or the scandalous bills run up by her new daughter-in-law.

140 ▲
141 ▶

There is a curious statue in the small garden of an old temple near Nagoya (*140*). Probably it represents Jizō (page 84)—the beloved bodhisattva is astonishing in his transformations and manifestations! His head has been covered with a red cap, and his body, partially, with a child's diaper. The astute bodhisattva, like an expert chorus girl, keeps the diminutive apron high on his breast, exposing to passers-by a well-shaped limb, exactly as the plaster mannequins do in a clothes' shop in Kyoto (*141*). Strangely, these mannequins come in half-bodies. A girl in a red kimono stands still a moment and unwittingly provides the other half.

The link between these two pictures may be purely visual, but for me they trigger deeper resonances, evoking the atmosphere of many humble and older neighborhoods in Japanese cities, with their network of alleys, shops, temples, and one-room factories—areas that abound in amusing and delightful encounters.

ART AND PEOPLE

▲ 142

▲ 143

Hatsutaiken (初体験; "first physical experience") reads the poster advertising a brash, sensational film in Kyoto *(142)*. Is the plump Lolita awaiting her "first physical experience"? Propped up on an elbow, with her chin cupped in her hand, she strangely resembles an ancient statue of Nyoirin Kannon *(143)*, a Buddhist deity elegantly balancing a wheel on a fingertip. The god also holds a jewel that symbolizes the celebrated sutra Prajnaparamita ("Perfection of Wisdom"). Since it was also known as the "Jewel of Wishes," on the popular level Nyoirin Kannon was believed to grant all sorts of material benefits. This interpretation, we are told by Alicia Matsunaga, is not entirely incorrect since material benefits acting as *upaya*, or intermediate goals, can ultimately lead to enlightenment. May we consider "first physical experiences" as a type of *upaya*? In former times, the fine medieval sculpture of Nyoirin Kannon was housed in the Hannya temple in Nara; when the buildings burnt down, the statues were abandoned in a yard.

Verlaine spoke somewhere of *les grands barbares blancs* ("the great white barbarians"). The Ainu chief enjoys a hearty joke in a hut at Kotan, on the shores of Lake Kutcharo near the center of Hokkaido, while sharing a goulash of bear meat with the author *(144)*. His paleolithic laughter is boisterously echoed by a *koma-inu* stone dog, squatting at the entrance to one of Japan's most ancient Shinto shrines, that of Oyamazumi on the island of Ōmishima *(145)*. Here we have been pulled back to the very earliest period of Japanese history. On the one hand, *koma-inu* ("Korean dogs"), introduced from the continent by wandering craftsmen, scholars, or Buddhist priests to guard temples or shrines; on the other hand, at the furthest points east, where Tokyo, Yokohama, and Kawasaki now stand—jungles of cement and steel with arteries turgid with oil and gas—*les grands barbares blancs*, the Emishi and Ezo warriors with bows and beards and a strange, archaic religion in which animals of the forest act as messengers between men and gods.

ART AND PEOPLE

146 ▲   ▲ 148

◄ 147

Crowds, crowds, everywhere, always! Crowds of
people at a gay fertility festival near Nagoya, waiting
for attendants of the shrine to throw them *mochi* ("rice
dumplings") (*147*), and crowds of Daruma dolls at a
country fair near Tokyo (*146*).   Daruma, the patriarch
Bodhidharma who came to China from India in the
sixth century, is said to have meditated for nine years
with his face turned towards a wall.   When he tried to
get up, he found his legs had rotted away; thus Daruma
is represented as an egg-shaped doll, all head and belly,
with two powerful, daunting eyes looking you straight
in the face.   A Daruma doll brings good luck; it inspires confidence and confers the same determination
as the master showed in his long meditation.   Crowds
of youngsters carry a palanquin during a festival (*149*),
and ranks of rice stacks dry in the sun (*148*).   This style
of stacking is typical of north Japan in the countryside
around Akita.   Often they look like an immense army
of samurai dressed in straw, silently waiting for the
order to march.

▼ 149

ART AND PEOPLE

151 ▲

◀ 150

152 ▶

This page is frankly a divertimento (*piccolo divertimento da camera per corpo umano, legni e spazio;* "a divertimento for bodies, wood, and space"). But *divertimenti* are often *upaya,* temporary steps, "skillful means," leading to some form of truth. The ancient, dry bone of a tree is a prominent feature in the entrance courtyard of Sambō-in, near Kyoto (*152*). In most other countries, the useless trunk would have been cut down and carted away long ago. Not so in Japan—and quite rightly! The trunk is splendid, pure sculpture; it has muscles and skin; it may also be seen as a monumental *ikebana,* or as a mysterious wooden ideogram. But above all it is dance, the very spirit of dance. The pretty geisha repeats with her fan the gestures of the tree (*151*), as do the enraptured crowds at Tokushima in their *Awa-odori* (*233*), or the fireman in his acrobatic exercises high up on a bamboo ladder during the annual display at Ueno Park in Tokyo, at the beginning of January (*150*).

ART AND PEOPLE

▲ 153
◀ 154

The overcrowding of fish in a small tank and the overcrowding of skiers on the broad slopes of Naeba, north of Tokyo.

Tank: water, liquid. Mountain: water, crystallized.

JAPAN

3

THE
IDEOGRAPHIC
SPACE

WRITING is a system of signs, intended to organize space and convey meanings.

Because signs have meanings, eyes scan them with curiosity and love and become docked to them like LEMs to interplanetary ships. A deep relationship is set up in childhood between eyes and signs. An age-long *ta-ue*, a transplantation of signs into eyes takes place. At the subconscious level there is a rigorous flourishing in the paddy fields of the mind. Finally eyes are saturated with signs and dictate aesthetic needs to hands. Signs reappear as objects in everyday life, buildings, furniture, posters, toys, hats. There is a continuous, complex flow from sign to eye and back from eye to sign, from eye to world; the taste of an age, a culture, a civilization is deeply affected.

Roman capital letters, as one can still see them on the facade of the Pantheon or on many of the ancient ruins in the Eternal City, are significantly related to the solid, rational, often unimaginative, buildings of the Republic and Empire. The A's and M's stand sturdily on the ground with their legs wide apart, as if to resist an assault; the I's are similar to columns; the T's and F's to lintels; the O's and C's remind one of some vault in an aqueduct, or in the Milvio Bridge, which still spans the Tiber, undaunted after twenty centuries of freshets, wars, and human folly. The spacing is harmonious, majestic, and assured. Gothic lettering, on the other hand, is nervous, sensitive, tendentiously baroque; the serrated vertical lines are intimately related to the gabled windows and roofs, to the fluted columns, to the general upward surge of the whole style. Gothic lettering is the product of the same eyes that loved elaborate tapestry, high steeple headdresses for ladies, and long, pointed shoes for pages and knights; the same eyes loved gargoyles and coats of arms, dragons and basilisks, slender adolescent nudes with threadlike arms and legs. Arabic writing, on the other hand, loses itself naturally among the tracery or ornamentation on the walls of a mosque or on the wood of a minbar; the untrained eye will hardly notice where the symbolism of the written sign ends and the more diffused symbolism of the decorative motifs begins.

Alphabets or syllabic systems of writing are comparatively simple graphic devices: the same elementary signs recur repeatedly. An ideographic script is infinitely richer: its possibilities are endless, even though they depend on the combination of a relatively limited number of graphic elements. In China and Japan, writing is absolutely central to culture. All roads lead to Rome, says an ancient Western proverb; all lines lead to the ideogram, one might say of the Far East. Writing is not only a medium to convey information and emotion but also a vast stock of abstract shapes that live in their own right, behaving often as echoes of shapes and mothers of new shapes. Norman Mailer sees a sexual orgy as an "aspect of technology." "The end result of an orgy," he says, "is to make people units, interlocking gears, coupling joints." In an ideographic civilization, a supreme, ubiquitous orgy of forms is perennially being enacted. Everything tends to become a smoothly interlocking gear, an elegant coupling joint.

Do not expect here a systematic enumeration of geometric classes, an Analytical Discussion of Correspondences. Let us leave that to some German *Japanologue*, industrious and *gründlich*, if he feels like it one of these days. He may, we hope, give us a paper entitled *"Die Bedeutung des ideographischen Schrift im Verhältnis zum Begriff des japanischen Formstruktur und Weltanschauung."* We Latins are much too lazy and disorganized for enterprises of such magnitude and consequence. We appreciate some fun. I wish to deal with this motif in the spirit of a divertimento following my compatriot, Giuseppe Arcimboldi from Milan, the sixteenth-century artist who delighted in making up strange faces with vegetables or animals, ingeniously compounding them into human likenesses. I believe that the basic idea of this chapter is valid and extremely fruitful in understanding many aspects of Japan, but I also believe that one can only approach it in a light vein, taking up some threads here and there, with gusto but unsystematically. I hope that the reader may become infected himself and start out on his own to discover families of forms and lines of correspondences between seemingly unrelated objects—unsuspected meetings of nature, architecture, writing, fashion, joinery, folklore, cottage industries, calligraphy, and cakes.

One important family of signs strikes one strongly, perhaps on very first contact with the Far East; it is composed of what may be called "pagodics." Let us define pagodics as lines that make one think of a pagoda. Pagodics, therefore, are all those ideograms that look somehow like a tiny building because they are covered by two diverging lines—a neat, dainty, sometimes quaint, little roof. "What a ridiculous idea!" someone might object. "It could only come from a foreigner." But a foreigner has the advantage of looking on to the *Forêt des Symboles* (the words of Bonneau) from outside; hence he perceives facts that may be too obvious to all those who are brought up within the system. Pagodics have no genetic relationship whatever with each other. In some cases the graphic device called *hito-yane* (人; "man-roof") derives from the radical sign for man, put on top instead of on the left side (*nimben*; 亻), such as in 会合今企金命念舍倉. In other cases it is part of the radical itself, as in 食登祭, or just an incidental development, 春陰琴. The class cannot even be said to have well-defined limits, which is the worst of all defects in any classification; it simply blurs off in many directions towards what a pedant might call "pagodoid"

会 合 今 企 金 命 念 舍 倉 食 登
au   *au*   *ima*   *kuwadateru*   *KIN*   *inochi*   *NEN*   *SHA*   *kura*   *taberu*   *noboru*

structures (such as 大 or 承) and towards the contiguous family of genuine roofs (the *ukammuri*; 宀), such as 家宮宴富.

Origins of the pagodic line may possibly be found in China. This would take us on a difficult trek to try and understand how and why Chinese roofs became tilted upwards at their eaves and developed that characteristic curve, which was subsequently imitated by the Japanese. A number of theories have been proposed, perhaps the most convincing being the one that considers it an imitation of the ancient Central Asian tent, stretched out and supported by wooden posts. Just as Greek architecture is supposed to represent a transposition in stone of a style developed for buildings of wood, here the transposition must have been from cloth or skins to masonry and tiles.

Whatever their origin, pagodics are immensely influential formal devices in the whole universe of Far Eastern appearances. Pagodics jump from ideograms to buildings and back. In Japan you find the pagodic line in temples and shrines (*155, 156, 162*), belfries, houses in the country (*164, 167–69*), and gates. Pagodics appear in stone lanterns (*ishi-dōrō*) (*160, 163*), in *torii* (gates to Shinto shrines) (*161*), in festival floats (*166*). They appear again with constant vitality in hats, caps, and in umbrellas of all types, fashions, designs, and sizes (*165, 171*).

Finally the pagodic line, simplified to a triangle (*170*), merges into the universal mountain shape— and leads us back to Mount Fuji (*173, 174*). An entire cycle has been covered and closed. From nature to architecture, to writing, to carpentry, to fashion, to gardening, and back to nature.

Japanese taste is not an easy thing to define or delimit. It varies according to time and place. It is enough to remember that the Katsura Villa and the mausoleums of Nikkō were conceived and built at roughly the same time, in the first half of the seventeenth century. One embodies aesthetic ideas of extreme refinement and restraint, trying to achieve a subtle fusion of man with nature; the other reveals a baroque excess, an extrovert pleasure in abundance, an overstatement of brillance and ornament, the aggressive affirmation of wealth and power. At the Katsura Rikyū one has to look for ornamentation in the hidden recess of a door knob; at Nikkō one is overwhelmed by gilt flowers, painted birds, Chinese sages, and dexterous monkeys giving Confucian lessons on behavior. Variations over the centuries are also very great. During the Nara and Fujiwara periods, curved lines and delicate, intricate designs were much in vogue. Symmetry was also highly thought of. Later trends brought about entirely different emphases. There are, however, some characteristics of Japanese visual arts that constantly recur, for instance a fundamental love of simplicity and at the same time elegance. There is an inborn feeling for the formal logic of design. Both characteristics are already outstanding in the rough, archaic frescoes at Chibusan in Kyushu, and they appear in Yayoi pottery and in *haniwa* figures of the same period.

The break, which occurred around two thousand years ago, between Jōmon and Yayoi pottery is like the sudden crossing of an ocean. Jōmon pottery with its luscious, often pointless, foamy germination of shapes, sometimes resembling a mysterious earthenware cancer, is the product of a mind completely different from the one that appreciated the clean elegance and logic of Yayoi dishes and vessels. Though there have been many contrasts in the history of Japanese art, as evi-

祭　春　陰　琴　大　承　家　宮　宴　富
matsuri　*haru*　*kage*　*koto*　DAI　SHŌ　*ie*　*miya*　*utage*　*tomi*

denced by the fact that a "Nikkō tendency" exists and has a vitality of its own, generally the opposite urge to search for bold simplicity and essential structure seems to prevail.   Shinto with its love of *meijō* (clarity and purity) can be considered an inner, guiding force in this direction.

It may seem strange that the Japanese, a people so seldom intellectually systematic, who have produced such an illogical language, should display such a splendid feeling for the logic of design. This takes us back to a basic theme: the Japanese, as non-dualists, live in the stream of life, and their logic comes out in action, construction, art, poetry, industry.   When they retire from life to consider the abstract, they are usually outside their normal mental habits and they become lost.

The universe of Japanese forms is dominated by bold lines.   Here, of course, the ideogram is master and king.   The ultimate semen of ideographic script, the first sign a teacher asks his pupil to write on paper, is the straight or horizontal line for *ichi* (一), "one."   Among the simplest signs are the three vertical strokes of *kawa* (川), "river," and the horizontal lines of the number three.   Horizontal lines sometimes grow into superb castles of flat stratifications, as in *kotobuki* "long life," both in its old (壽) and modern (寿) versions, in *koto* (事), "thing," or in *kaku* (書), "to write."   Vertical lines are less distinctive, though there are some thickets of strokes spouting gallantly upwards, as in *nira* (韮), "leek," or *mizu* (瑞), "freshness."

Simple vertical and horizontal lines are a constant accompaniment throughout the Japanese day, suggesting a gentle feeling of purification rather than the cold aloofness of abstraction.   The home is a symphony of straight lines, and this is more out of respect for the flesh of wood than through a Pythagorean cult of mathematical harmony.   *Shōji* ("screens"), with their lattice of wood and paper, have the finality of abscissa and ordinates in a graph, but they retain all the gentleness of a light screen between moonlight and the tender rendezvous of love.   *Tatami* ("matting") look like a lesson in perspective by Brunelleschi, but they are also (when new) the source of a delicate perfume that takes us directly back to the woods in summer.   The posts of a *tokonoma* ("alcove") have the essentiality of a shell picked up along the shore, but also the warm elegance of young limbs, the charm of a girl's nape.

The feeling for lines and their value is always alert in the Japanese artisan.   It may suddenly appear in costumes (*175*), in the curious bridge of a garden (*182*), in the gigantic fantasy of a dragon-lion (*shishi*) (*181*) brought to life by a whole team of youngsters during a spectacular festival. Lines are also seen in the chance arrangement of fabrics drying in the sun along a riverbed in Kyoto (*185*), in the compact list of temples affiliated with the head institution (*186*), in rows of lanterns (*183*), or drying cuttle-fish (*184*).

In calligraphy, vertical and horizontal lines are accompanied by diagonal ones, which adopt different shapes and names according to their position.   The ideogram *nagai* (永), "long," is considered to include all the most important strokes and is one of the first that a pupil must practice.

There is a fascinating elementary stroke called *shikigamae* (弋), a powerful, downward, slashing sign.   It appears rather timidly in the ideogram *nagai*, where its assertiveness is inhibited by the general balance of the design.   But in such compositions as *utsu* (伐), "to strike," *shiro* (城), "castle," *BU* (武), "military," *GI* (義), "justice," it appears in its full splendor, a decisive, imperious gesture—down and right, with its final check and peremptory hint of a return upwards.   It suggests a pow-

一 川 壽 寿 事 書 韮 瑞 永 伐

ichi *kawa* *kotobuki* *kotobuki* *koto* *kaku* *nira* *mizu* *nagai* *utsu*

126

erful skier swinging down a slope to come to a sudden stop with an elegant turn (see page 103).

Other more gentle lines run in the opposite direction, as one finds in *aru* (有), "to be," in *mairu* (参), "to go," in *mezurashii* (珍), "strange" (see page 148). The delightful, if rare, *RYŌ* (寥), "lonely," seems to suggest the branches of a weeping willow. There is something firm, an echo of Bach, in the repetitive chords of *kuwa* (桑), "mulberry tree," or of *KYŌ* (協), "cooperation."

The circle, and curves in general, might be thought to have no counterpart in the ideographic world, and this is true in a certain sense. Curved lines existed in the primordial period of Chinese writing, when signs were cut into materials like bone or bronze, but in the Han dynasty the brush was invented and required a completely new style of writing. All curves had to become angles; all circles were transformed into squares or rectangles.

Soon, however, this boxlike writing became simplified and softened when it was used on informal occasions or in a hurry. Next to what the Japanese call *kaisho* ("square hand") appeared *gyōsho* ("running hand") and *sōsho* ("grass hand"). Single strokes were fused one with the other, connected into chains and garlands, into long tendrils. Curves came into their own again. An amazing universe was born with flying loops, with threads and cartouches entangling one another. All formal rules were waived. Personality took over and reigned supreme. These could be the jottings of fools, but they could also be the signatures of great masters. Pretences became impossible. A final nudity of the soul had to be accepted. Moments of lucidity and great power were faithfully registered, but so were uncertainty and weakness. Shapes changed beyond recognition. Reading often became a desperate labor of interpretation. Sometimes it became impossible to connect beauty with a meaning that had become indecipherable; one had to look for it in abstract values, in the music of lines and space.

The Japanese developed this aspect of calligraphy in a direction that had no counterpart in China. The nature of their language—inflected, not monosyllabic—compelled them to invent an alphabet. The ideogram could give the fundamental ideas of a phrase, but the inflections of words, their varying terminations, and all the particles had to be written with purely phonetic signs. Two alphabets were developed. *Katakana* ("hard" *kana*) was angular and spiky, but *hiragana* ("plain" *kana*) was soft and full of curves. The brush caressed the paper, often leaving white spaces where it leapt and briefly suggesting a connection that was not entirely "said" by the brush. This is typical of *u* (う), *ko* (こ), or *i* (い), for instance. *Hiragana* often looks like seaweed dancing in a submarine current or resembles the hair of ancient beauties depicted in *Yamato-e* scrolls. Women in those times were not supposed to learn the solemn, powerful, towering *kanji* Chinese ideograms, so they became skilled masters of *kana*. Some of the greatest novels of those times (Murasaki Shikibu's *Tale of Genji*, for instance) were written almost entirely in *hiragana*.

Apart from writing, the circle is used with great sophistication in Japanese life whenever it can act as a point of reference, as a center for lines otherwise scattered. It may appear as the frame of the *mitsu-domoe* (good-luck sign) on a lantern (*177*) or on the back of a costume worn at a festival (*178*), as it may be seen in the robust heads of nails that fasten iron plates to a gate of a medieval castle (*176*). Occasionally a window may be round (*180*) or a small stone basin that contains water to rinse and purify one's mouth when visiting a temple (*179*).

城　武　義　有　参　珍　寥　桑　協
shiro　*BU*　*GI*　*aru*　*mairu*　*mezurashii*　*RYŌ*　*kuwa*　*KYŌ*

Mother of all straight lines is the rice field. In early summer, after the *ta-ue* ("rice planting") ceremonies, paddy fields all over Japan are like vast mirrors of water, reflecting the sky with its heavy clouds full of rain, the trees in their greenest foliage, children running along with fishing rods. Incredibly clean lines of rice sprouts, planted in row upon row by patient hands, are inscribed in the mirror. Lines, unending lines, crisscross the Japanese countryside at this time of year, turning it into an abstract design. If one travels by train and concentrates for a while on the fields spinning by along the track, one's head, too, soon begins to spin.

The rice field brings us to the sturdy ideographic family of squares. *Ta* (田), "field," is one of the few clearly realistic ideograms to have survived millennia of evolution and change. There it stands in its elemental simplicity, together with many other forms that are totally unrelated etymologically, but that are all part of an exceedingly clannish reunion. Here are *kuchi* (口), "mouth," and *mawaru* (回), "to turn"—ideograms with an Assyrian solidity. Once upon a time the ideogram for *kuni*, "country," was written 國, elegantly uniting an interior rhythm with a feeling of protected unity; now the more brutal form (国) has been adopted, with much aesthetic loss I fear.

The square world develops formally into all sorts of directions. Small mouths combine to form *shina* (品), "thing," and cluster into the delightful *utsuwa* (器), "container." Sophisticated rhythms appear in *A* (亜), used phonetically, *MEN* (面), "face," and *omi* (臣), "minister." *Deko* (凸) and *boko* (凹) are very much two hippies, although they belong to the square class of ideograms. I remember visiting a small temple in Shikoku, called Deko-boko-ji, which turned out to be a sex museum; *deko* and *boko* suddenly became hilariously relevant concrete abstractions.

The square world takes us into the very heart of Japan, to some of its most exquisite formal refinements: stones set in a carpet of moss at Katsura (*189*), awaiting the bare feet of a goddess; an *obi* (*190*), perhaps inspired by a famous chequered motif on the *shōji* of a tea hut in the Katsura garden; the lone square stone in the Ryōan-ji garden (*191*); the small windows used for ornamentation and observation in the walls of Himeji Castle (*193*); or a square *tate* screen at the entrance of the Sanzen temple near Kyoto (*192*); or just a simple *futon* put out of the window to air in a village of Hokkaido (*194*). Squares may be flattened to rectangles and compose a motif of Palladian elegance in one of the stairways of the Imperial Palace (Gosho) in Kyoto (*188*).

Lines meeting, crossing, tiers of lines, counterpoints of lines, families of rectangles and squares— we are deep in the ideographic forest, and in the living tissue of Japanese life at the same time. I will just mention a few ideograms as representative. Here is *KA* (華), "flower," incidentally the very ideogram used by the Chinese when they name their country "The Middle Flower." It is a subtle but peremptory statement in lines, with its long, slender stem. Here is *yutaka* (豊), "abundant, rich, fruitful," somehow suggesting a stylized vase full of ears of corn or flowers. Here is *wa* (輪), "wheel," and *aganau* (購), "to buy," both magnificent constructions, powerfully welded into an iron skeleton, like the frames of skyscrapers. Space is here slashed into minute fragments with merciless precision.

Space is similarly disciplined with elegant sobriety around plate, chopsticks, dish, bowl, and cup, on a tray with the evening meal in a Japanese restaurant (*196*). Only the ideographic eye could have suggested to some unknown artist the perfect design of lacquered trays that fit one into

田　口　回　國　国　品　器　亜　面　臣　凸
ta　kuchi　mawaru　kuni　kuni　shina　utsuwa　A　MEN　omi　deko

the other to form an interlocking unit (*197*). The same need for precision seems to dictate the strokes of *tsutsushimu* (謹), "to respect," or *kōjiru* (講), "to lecture." Even the painted drums of a ceiling in Kyoto's Nishi Hongan-ji (*195*), with all their flow of silken scarves, fall neatly into a frame of squares.

A growing complexity leads us to asymmetric, dynamic ideograms—ones that whirl, jump, swim, sprout, and seem to carry our whole body along in a sudden desire to dance. How far away seems the static territory of straight lines, vertical or horizontal, of squares and their relatives. It is like discovering a new dimension to reality and experience. Take, for instance, *hikari* (光), "light," a firework of lines darting out from an imaginary center (see page 62); take that fascinating tower of stratified levels, interrupted by flying dots and darts, that is the castle of *ai* (愛), "love"; take the simple, flowing tent of *kaze* (風), "wind," or the splashing ebullience of *umi* (海), "sea." It is curious that so many of these asymmetric, dancing, mobile, fluid characters have meanings that are entirely consonant with their formal structures. Is it mere chance?

Japanese life all around us is rich in the flowing lines of things that swim in the wind, like the colored flags set up for a festive day in the north, as it is rich in animals that swim in lakes or in the sea. The wind makes flags flutter, but it also carves rocks into myriads of eyes. Roads flow and repeat the silvery curves of mysterious fish from the depths; fields flow and repeat the furrows of rocks that tell the story of our planet in millions of years. Years flow through trees and leave lines on wood; blizzards pass over snow and trace designs; insects, too, eat designs into the old statues of a temple. Waves, immense waves, threaten a miserable boat which is finally saved by the grace of Kompira-sama, as we can surmise from the *ema* ("votive painting") the captain offered on his safe return to land (*200–213*).

We have seen that Japanese philosophy, even in its most archaic and intuitive stage, recognizes two opposite temperatures of the human spirit: the one calm and static (*nigi-mitama*), the other powerful, dynamic, stormy, and dangerous (*ara-mitama*). Also in the world of forms, provision is made for complexity, intricacy, knotty snarls of lines and shapes, as well as for simplicity. In the neat world of things Japanese, one generally finds that intricacy is circumscribed. It may be a *bonsai* ("dwarf tree"), looking a thousand years old, set in the immaculate space of a *tokonoma* ("alcove"); it may be a *mon*, "family crest," incorporating the tangled design of flowers, insects, monsters, or imaginary beings, and set off against the monochrome tint of a kimono. It may be an ancient rock laid down like a jewel in a small desert of carefully raked sand; it may be the snakelike branches of an old wisteria tree; or it may be a precious tapestry, a sculpture of dragons. Here, too, we shall be led back to nature, to the ultimate foundation of mandala Japan; to roots in the forest of Kurama or to roots emerging from the carpet of moss in the Ryōan-ji garden, like a dinosaurus slowly waking from his aeon-long sleep, or to the contorted branches of an old pine tree (*220–26*).

Dragons have their rightful privileged place in art, legend, myth, theatre, in folk dances, in festivals, and among the ideographic signs. Tension is most simply and splendidly evoked by

凹　華　豊　輪　購　謹　講　光　愛　風　海
boko　hana　yutaka　wa　aganau　tsutsushimu　kojiru　hikari　ai　kaze　umi

yumi (弓), "bow," or by *hiku* (引), "to pull" (a bow with its string), but it reaches a full balance of thrust and weight combined in the most beautiful of all signs, *tatsu* (龍)—the dragon himself, now lamentably demoted to 竜, which looks like a scorpion.

With the dragon sign we are near the level of maximum circumscribed complexity. Lines crisscross, mince space into a salad of shapes, creating delicate, uncertain, explosive balances. Sweeping strokes of great force and structural meaning are united with pedantic games of pointillism. A great number of ideograms are found at this level. Many are—let us admit it—not very successful, and some are downright ugly. Take, for instance, *uruwashii* (麗), which ironically means beautiful. It is disorderly—heavy on top without being either light or strong at its base; it has no center and at the same time is not asymmetrically dynamic. Take *kisoi* (競), "competition," with its childish repetition, the "two men running." Many are just complicated, fat ideograms that have overeaten themselves into a ponderous, middle-aged, tottering mechanism clumsily put together, reminding us of some old car or some prehistoric expresso coffee machine.

But others are superbly integrated, wonders of mechanical precision. One can imagine them as three-dimensional objects, things to be held in the hand as abstract sculptures, to be admired for hours without ever becoming tiresome. For instance, *oru* (織), "to weave" which seems to weave space into a brocade of lines, subtly and harmoniously related. Or *kura* (蔵), "storehouse, treasure house," a tracery of lines and balanced spacings, suggesting the work of goldsmiths; or *hata* (機), "loom," now used for machines in general, a sign that transmits straight to one's fingers the interlocked complex of cogwheels, shafts, and gears. *Kusamura* (叢), "bush," is an admirable counterpoint of space and lines. The enormous hat above and the powerful base below are joined by the wasplike waist of a bare shaft in the midle. Here again meaning and form have nothing to do with each other. This well-balanced sign ought to stand for some scientific concept or some ingenious apparatus, for some jewel, or at least for a potent philter. Nothing ever looked less bushlike, more orderly and mathematical. If I had invented it as a piece of abstract art, I would have called it *"Hommage à Euclide."*

May I confess a predilection for ideograms that are top-heavy? There is, for instance, that lovely thing *DŌ* (堂), "hall," with its impressive covering that looks like the strange thatched roof of an unknown architectural style. Or *odoroku* (驚), "to surprise," in which the entire framework is precariously balanced on the asymmetrical dots at its base; the slightest error and it will topple over disastrously. There is *imashimeru* (警), "to admonish," much more stable than *odoroku*. And there are *kusuri* (薬), "medicine," *nori* (憲), "law," and that delightful *ko* (子), which means both child and female, carrying in its slender simplicity all sorts of secret, endearing messages.

Top-heavy ideograms, standing on their feet as if ready to be picked, give one the same feeling of power and poise as a large bird perched on a roof ready to take off and fly *(228)*. They also make one think of flowers in a vase, like the seven herbs of autumn set on a dais in front of an open window in honor of the September moon, the most beautiful one of the year according to Japanese tradition *(230)*. Or they may remind us of the elaborate bracketing by means of which the eaves of a temple are supported *(229)*. And there is the human body in ritual and dance, balancing its weight on that slender, fascinating bundle of bone, sinew, and muscle—the ankle *(231, 233)*.

弓　引　龍　竜　麗　競　織　蔵　機　叢　堂　驚　警　薬　憲　子
yumi　*hiku*　*tatsu*　*tatsu*　*uruwashii*　*kisou*　*oru*　*kura*　*hata*　*kusamura*　*DŌ*　*odoroku*　*imashimeru*　*kusuri*　*nori*　*ko*

The ideogram *nagai* (永) and its brushstrokes.

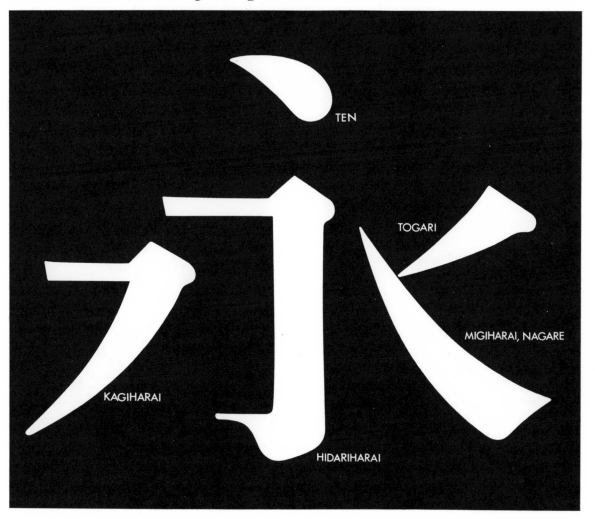

TEN

TOGARI

MIGIHARAI, NAGARE

KAGIHARAI

HIDARIHARAI

"Written boldly in four Chinese characters are the syllables *Sha-ka-mon-butsu*, the transliteration of the name of Śākyamuni Buddha. The signature beside it reads Ōbaku Ingen (or Huang-po Yin-yüan) and belongs to the Chinese monk Yin-yüan, who had come to Japan in 1655 .... This example by Yin-yüan, however modest in scale, is written with great vigor in the grass-writing style, when great liberties are taken with the basic structure of the characters. After writing the radical for *sha*, the first character, Yin-yüan recharged his brush with ink and then, in a single brilliant, uninterrupted stroke, wrote the rest of the *ka*. He then completed that character with two strokes, in the last of which the ink was depleted and left a dry-brush effect. He used the same method in joining the next two characters, *mon* and *butsu*." (Powers Collection, New York)

会 塔 企

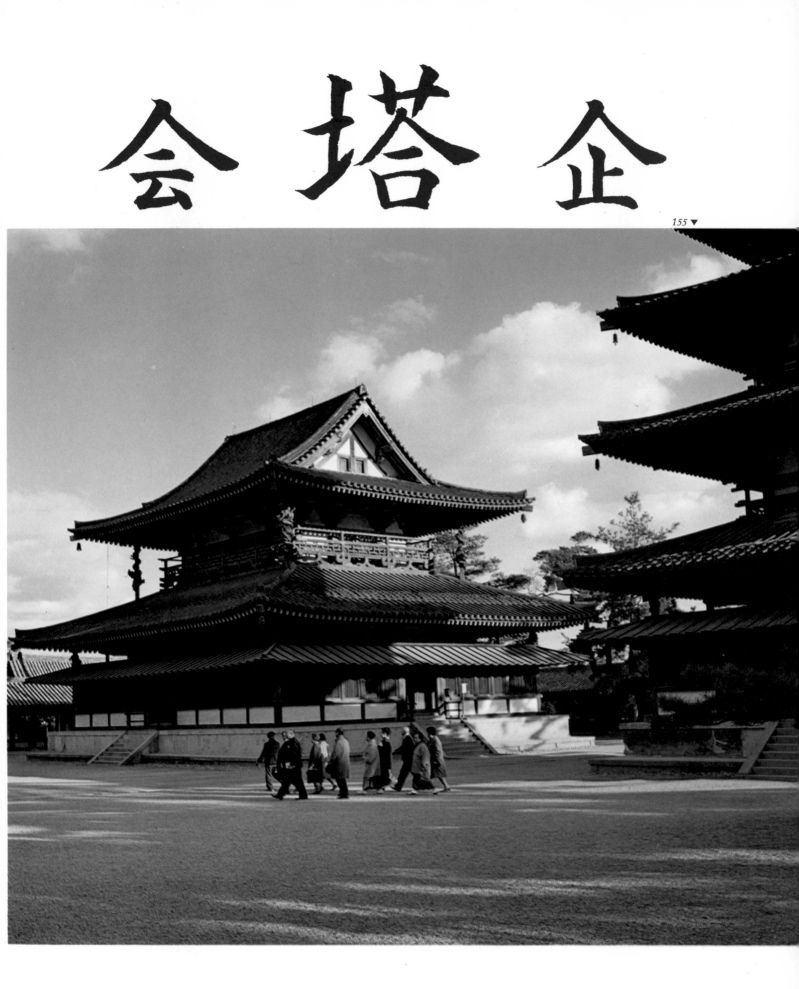

THE IDEOGRAPHIC SPACE

JAPAN

No civilization can develop an ideographic script without tremendous consequences. The formal richness and variety of characters provides innumerable visual centers of gravity towards which all sorts of lines, forms, rhythms, spacial relationships become irresistibly attracted. An ideographic universe is born. Ideograms send out tentacles and take possession of buildings, instruments, objects in daily use, decoration, clothing, fashion, gesture, taste, possibly even nature, through discrimination and elimination. In the Far East, one fundamental graphic device is what may be called the "pagodic"—two slanting lines forming a neat little roof as seen in 会 (*au*; "to meet") or in 企 (*kuwadateru*; "to plan"). Etymologically, this sign is not a roof, and its origins are varied, but graphically it appears distinctive and dominating.

Real etymological roofs (宀 冖 亠) are also dynamic molders of forms. 亭 (*TEI*; "pavilion") has all the grace of a small wooden building with a fanciful roof. In its cursive version it seems to echo the quivering reflections of water.

THE IDEOGRAPHIC SPACE

Japanese ideographic space is filled with pagodics. In architecture, they are lifted gloriously to the sky and given heroic proportions (*155, 156, 162*). Humbler pagodics may be noticed as the crowns of *ishi-dōrō* ("stone lanterns") in the precincts of temples and shrines or in gardens, for example the one standing beside the mountain path above Katsuo-ji at Mino-o (*160*). Many more important shrines, such as the Kasuga-jinja in Nara, have a prodigious range of lanterns, and hence

provide vast inventories of pagodics. The lone *torii* gateway in the open country of Okayama (*161*) is striking for its graceful line and for its fine old crossbeam.

The first ideogram of the maker's name on casks of saké wine offered to the gods at Kotohira Shrine in the island of Shikoku (*159*) is 金 (*KIN*; "gold"), which we might choose together with 舍 (*SHA*; "hut") and 釜 (*kama*; "kettle") as a sample of the constantly recurring pagodic line.

▲ 161

舍 釜

THE IDEOGRAPHIC SPACE

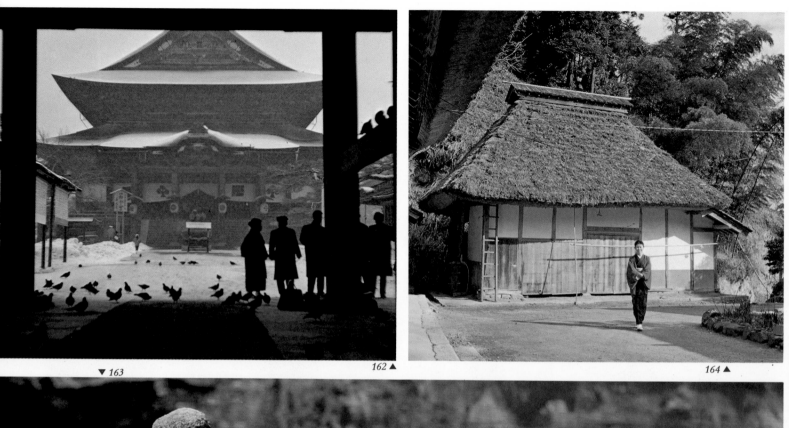

▼ 163   162 ▲   164 ▲

JAPAN

▲ 165

166 ▼

Snow falls silently on Zenkō-ji, a famous Buddhist temple in Nagano. High above the wintry desolation of the court, vast roofs embody a powerful pagodic thrust; down in the foreground, pigeons peck away at seeds thrown by visitors (*162*). *Tori*, "bird," usually written 鳥, may also be 禽, which by an amusing coincidence seems to reiterate the essential outlines of monumental Zenkō-ji. A similar, though less ponderous, pagodic line shapes the roof of a float in the Gion Festival procession, held every year in July in Kyoto (*166*).

傘 (*kasa*; "umbrella") can be designated a true pictograph. Its frank pagodic crown, as a locus of lines, allies the thatched roofs of a cottage near Yano, north of Hiroshima (*164*), the wide straw hats worn by *yamabushi* ("mountain hermits") during an esoteric fire ceremony in the Ryūan-ji, near Mino-o (*165*), and the delightful stone cap of a small lantern in the garden of the Katsura Villa (*163*).

◀ 168

JAPAN

169 ▲

Japan was once a country full of thatched roofs, those symbols of serenity and unpretentious warmth that we can still find covering the small Giō-ji near Kyoto (*167*), the gateway to Kyoto's Hōnen-in (*168*), or some of the cottages in the countryside (*169*). Now they are being increasingly replaced with metal or, at best, blue and brown tiles. Soon perhaps, only some allusive pagodic ideograms will remind one of much vanished beauty.

THE IDEOGRAPHIC SPACE

▲ *170*

172▶

▼*171*

JAPAN

▲173

174▶

When the pagodic line starts to lose its outer curl, it becomes a mere shadow of itself. It may still appear playfully in a procession of umbrellas under the rain, as seen during the Sumiyoshi Festival (*171*), or it may confer a certain dignity on boards commemorating donations of a hundred thousand yen to Kotohira Shrine (*172*). But when we look at a pretty, dwarf azalea tree (*bonsai*) in full bloom, ready to be put out on a windowsill (*170*), the line has mislaid its special identity, and is converging toward the simple universal pyramid or cone of a volcano. A first ramble through Japanese ideographic scenery has thus led us back to Mount Fuji: from nature to art, from art to writing—and back to nature! An arrow on the road crossing the Hakone hills threatens to belittle the distant volcano (*173*); Fuji, however, manages to emerge triumphant from the greater threat of the host of factories and chimneys and pollution at Numazu on its south flank (*174*).

韮山三川

▲175

176▶

儒

THE IDEOGRAPHIC SPACE

▲179

◀180

お

▲181

182▶

瑞

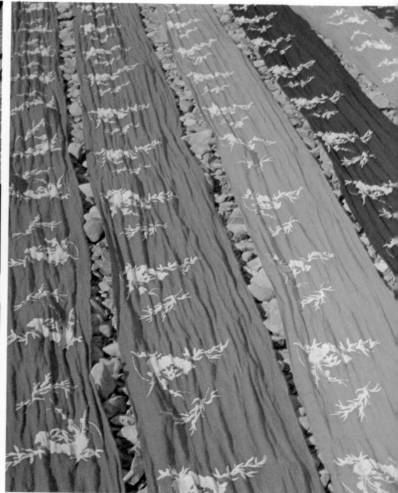

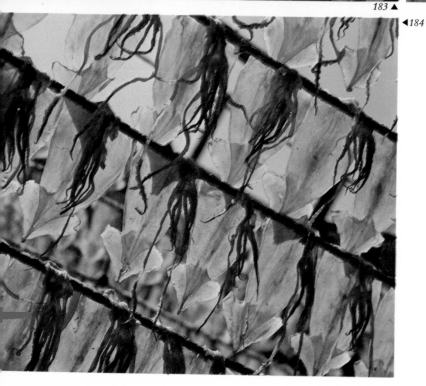

A gallant empire of lines extends all over Japan. Thin, precise parallels echo from the ideograms of river (川) and mountain (山) to the wooden gratings over Kyoto windows (177), from the battery of horizontal ribs of 韮 (nira; "leek") to the delicate tracery of sliding shōji panels in the home.   The vigorous linear statement of 儒 (JU; "Confucianism") reappears peremptorily in the iron-clad gates of Kyoto's Nijō Castle (176) and on the short gowns of palanquin bearers in the Gion Festival (175); in the same way, 瑞 (mizu; "freshness") harmonizes graphically, musically, and in meaning with the bridge over a pond in Ritsurin Park near Takamatsu (182), or with the gigantic body of a festival

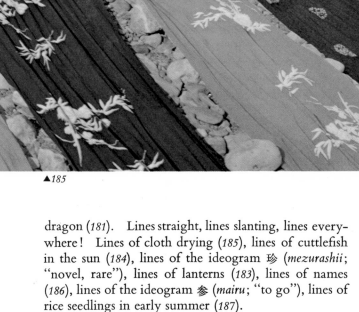

▲185

▲186

▲187

dragon (181). Lines straight, lines slanting, lines everywhere! Lines of cloth drying (185), lines of cuttlefish
in the sun (184), lines of the ideogram 珍 (mezurashii;
"novel, rare"), lines of lanterns (183), lines of names
(186), lines of the ideogram 参 (mairu; "to go"), lines of
rice seedlings in early summer (187).

As for circles, loops, rings, the *hiragana* alphabet provides an inexhaustible repertoire. The elegant and
rounded letters of *a* (あ) or *o* (お) and the syllables *no*
(の) or *nu* (ぬ) find a family atmosphere in the *mitsu-
domoe* emblems on the backs of *happi* coats (178),
among windows of a room (180), or stone basins for
lustral water (179).

▲188

口 回 国 田 固

亞 凸 凹 品 器

JAPAN

The square world is masculine, objective, orderly. Hesitancy, doubts, deviousness are forbidden. These are fundamental blocks of space, atoms of formal discipline! Mondrian, one dares to think, would have approved of the wooden stairs of the Imperial Palace in Kyoto, rising in a white reiteration of rectangles, seemingly suspended in a void (*188*). He might also have liked the stepping stones set in moss in the garden of Katsura Villa (*189*), or a *futon* quilt put out to air in the sun of Hokkaido (*194*); and surely he would have been enthusiastic for the window loopholes of Himeji Castle (*193*). The bold check motif in the *obi* of a girl in Kyoto (*190*) recalls some elementary ideographic ideas: 田 (*ta*; "field"), 器 (*utsuwa*; "container") and, on a more sophisticated level, 畳 (*tatami*; "mat") or 画 (*GA*; "picture"). A small standing screen in Sanzen-in near Kyoto (*192*) or a stone from the Ryōan-ji garden (*191*) reminds us of other basic ideograms in the square family: 口 (*kuchi*; "mouth"), 回 (*mawaru*; "to turn"), 国 (*kuni*; "country").

THE IDEOGRAPHIC SPACE

▲191

◄192

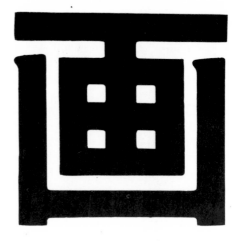

JAPAN

▲193

194 ▶

THE IDEOGRAPHIC SPACE

196 ▲

As squares meet circles and diagonals, the graphic complexity and beauty in Japanese life become apparent. A pleasing music of shapes, lines, textures, a subtle counterpoint of proportions may accompany as lowly a thing as a meal on a tray (196). Somewhere on parallel ideographic planes, a growing formal richness requires increased attention to the interplay of lines and intervals. The equilibrium of an ideographic edifice depends on the perfect balancing of stresses. 春 (*haru*; "spring") looks innocent enough, but if you try to write it, it reveals many delicate problems; it must stand solidly, yet it is not quite symmetrical. A closely related interest in delicate balances seems to have guided the hand of the artist who painted a ceiling with drums in Nishi Hongan-ji in Kyoto (195). Lacquered trays (197) in the cavernous kitchen of Hōkō-ji, north of Hamamatsu, interlock as neatly as the elements composing the orderly little ideographic cupboard of 興 (*okoru*; "to rise"). Cotton yarn drying in the sun (198) and a *shōji* sliding door (199) are familiar Japanese sights with a particularly linear flavor.

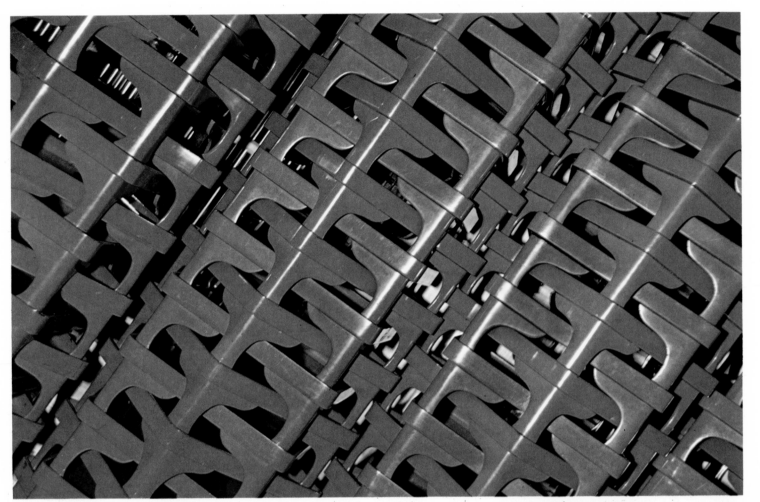

▲197

◀198

▲199

THE IDEOGRAPHIC SPACE

A major portion of life's flowing, dynamic richness would escape if ideograms were always written in the stiff, lapidary style called *kaisho*. However, long ago, on informal occasions, ideograms began to be written with a more cursive style. As calligraphy became freer and more personal, separate strokes fused into sinuous, sensitive lines, causing entire new chapters of graphic shapes to be created and finally enabling life, with all its magic and elusive fluidity, to be reflected in ideographic writing. The progressive simplifications and suppleness of 風 (*kaze*; "wind") seem to capture the essence of all that flows, flies, waves, swings, swims around us. Contact is established between writing and the long, gorgeously colored banners put up for the inauguration of a gasoline station near Sendai (*200*), the movements of live fish in a pond (*201*), the forms of dead fish in a basket (*202*), the light and shadow at the foot of a wooden *torii* pillar (*204*). Even rocks, etched by the wind (*203*) near Cape Ashizuri, seem akin to the fluid, rather than to the solid, family of forms.

THE IDEOGRAPHIC SPACE

205 ▲

◀ 206

愛媛

JAPAN

207 ▲

208 ▶

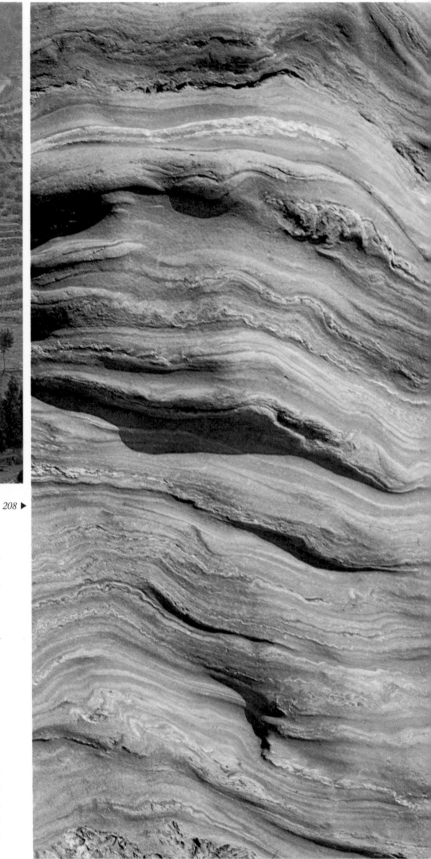

Ideographic fluidity is not exclusively the attribute of cursive writing. There are developments in the more formal and structurally obvious style that can be deeply evocative, abstractly symbolic. The two characters opposite this page, 愛 (*ai*; "love") and 媛 (*hime*; "princess"), suggest flow and movement not by formal and literal statement, nor by meaning, but through delicate balances in asymmetry, through the harmonious interplay of slants and gently curving lines that taper into nothing. Both characters have more than one center out of which lines gush and dots explode and fly. There are legs posed as if in a dance, and scarves that threaten to whirl off in the ideographic wind.

The two signs (in this case read *Ehime*) happen to compose the name of a distant and still partly unspoilt region of the island of Shikoku, where the flowing highway (*205*), the flowing terraced rice fields (*207*), the flowing lines of silvery fish (*206*) and of green monolithic rock (*208*) were seen and admired.

THE IDEOGRAPHIC SPACE

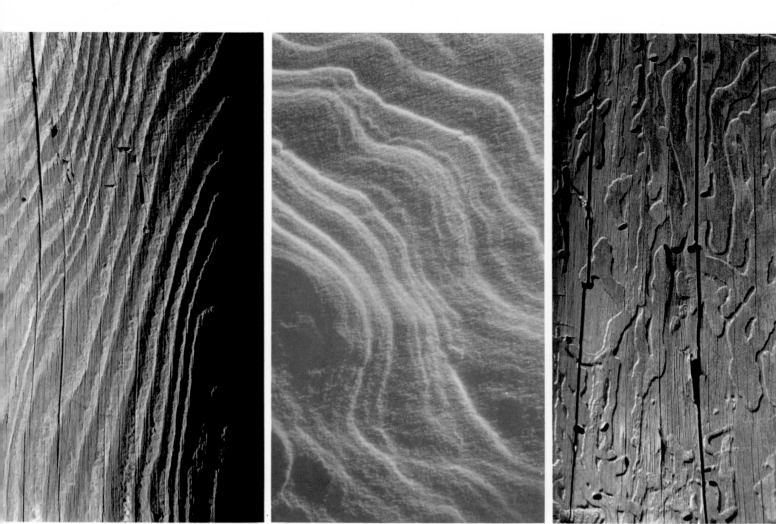

209 ▲ ▲ 210　　　　　　　　　　　　▲ 211

The word hair has recently acquired heavy sexual connotations by being the title of a much-banned play. Perhaps hair as wave and current, the hair of Leonardo da Vinci's sketches, in which it gradually merges into dreams of water, is nearer to nature—to the veins of wood in the pillar of an ancient temple (209) or in a door in Kyoto (214), to the traces of wind on the snow on Mount Fuji (210), even to the burrowings of bugs in the back of an old Buddha (211). The ideogram 髪 (kami; "hair") is a delightful edifice—asymmetric, polycentric, elegant and powerful, happy and jocular, with feathers, streamers, windsocks flying, the whole poised on light feet striding the wind. It captures the essence of hair without prosaically reproducing the appearance of hair. It seems to epitomize all looping, flowing things, from the magically colored fields of Asuka in early spring (212) to the frightful billows out of which some sailors must have once been saved since in gratitude they presented this picture of the ordeal to the god of Kotohira Shrine (213).

▲ 212   213 ▼   ▼ 214

THE IDEOGRAPHIC SPACE

217 ▲

豊 勢

◄ 215
◄ 216

Two splendid characters, 豊 (*yutaka, toyo*; "abundant, rich, fertile") and 勢 (*ikioi*; "vigor, energy"), have a more sophisticated graphic complexity. *Yutaka* is thought to have originated in China as the picture of a sacrificial vessel in which is placed "a bunch of green branches for decoration; symbol of plenty" (L. Wieger). The ideogram rises from its base as a solid tower of strokes developing and spreading to reveal a counterpoint of intervals and repetitions up to its final terrace. Abundance in food may be represented here by succulent seaweed (*konbu*) drying in the sun at Nemuro (*216*); abundance in goods, by lengths of cotton and silk waving in the wind along the Katsura river near Kyoto (*217*). *Toyo* is a word much cherished for names of places, people, shrines, and gods. It fully expresses the Japanese commitment to this life as the ultimate reality.

势 勢

Ikioi has the dynamics of asymmetry. The head-gear of Gothic intricacy is supported by a puny base, and it makes one think of those Renaissance coats of arms in which a small escutcheon is proudly surmounted by a towering helmet with its lambrequin and crest of feathers. *Ikioi* as a concept conveys Japanese optimistic vitalism, reflected so brilliantly and colorfully in the cotton carps raised in the spring breeze to celebrate the Boy's Festival in May (*215*). Carps embody *ikioi*; they swim against the current in rivers and even leap up waterfalls. Japanese festivals are full of *ikioi*: a youth leads a procession, brandishing a flamelike trophy of wood and paper (*219*), or a group of young men in red cloaks drum evil away during the Imamiya-sai at Kyoto in April (*220*). Even the mysterious old *yamabushi* hermits and shamans, lighting a *goma* fire in the mountains, are seeking secret, magical forms of *ikioi* (*218*).

THE IDEOGRAPHIC SPACE

◀ 221

222 ▲

Tension is muscularly expressed by 弓 (*yumi*; "bow"); and tension, contortion, and mystery by 龍 (*tatsu*; "dragon"). The unpredictably dangerous and beneficial genie of Far Eastern myths haunts nature, painting, sculpture, embroidery, language, and plunges into calligraphy with an entire radical of his own (the two hundred and twelfth), a majestic monogram with contracted scales, wings, snakelike body. The sign stands gloriously on its own merits as a monumental abstract statement of power, dignity, fury, and cunning, in spite of its literal pictorial aspects. Dragons often appear carved in wooden panels, such as this one from Zempō-ji near Yuatsumi (*224*), but the menacing creatures in the tapestries put out for the Gion Festival in Kyoto (*221*) are probably Chinese. Dragons seem to have become part of the forest among the *sugi* trees above Kurama (*223*), and a pine tree in the garden of an old samurai's house near Daikaku-ji in Kyoto has been pruned to form a seething nest of snakes in the sky (*222*).

▲ 223

▲ 224

▲ 225

Fuji, the wisteria vine, is memorable in all seasons, even when its indolent, leafless branches droop toward somber waters from the trellis of an old stone bridge in Kyoto's Sentō Gosho Imperial garden on a misty autumn day (225). Something feminine, elegant, withdrawn, permeates both the creeper and its ideographic statement. As a formal stylization, the ideogram 藤, with its shower of dots and interwoven lines, evokes the clean fragrance of the spring blossom; as a cursive series of loops it bears ready comparison with the twisting convolutions of the leafless tendrils. Moss, as it is in the Ryōan-ji garden (227), and an ancient potted juniper tree (226) seem to promise us further revelations about jealously guarded secrets of Japanese beauty.

JAPAN

▲ 226

藤蔓

▼ 227

With 構 (*kamae*; "construction") we return to solid male objects in the sun. Space is apportioned with competence and nicety. Lines are riveted into miniature palaces according to the highest professional standards of ideographic joinery. There is also what seems like solid etymological backing: the right part of the sign, L. Wieger tells us, "is a primitive whose straight and crossed lines represent graphically the timbers in the framework of a house, as they interlock and cross each other; hence the idea of a network, an ordering, a combination." Exactly this can be seen in the wooden

 230

構筆

masugumi eaves of a Buddhist temple near Matsue (*229*)! Construction in Japan (a civilization of wood) is rarely heavy and massive. There are always light and elegant touches, for instance a phoenix that is perching on the highest gable of the roof of Byōdō-in at Uji (*228*), or the offering of flowers, wine, and fruit to the September moon, on the doorstep of a home near Osaka (*230*).

Incisive graphic entities, slim and long-stemmed, rise in the ideographic air like the phoenix or expand like the bunch of flowers. 華 (*hana*; "flower") is a prince of this class, as are 筆 (*fude*; "brush") and 葦 (*ashi*; "reed").

THE IDEOGRAPHIC SPACE

▲ 231

◄ 232

The characters on the previous page lead us to the human body in movement; just as they confidently bear elaborate crowns on their tapering stems, the girls in the *Awa-odori* (that collective madness that takes hold of the city of Tokushima every August) gracefully balance a continuously shifting weight on the tips of their sandals (*233*). However, there are even more baroque and alarming constructions, such as 驚 (*odoroku*; "to surprise"), where the entire framework of strokes is precariously poised on the fragile dots at its base; the slightest error in graphic etiquette and it would topple over disastrously—exactly as might happen to the pretty *maiko*, in Kyoto's famed Gion quarter, when she ventures out on her high wooden clogs (*231*). The bizarre headdress of a beauty, ceremoniously holding rice seedlings before her (*232*), seems neatly transposed by 叢 (*kusamura*; "bush"), shown on the following page. Here, too, a hat that is almost grotesque is joined to the brocaded, bosomed body by the sensuous neck of one neat, downward stroke of the brush.

THE IDEOGRAPHIC SPACE

▲ 234

236 ▲

◀ 235

The curious flowering of paper horoscopes tied to branches around temples and shrines all over Japan (235) or the offerings of *sembazuru* ("thousand cranes") of folded paper (236) testify to the constant human hope of penetrating the veil of mystery that hides ultimate meanings. The blossoming cherry trees, as seen here in the garden of Kyoto's famous Tenryū-ji, near Arashiyama, (234) are often considered by Japanese poets to mark, in a particularly poignant fashion, the fateful passing of time.

4

THE FUTURE
of
THE PAST

EVERYBODY is aware of Japan's success story in the modern world: from hermit nation to *Troisième Grand* in one century.

At this point it is always effective to mention statistics, and I would love to give pages full of them, but with Japan it soon becomes quite hopeless. The latest information concerning the production of steel, cement, ships, television sets, pianos, or toys is invariably and immediately superseded by a newer and more impressive table of data. Statistics in the case of Japan should be conveyed by something more dynamic than the old-fashioned printed word—perhaps a moving graph transmitted by television.

This very impossibility of obtaining a well-focused image of Japan's advance on paper may be the final and most impressive result of all. We are confronted with the metabolism of a bamboo sprout visibly growing under our noses. The question now is: will the bamboo behave like Jack's beanstalk? Will it turn into an unheard of cross between a bamboo and a sequoia? Will it find a more normal maturity? Will it perhaps explode? Or collapse under its own weight? Or is it going to disappear beneath the mountains of its own discarded slag and dross, poisoned to death by its own pollution?

Professor Herman Kahn of the Hudson Institute[1] and Hakan Hedberg[2] are keen proclaimers of the theory that sees the Japanese bamboo becoming a great twenty-first century sequoia. They periodically startle the world—and the Japanese themselves—with predictions both awesome and splendid, which are extrapolations from the curves of the growth of Japan's economy. They may be right or they may be wrong. If, however, by some chance, the twenty-first century does become the "Japanese century," statistics will only be the outward manifestation, the most superficial symptom of a passionately interesting feat of human achievement. It will then be rewarding to examine not so much what happened to things and money, but what took place in the secret gardens of human ideas and emotions, in the soil from which the sequoia took its nourishing saps.

---

[1] See Herman Kahn, *The Emerging Japanese Superstate* (New York: Prentice-Hall, 1970).
[2] See Hakan Hedberg, *Le Défi Japonais* (Paris: Denoël, 1970).

If looking ahead towards Japan's future has the thrill of great expectations, looking back towards Japan's modern and modest origins strikes one with an impact of wonder and delight. It is like reading the biography of some collective Ford or Matsushita, starting off to build their business empires on fifty dollars' capital. It was only yesterday really, in March 1860, that the seventy-seven samurai of Japan's first embassy to the United States happened to pass the night in a hotel in San Francisco, California. "The beds were always left in the room," noted one of the party in great astonishment, probably remembering the way his womenfolk put away carefully every morning the *futon* on which the family had slept during the night. And there was more about this matter. "One of my friends," went on the diarist, "who could not find the pillow, though he searched the room, found a clean white jar under the bed, which he used as a pillow and was happy. As it was hard, he slept well."[3] The robust samurai, used to supporting his neck on a small, solid pillow of compressed rice chaff, found the chamberpot an excellent substitute!

In 1856, the American, Townsend Harris, and his Dutch assistant, Henry Heusken, landed in the little port of Shimoda, on the southern point of the Izu peninsula, to settle there and open the first foreign consulate on the soil of Japan. The nearest equivalent to a Foreign Ministry at that time was a Committee for Maritime Defense, a rather minor branch of the Tokugawa *Bakufu* ("Military Government"). An interminable exchange of letters seems to have taken place between the local authorities in Shimoda and their senior officers in the capital, Edo (Tokyo), concerning such matters as: permits for the Americans to keep a cow (originally refused), a license to lodge a courtesan in their home (granted), permission to handle local currency (at first refused and later granted). Reading the diaries of Harris and Heusken today, we feel we are setting foot on another planet rather than entering a world that is barely more than a century past.

How did such a rapid, incredible, miraculous transformation occur from *that* Japan to *this* Japan? Explanations can range anywhere between two extreme propositions. On the one hand is found the simple, and rather naive, theory of pure Westernization, according to which Japan has reached its present position of material and cultural advancement simply by copying the West. The course of Japan's development, during the last hundred years or so, is seen as a very active and earnest job of adaptation not only of gadgetry and technology but also of science, law, education, styles of art, theories and principles of literature, forms of music, sports, the calendar, measurements, manners, customs, fashions—in short, practically everything except the alphabet and religion. The West, it is implied, has its own unchangeable course, like a majestic river indifferent to small undulations of the surrounding countryside; it must be considered a cultural absolute, in fact Culture itself. The process of Westernization may thus consist in the progressive approach to, and eventual identification with, this central axis of human advance.

The opposite extreme is represented by theories, such as the one advocated by Professor Umesao Tadao, that consider Japan's modern century to be the result of an "autonomous process merely paralleling modernization in the West,"[4] something to be explained entirely in native terms.

In between fall all other theories—and they are infinite in number—which combine the influence of the West with indigenous development in relationships of varying reciprocal impor-

---

[3] J. Fukuyama and R. H. Jackson, translators, *The First Japanese Mission to America (1860)* (New York: F. A. Stokes, 1938), p. 24.

[4] Tadao Umesao, *Bummei no Seitai Shikan* ("Introduction to an Ecological View of the History of Civilization") (Tokyo: Chūō Kōron, 1957), pp. 32–49.

tance.   Here, in an entirely different context, we may find repeated that historic debate between the supporters of heredity and those of environment as an essential factor in biological evolution.

The success of Japan in the modern world is not due to any great endowment either from the gods or from "the eight myriad *kami*" as regards land and natural resources.   It has been observed many times that Japan, with an area the same as California, must find space for a population five times as large.   Moreover, most of the country is mountainous, and barely fifteen to twenty percent of it can be used for cultivation and settlement.   A country of this sort is expected to make a decent living perhaps, but not to become the subject of a spectacular success story.

The reasons why the United States or Russia occupy their respective positions in today's world are easy to understand: both these countries spread over the breadth of an entire continent; both are endowed with every imaginable natural resource; both have a population that is large enough to ensure development, but that is not gigantic or unwieldy.   As for the runner-up, if it were China, India, Brazil, Germany, South Africa, or Indonesia, there would be some geographical sense in the situation.   In the case of Japan, one is flabbergasted.   Is this "an ugly fact that spoils a beautiful theory," or is it the beautiful fact that lays a lot of ugly theories to rest?   However one looks at it, Japan's success story is foremost a story of human achievement and one that must be explained in human terms.

What is meant exactly by Westernization?   Essentially, I would say, the acceptance of the values and ideals of the West, not merely of technology and science.   In this sense Westernization is a convergence towards Western ways of thinking, towards a Western outlook on life and on the world.   Modernization, on the other hand, involves, more than anything else, the adoption of technology, which is ideologically neutral.   A plane can take Reds to Rabat, or a pope to Pago-Pago; a newspaper can print exhortations to world revolution, or prayers for world peace—indifferently; neon tubes can be twisted into hammer and sickle signs, crosses, stars of David, commercial advertisements, or political slogans.   In fact, modernization may strengthen local traditions or ideologies and become a powerful force resisting or opposing Westernization.   A typical example is the way the caste system in India has grown stronger in recent years, owing to the skillful use of mass media by sectional politicians.   The Meiji leaders understood this very well when they preached the idea of *wakon-yōsai* ("Japanese spirit and Western technology").   The whole development of the early Showa years up to World War II took place with modernization acting in what was fundamentally an anti-Western spirit.   Looking at the Far East, it may be postulated that, while Japan is more modernized than Westernized, the Philippines are more Westernized than modernized.   Accepting a religion deeply imbued with Western thought and values, as the Philippines have done with Catholicism, has opened the very core of local civilization to structural change and made it draw significantly closer to the West.

In considering Japan's modern century, one certainly cannot exclude Westernization, and I am not thinking of it only as a stimulant but as a vast process by which innumerable objects, techniques, words, ideas, values, and attitudes have been taken over and incorporated into the Japanese

177

way of life. It is often extremely difficult to say where Westernization ends and modernization takes over, or vice versa. Inventions, such as printing, the radio, television, the car, the steam engine, penicillin, atomic power, are entirely neutral: their adoption and diffusion is pure modernization. On the other hand, when scholars of the early Meiji period concocted the word *kenri* to express the concept of right (traditional Japanese thought lacked the idea and the word), or when the philosopher Nishi Amane adopted the term *tetsugaku* for philosophy as distinct from knowledge or wisdom, they were both performing acts of genuine Westernization.[5] Wearing trousers instead of *kimono* or *hakama* looks very much like an act of Westernization, but it is not necessarily one at all. Many a fiercely anti-Western thought has been conceived beneath a bowler hat, or by gentlemen sitting in armchairs and wearing Saville Row suits.

Let us look at things the other way round. Does a Westerner suddenly feel his eyes assuming an almond shape and his thoughts becoming Buddhist simply because he drinks tea? Does he think of himself as Ethiopian because he sips coffee, or Red Indian because he smokes tobacco, Chinese because he writes on paper, Inca because he eats potatoes and tomatoes? In practice, material acquisitions are absorbed immediately and easily into any culture, and soon lose all reference to their origin. Coca-Cola's Americanizing influence seems an exception. But "Cocacolonization" is not due to the actual drink but to some of the advertising that goes with it, to the pictures, the slogans, the apparatus that accompanies the liquid and acts on a purely ideological level: those glorious, blond, tennis-playing girls, those young couples relaxing near a swimming pool! Here is a whole bible of Americana making its way through the eyes into the softer parts of the soul, the real "Cocacolonizable" parts.

Even at this level, however, nearer to what is considered the core of man—his spirit—it is easy to notice how all sorts of habits can be absorbed with the greatest aplomb. *Il calcio* ("football") is the national sport of present-day Italians, but not one in a million of the Sunday *tifosi* ("fans") ever stops to reflect on its British origins; in Japan the same can be said about baseball, which has become *yakyū* ("field ball"), or golf—that most important status symbol. Skiing may have originated in Norway, but it has become totally indigenous to the Alps and to other mountain regions of the world. It takes a fanatical racist to remember that jazz was originally a form of negro music, or a very staunch adversary of *les anglo-saxons* to object on seeing Christmas celebrated with a decorated tree instead of a *presepio*—the traditional Mediterranean manger with ox and donkey.

Most cultures, especially if vigorous, can stand an enormous amount of battering and can absorb a seemingly endless flow of intrusions from outside without losing much of their objective identity, and, what is more, without its members feeling aware of any loss of their own identity. There probably exists a limit beyond which cultural identity is finally shattered, either because of fusion with another culture or through sheer chaos and disintegration. This may be the case with small, primitive ethnic groups, such as the Australian aborigines, some of the American Indians, and to some extent the Ainu. Such a situation does not apply, even remotely, to the Japanese. Their ethnic and cultural identity is vigorously, often aggressively, asserted in every imaginable field. There may have been periods of spiritual bewilderment—after 1870, and after 1945—but they were very brief.

---

[5] See G. B. Sansom, *The Western World and Japan* (New York: Knopf, 1950), p. 472, and Gino K. Piovesana, *Recent Japanese Philosophical Thought: 1862–1962* (Tokyo: Sophia University, 1968), p. 41.

A Japanese feels entirely and unequivocally himself, though he may sleep on a bed (and not between *futon*); though he may walk on the carpets of an apartment in a many-storied building of steel, concrete, and glass (instead of on the *tatami* matting of a small one-family house of wood, paper, and straw); though he eats cornflakes, eggs and bacon, sips milk and coffee for breakfast (instead of *miso* soup, rice, pickles, and fish); though he slices a beefsteak for lunch and has a French, American, or Italian dinner (instead of *tempura*, *sushi*, *sukiyaki* or mixed fare of fish, both raw and cooked, vegetables, and pickles).   Wearing a Western suit (*sebiro*) as we have seen, playing golf, going to cocktails—all are habits that have practically no effect on the basic sense of identity.

The most alarming object in the domestic scene is that simple, sometimes vaguely ridiculous piece of furniture—the chair.   The entire concept of interior space is upset by the mere fact of raising the level at which one works or eats a foot higher; aesthetics must be entirely revised with such a change in the level of viewing things.   Furthermore, chairs chase away *tatami*, which they would break through with their legs, and shoes have come into the house.   Chairs effect positions of the body, and in the long run they influence growth and anatomy, movements and habits. Professor C. P. Fitzgerald has shown, with delightful erudition, how the introduction of the chair in China during the early Sung dynasty not only modified Chinese domestic life but had a profound effect on Chinese architecture and arts.[6]   Something similar is taking place now in Japan. There is no reason, however, to think that this revolution, which did not disturb the stability of Chinese civilization, will really affect the Japanese ethnic identity.   The Turks have been able to absorb a much more drastic change—the substitution of the Arabic alphabet for Roman letters.

The Japanese are taking Western marriage customs in their stride with the greatest ease—white veils, the wedding march, orange blossoms.   When one considers that many such marriages were probably arranged by the families according to the traditional *miai* custom, one sees the ceremony not as a case of Westernization, but as the adoption of a form of technology, the social technology of uniting a man and a woman.   The Japanese are absorbing Christmas too—perhaps as an aspect of the technology of salesmanship?

There are photographs of Mishima Yukio—the arch *bushidō* hero, neo-samurai, emperor-worshiper—taken in his home in which he looks exactly like a rather well-to-do British squire, or Bostonian aristocrat, sitting on a sofa under pictures of schooners in full sail, with a pipe in his hand, and a bottle of whiskey on the mantlepiece nearby.

On the other hand, why should this appear strange?   Has anyone ever felt it bewildering to notice that a German, a Russian, an Italian, lives more or less as English-speaking people do, at least in the outward fixtures of their daily lives?   One may answer that Western uniformity has been achieved for centuries, goes deeper and is therefore taken for granted, while Japanese conformity to Western standards is something recent, rather startling and still in progress, though very far advanced in most instances.   A Japanese friend once told me, "Now that we are really alike, we can start being different!"   There is much truth in this.   The Westernization-modernization process levels off a lot of details of our daily lives (clothing, home, food, transportation, work,

179

---

[6] See C. P. Fitzgerald, *Barbarian Beds: the Origin of the Chair in China* (London: Cresset Press, 1965).

amusements, fashions, sports), which may seem very important but evidently have much less weight than is usually imagined. Once uniformity has been reached, then the fundamental and meaningful differences may become manifest.

⸻

Shall we then be forced to conclude that the entire cultural process that has taken place in Japan during this last century or so has been exclusively one of modernization? Definitely not. There has been a lot of genuine and subtle, often unconscious and therefore deeper, Westernization, just as there has been and there is in progress a lot of subtle Easternization of the West.

However, it is not easy to pin cases down. It occurs to many that the remarkably successful adoption of a substantially democratic system of government may be mentioned as a good example of genuine Westernization. There is a lot of truth in this; on closer examination, however, one soon finds out that the Japanese version of democracy is very different from what goes under this name in countries with British and American traditions. The way factions maneuver to stay in power, the relationship between individuals and groups, the eternal search for compromise solutions to avoid a so-called tyranny of the majority reveal that democracy has been very much Japanized, rather than Japan having turned genuinely democratic. Apart from this, democracy in a wider sense of the word is only partially a new importation. Provided that a certain degree of deference is maintained by the *shimo* (the lower orders) when dealing with the *kami* (the higher orders), collaboration between different sections of the population, which is the essence of a democracy, appears to be something as old as the hills in Yamato.

Industry and commerce, fields in which a high degree of Westernization is often assumed, are not only very sparsely Westernized but may be considered important examples of a parallel tradition growing up next to the Western one and now showing its worth. A whole literature exists on this subject; some works are serious and valuable; others are facetious—and also valuable.

True Westernization of a very high level is more manifest among scholars, artists, and the intelligentsia in general. Here, of course, it is something extremely difficult to evaluate; we are dealing with intangibles, with a certain perfume of the personality, and indefinable hue—qualities that the instinct appreciates, but the mind cannot put into maps and formulae, partly because human beings change and develop continuously. When a student has grown up reading Western authors nearly exclusively, studying Western thought, pinning portraits of Descartes, Kant, Schopenhauer (abbreviated to *De-kan-shō* in an old school song), of Marx, Sartre, and Che above his desk, when he is constantly listening to the music of Bach, Vivaldi, Gershwin, and the Beatles, and looking at reproductions of works by Michelangelo, Leonardo da Vinci, Blake, Van Gogh, and Picasso, then there is no doubt a high degree of Westernization. This is all the more impressive when one remembers that a corresponding knowledge of Chinese and Indian classics, of Buddhism, Confucianism, of Khmer or T'ang art, may be virtually non-existent. The situation, however, does not usually produce any loss of identity, partly because it is general and partly because the foreign elements are subtly and immediately Japanized.

Sometimes one may frankly doubt if there is any real Westernization in this process. One starts thinking of some horrendous term, such as "mondialization," to express the essence of a totally new but very important process. Perhaps there is no genuine veering of the Japanese mind and spirit toward the West but only a slight movement towards a neutral territory, now in the nothingness of nowhere, which at some distant time in the future will take shape as a world culture. Such a culture, on becoming recognizable, will not be exclusively but only partly Western. The West, too, will have moved towards it from its own closed gardens of thought. There will be a polyphonic richness of many voices in what is now a mere point in space-time, rich only in potentialities.

If language is a mirror of thought, then there are many signs of a definite, though subtle, trend toward straight Westernization and toward a future, undefined world culture.

Many of the innumerable foreign expressions that drift in and out of modern Japanese have little importance. People may use *pāma* (for permanent hair wave), *karafuruna* for colorful, *hotto tsū* for two cups of hot coffee, *ankēto* for "opinion poll" (from the French *enquête*), *interi* for "intelligentsia," *teki* for "beefsteak," *sararīman* for "salary man," *betto* for "bed," *abekku* for "in the company of someone of the opposite sex" (from the French *avec*), *infure* for "inflation," with practically no aftereffects. They may coin new hybrids, such as *gebabō* (*gewalt-bō*, "power-stick," a German-Japanese combination for the sticks used by students when fighting the police), or *erodakushon* ("erotic film poduction"); they may turn simple beer into *o-bīru* ("honorable beer"); they may prefer "open" to the native *eigyōchū* — it is all part of a complex and changing world. Some modifications in grammar and style are perhaps more significant. "*Anata wa ima anzen-unten o shite imasuka?*" ("You, now, are you driving carefully?") says a sign with enormous ideograms, often seen along the roads. Here is a definite Western way of thinking in the use of the pronoun, the direct approach, the entire styling of the phrase.

The really momentous innovations have a deceptively Japanese look about them; they harmonize with the rest of the vocabulary. *Kenri* ("right") has been mentioned, but there are dozens of other such terms introducing Western concepts or Western ways of interpreting concepts, for instance *kakumei* ("revolution"), *shakai* ("society"), *keizai* ("economics"), *seisan* ("production"), *bōeki* ("trade"), *eisei* ("sanitation").[7]

In addition, new meanings are read into common, old words, and this is also significant. Typical, for example, is *kami*, employed to mean God—good old Western God, the Father, Creator, Judge, with beard and all. *Ai*, which used to mean love in the sense of parental affection, or charity, is now used as a natural and full translation of the Western "love," including much of *koi*, "passion." One may also think of *bijutsu* ("art"), *shizen* ("nature"), and many other abstract terms. Father J. Spae writes, "I am convinced that there is a remarkable linguistic evolution going on in this country due to the ever-growing acceptance of originally Christian meanings which penetrate irresistibly into Japanese parlance and literature."[8] I think he is perfectly right. Of course, there is also a corresponding influence of Buddhism on English, a fact that makes us look with hope toward some degree of spiritual exchange and enrichment in the future, not only to that one-way traffic that may seem desirable to missionary zeal.

The Western system of counting years (B.C. and A.D.) is slowly being adopted, especially in

181

[7] R. A. Miller, *The Japanese Language* (Chicago: University of Chicago Press, 1967), p. 261.
[8] Father J. J. Spae, *Japanese Religiosity* (Tokyo: Oriens, 1971), p. 204.

historical contexts. The former system of *nengō* (short periods, sometimes lasting only a year or two) is extremely inconvenient as soon as one goes back to the distant past. As in the case of Christmas, no particular connection with Christianity is implicit in this change. It is merely a case of *gōrika*, "rationalization."

A curious and unexpected detail is that Westernization seems particularly easy to detect in attitudes toward nudity and sex. Visitors to Japan before 1900 noticed everywhere a total innocence concerning the nude human form, both male and female. The reactions of these worthy Victorians or of their contemporary French, German, and American colleagues were always extreme. Sometimes they took the form of ecstatic admiration; more often they reflected a scandalized prudishness or outright horror.

Albert Tracy (*Rambles through Japan*: 1892)[9] describes with lyrical admiration an encounter with some girls who were evidently practicing *mizugori* (religious purification under a waterfall).

> The young women were actual types of beauty.... The sight of these living statues, with water streaming over them, against a background of dark rocks and green ferns and foliage of trees, was certainly, from an artistic point of view, exceedingly picturesque.... By turns they stepped lightly upon a block of stone under one or other waterfall; the long hair, loosened, was streaming down the back; the head was bowed; the hands clasped in attitude of prayer; the lips murmured the invocation; until suddenly, unable to endure the penance any longer, the light form sprang from beyond the reach of the cascade with a merry laugh, and another took her place. They seemed as all as unconscious of impropriety as so many water nymphs—in the fairy days before nymphs left this degenerate world.

Anne d'Aguilar (*A Lady's Visit to Japan*: 1863) was, on the contrary, very much disgusted by the "absurdly indecent scene" of a public bath.

> At the further end of the room... numbers of men and women were bathing *in puris naturalibus*. A thick vapour rose about them, and a strong sulphurous odour pervaded the place. They were dancing about as though half-mad. Whether this arose from sensations of joy or of pain, I cannot say, but I know they reminded me forcibly of a representation of souls in purgatory I once saw outside a church in Antwerp.

Even a sailor visiting a bath house (J. D. Johnson, *China and Japan*: 1873) though admiring "several finely formed and really handsome young women," felt he must anticipate the reader's reaction by noticing how they appeared "utterly unconscious of any thought of impropriety in this indecent exposure of their persons."

My own memories go back only a limited time, but I definitely remember that in this respect conditions before World War II were very different from now. Mixed nude bathing was the rule at all *onsen* ("hot springs"). At Kamakura students bathed naked, and in Hokkaido I have seen an entire school of girls descending into the sea wearing only diminutive panties, breasts bare to the sun. These must have been the very last traces of Yamato innocence.

Now an impressive prudery has taken hold of the nation, especially among the young. Bathing

---

[9] I owe this and the following passages to a very amusing selection compiled by A. Maclean and published under the title *The Truth about Japan* (Tokyo: Watts Press, 1967).

naked is looked upon as most boorish.   Boys wear th chastest of trunks; girls may don bikinis, but they would feel desperate if they had to go around bare-breasted.   Mixed bathing is now forbidden at most hot springs.

Together with this prudery in actual life, interest in the nude as an object of sexual arousal has rapidly developed.   In the old order of things, a naked woman was just a naked woman; now there is a piquant taste of a newly forbidden fruit, as one may easily appreciate on seeing the ubiquitous presence of erotic magazines, nude and *sutorippu* (strip) shows.

Undoubtedly, these facts reveal a movement toward traditional Western views.   The motive force, of course, has been entirely traditional and entirely Japanese, being principally national pride and the fear of being considered provincial or backward.   By an amusing coincidence, while nudity in everyday life seems to be on the way out among the Japanese, throughout most of the West it appears to be very much on the way in.

A form of Westernization is also to be seen in the acceptance of kissing.   Just before the war, kissing was proscribed as a disgusting Western habit.   American films were often rudely censored; one would see the leading actor approaching his partner, only to jump away suddenly with a jerky movement.   Ten inches of celluloid had simply been lopped off by the censors!   Now young couples walk happily arm-in-arm along public avenues, and nobody makes any objection.

Neither Westernization nor modernization, separate or combined, seems sufficient to explain fully the nature of Japan's success in the modern world.   Both help one to understand the mechanics of the process, but somehow the deeper levels of motivation seem to remain obscure.   After all, Turkey, Iran, India, Thailand, and Indonesia have been exposed to the same influences in varying degrees, in some cases for a much longer time, with final results that are impressive for their difference.   There must be something in the local soil that has nourished foreign seeds so healthily.   To reiterate our first point, Japan's success must be explained in human terms and, one must add, predominantly in Japanese terms.

Here a brief look backwards and Westwards may be rewarding.

There is no doubt that the scientific and technological revolution is the European gift to the human species.   Professor J. Needham, in his monumental *History of Science in China* (a work that has been compared by George Steiner to Proust's *A la Recherche du Temps Perdu*, in as much as it is a superb "re-experienced structuring" of an entire society of the past, accomplished with "total imaginative penetration"), has shown how far East Asia has progressed on the technological level, and he has also analyzed the reasons why it failed to give birth to real science, similar to what evolved in Europe in the Renaissance.   In Europe, the very first awakening of the scientific spirit can be detected in the drawings and jottings of Leonardo da Vinci, just as the very first signs of scientific insight appear in the work of Copernicus, otherwise a "Polish ecclesiastic of unimpeachable orthodoxy."[10]   Both trends met in the work of Galileo, Kepler, Tycho Brahe, Francis Bacon, and, of course, Newton.   "By 1700 the mental outlook of educated man was completely modern."[11]

[10] Bertrand Russell, *History of Western Philosophy* (New York: Simon & Schuster, 1945), p. 512.
[11] Ibid., p. 522.

183

Passing from chipped stone to polished stone and pottery, graduating from hunting to agriculture, building the first cities and founding the first empires were all steps of momentous importance in the history of human development; but the advent and diffusion of science and of the technology derived from science were possibly even more decisive and pervading in their effects on every aspect of our lives. Whatever happens, we shall never be the same again.

Entire libraries have been written on the philosophy and methodology of science, on the relative importance of induction and deduction, on the ultimate value of these instruments of inquiry, but essentially the step was simple. It consisted in approaching problems with a completely open mind and letting nature supply the answers. Nature and experience became, at least in certain fields, an ultimate fountainhead of truth. Previously the accredited fountainhead had been either the great thinkers of the ancient world or some relevant point of divine revelation. In practice, authority lay in books. The scientific revolution consisted primarily in taking men out of the library and into the open air, into the actual stream of life.

This authentic mutation in human history, which was accomplished in Europe, subsequently spread from its original home to other parts of the world and to peoples whose philosophic and religious backgrounds had matured in entirely different circumstances.

In Europe itself, the response to this mutation taking place in its very heart was far from enthusiastic; indeed, those wishing to call it definitely negative have many arguments in their favor. European civilization as it has developed since the age of the great German emperors and the crusades, as it flourished in France, Burgundy, Italy, Spain, along the Rhine, and in England, between the tenth and fourteenth centuries, presented a very definite character. Men were organized into kingdoms, republics, a vast empire; these may have been all too often torn asunder by wars, but nevertheless the people were tightly bound and united by a common religion, by a common culture, by systems of economic production and political administration that were remarkable in their uniformity. Manor, monastery, village, and town; feudal lord, monk, peasant, and burgher; all had slowly developed along parallel lines from England to Sicily, from León to Denmark, from the plains of Lombardy to the hills of Palestine, where the *familles d'outremer* extended Europe along the shores of Asia.

Europeans of these ages had very clear ideas of right and wrong. Man and his relation to God, the universe, the world (past, present, and future)—everything was clearly mapped out and catalogued. There was to be one pope and one emperor; there were seven arts and seven planets; logicians specified a definite number of correct syllogisms; and theologians counted 266,613,336 angels, divided into nine classes. Jerusalem was the center of the world, which had been created in exactly 3761 B.C. There were four temperaments and seven virtues, just as there were seven deadly sins and four seasons. St. Thomas Aquinas and Dante had the genius to sum up the entire knowledge of their times, the one in a cathedral of thought and definitions, the other in a world of imagery and poetry.

Science exploded in, and upon, this particular world. The scientific revolution would have been perfectly acceptable if it had involved only the building of better ships, the invention of weapons more effective in their threat and power to kill, the planning of cities easier to defend, the concoction of medicines of a more dependable quality, or the manufacture of clocks that would keep better time. Unfortunately, the scientific method was revolutionary just because it led straight to fundamentals, just because it upset the most cherished ideas. Soon a headlong clash between this new thing called science and the old, established traditions became inevitable.

This is not the place to remind the reader of the details of a confrontation that has lasted now for centuries. Galileo's tragic story is known to everybody: the old scientist, nearly blind, was condemned by the Roman Inquisition, first in 1616, then publicly in 1633, when he had to recant his discoveries. "The inquisition," Betrand Russell reminds us, "was successful in putting an end to science in Italy, which did not revive there for centuries. . . . Fortunately, there were Protestant countries, where the clergy, however anxious to do harm to science, were unable to gain control of the state."[12] The development of modern finance was greatly retarded by metaphysical notions concerning capital and interest, then called usury. Later on, the theory of evolution met with wild, and in some cases hysterical, opposition. Criticism of the bible and the demotion of so-called sacred history to a simple branch of normal history were fought with every imaginable means and are still looked askance at in many quarters.

It can surely be said that first Europe, and later the more extended West, has offered a very poor historical background for the development of science. Every step forward was the result of a hard-won victory against the powerful and often organized opposition of established traditions, doctrines, churches. Advance was often due to the voracious pull of the technological necessity of war, of seafaring, of exploration, and of colonization. Basic science, upon which all real advance depends, won general acceptance in universities and among the public only during the nineteenth century. It is rather disappointing that the very first chairs in purely scientific subjects to be supported by the state were in Germany when Bismark understood the importance of nourishing with research the expanding industry and military power of his country.

185

In the case of Japan, a series of historical circumstances and some extremely lucky coincidences place its civilization in a most favorable position as regards the scientific mutation. The scientific revolution is not necessarily confined to the West, any more than Buddhism was confined to India, Christianity to Palestine, or communism to Germany. In fact there seems to be a curious destiny awaiting great human movements, for they often develop more successfully far away from the people and the place of their origin. Powerful clusters of new ideas, inspiring thoughts and actions may arise or be performed in one spot of the planet, but they belong to humanity in general, and the seeds they sow finally germinate most fruitfully where they find the best soil.

Negative forces, retarding the acceptance and development of scientific thought, of a scientific attitude to reality, were conspicuously absent in Japan.

Japan's intellectual history is highly complex. Buddhism, introduced in the sixth century A.D., found a native system of religious beliefs that was not so primitive as to be swept away. "It was just when Shinto was first assuming the features of a more homogeneous and developed religion that the arrival of Buddhism caused it to be relegated to a position of minor importance

[12] Russell, *History of Western Philosophy*, p. 520.

for many centuries."[13] A third system of thought, Confucianism, added depth and further voices of great authority to the philosophical debate—a debate that has continued until the present day.

Such a composite picture, in which no one view of the universe and life prevailed with absolute and final exclusiveness, has planted an attitude of tolerance deeply into the Japanese mind. There has always been room for dialogue, for a concert of intellectual powers. Each system of belief or thought was considered a Way (DŌ, *michi*), literally a "path," towards the summits of wisdom, of spiritual achievement, of inner illumination, of cosmic integration. The mind has been permitted to examine dispassionately any system of thought, belief, or values, any Way that might present itself on the spiritual horizon, provided its credentials are impressive.

G. B. Sansom has noticed how the Copernican theory was easily accepted in Japan,[14] and J. Z. Bowers has followed in detail the comparatively smooth acceptance of the dissection of human corpses for medical and anatomical research. Even though particular groups may have objected to the introduction of certain theories, or teachings, or methods, there was never a united front, and the state, in its Confucian mold, was luckily agnostic.

Of course, it was not indifferent when political matters came to the fore, and here we encounter what looks like a frightening example of intolerance: the proscription of Christianity in the sixteenth and seventeenth centuries and the persecution of its believers, many of whom died miserably as martyrs. Historians generally agree, however, that this was only marginally a religious persecution; the authorities took no interest in the doctrines of Christianity as such, but they saw in it a possible subversion of the state and the birth of new loyalties that might prepare the way for the intervention of foreign powers. In this case, the authorities went to seemingly absurd extremes of fanaticism. The fear of Christianity as a political force was such that in 1673 a British ship was not allowed to enter the port of Nagasaki, simply because it was learned that the king of England was married to a Portuguese princess.[15]

Again, during the late thirties of this century, a climate of frightening political intolerance took hold of the nation, and its shadow extended even to matters of purely academic interest, such as history. The author personally suffered persecution during those years for his liberal views and can recall many episodes of bigotry. However, once the political fetters are removed, as they were on the fall of the Tokugawa regime in 1867 and with the end of the military dictatorship in 1945, the Japanese personality appears signally devoid of intellectual blinkers, and of the intolerance that derives from them.

The only eminent Japanese in whose words and thoughts one can detect genuine intellectual, religious intolerance is Nichiren (1222–83). "Those who practice invocation to Amitābha are due to suffer continuous punishment in hell; the Zen sect is the devil; the Shingon sect is the ruiner of the country; the Ritsu ... sect is the enemy of the country."[16] Unfortunately some of his modern descendants seem to have inherited not only his passion and fire but also many of his atypical limitations.

However, these are exceptions. The normal attitude to thought is tolerant, and this is encouraged by the fact that the idea of revelation is weak in Japanese religious tradition. There is not even a common word for this concept, which is absolutely fundamental to the West, and without

---

[13] R. Tsunoda, W. T. de Bary, D. Keene, *Sources of Japanese Tradition* (New York: Columbia University Press, 1958), p. 24.

[14] Sansom, *Western World and Japan*, p. 196.   [15] Ibid., p. 175.

[16] Hajime Nakamura, *The Ways of Thinking of Eastern Peoples: India—China—Tibet—Japan* (English translation edited by P. P. Wiener) (Honolulu: East-West Center Press, 1964), p. 483.

which it is impossible to make any sense of Western personality and attitudes. An expression such as *kami no shirase* simply means "information from the gods." More technical terms, such as *tenkei*, are better translated by "oracle." *Keiji* approaches the Western "revelation" in meaning, but it is certainly not a term that is used every day or understood at every street corner.

In Buddhism, the concept of revelation makes little sense, and it is the idea of illumination that forms the starting point and the goal. Buddha's message is not "news from the gods," but a sort of sudden implosion taking place in the human spirit, a sudden contact with ultimate reality, which his followers are encouraged to repeat. In later, more elaborate Mahayana works, revelation has a place, but it is never as central as it is in the cluster of Western religions.

Shinto has always made great use of oracles. In A.D. 770, for example, the Japanese imperial system faced one moment of supreme danger when the monk Yuge no Dōkyo tried to persuade Empress Shōtoku to declare him successor to the throne, thus breaking the dynastic line. The decision was so grave that oracles were sought from the god Hachiman, who eventually said no and affected the whole course of Japanese history. But an oracle, though akin to revelation, is somehow humbler and more circumscribed in its effect. Moreover, the sacred scriptures of Japan (the *Kojiki*, the *Nihon-shoki*, the *Engishiki*) do not have the character of revelation, though they can be seen in that light and were so in part by the Kokugakusha (a loose group of intensely patriotic scholars) during the eighteenth and nineteenth centuries, and later by extreme nationalists.

In the West, the idea of divine revelation has been a pivot around which thought and history have revolved for twenty centuries. It has caused wars to be fought with bestial fury; it has justified persecutions and horrific massacres, as it has also inspired the greatest art, music, and literature. It has tortured the Western soul; it is torturing it still. Japan and the Far East in general have been spared much of the uglier influences of the concept of revelation. It is also possible that some higher and more brilliant flames of such demonic fire may have been lost, but assuredly there has been less persecution, fighting, maiming, and less suppression of fruitful ideas because of what was written in some ancient book or because of interpretations thereof.

Japan, therefore, appeared on the modern scene with a mental outlook particularly adapted to accept in full the essence of the Western scientific cultural mutation and of its dependent technological revolution, leaving behind all the antagonistic and retarding elements that were, and still are, so deep a part of Western civilization.

187

This absence of strong negative forces is only one aspect of the total picture; it is perhaps not as important as the presence of positive forces.

One of the lucky coincidences mentioned already is that the essence of Western scientific thought and the essence of some of the major traditional Japanese attitudes to the world and life happen to move along the same lines and in the same general direction, though on entirely different planes.

Let us first consider the very ancient Japanese belief that this world, comprising both nature and man, is essentially divine. In the primitive layers of tradition, the very land on which man dwells was generated by the gods in a straightforward sexual process.

"How is your body formed?" Izanagi asks his spouse, Izanami.

"My body," she replied, "formed though it be formed, has one place which is formed insufficiently."

Izanagi then suggests, "My body formed though it be formed, has one place which is formed to excess. Therefore, I would like to take that place in my body which is formed to excess and insert it into that place in your body which is formed insufficiently, and [thus] give birth to the land."[17]

After some fruitless attempts, the gods generate the islands of Awaji (the hilly strip of land that closes the bay of Osaka to the West), then Iyo (now Ehime), Tsukushi (now Kyushu), and subsequently all the Ōyashima archipelago (Japan). Later came rivers and seas, the wind, trees, mountains, and so on. Last to be born is Fire, who cruelly destroys his mother, Izanami.

This is a delightful and grandiose childish myth, but the ideas and emotions behind it can be the starting point for an entire philosophy of life; this is exactly what has taken place in Japan.

What is explained on the mythological level by sexual generation, on the religious level becomes a fundamental feeling of unity between gods (*kami*), man, and nature. Finally, on the philosophical level, it can be expressed by one simple, though absolutely basic, affirmation: this world is the ultimate reality. The belief that the phenomenal is actually the real is deeply rooted in tradition, as we are repeatedly told by Professor Nakamura and all other authorities on Japanese thought.

The consequences of a solution of this sort, once it has instinctively been chosen by a civilization, envelop the whole of life and society. If all is sacred and ultimately divine, then man is not simply master of a soulless, passive, dead, material world but part of a more intimate, organic universe. Fujisawa Chikao speaks of a "consanguineous kinship with plants and animals" and of *shinjin gōitsu*, "spiritual coalescence," with all things.[18] *Kami*, man, and nature are essentially interchangeable actors in a great cosmic play. Man is the Kami-stuff (*jinmotsu*) of the world," as the author of a famous medieval history, the *Jinnōshōtōki*, expresses it[19]; and Arai Hakuseki adds, "In ancient times, what was called Kami was man."[20] A deep spirit of harmony and brotherhood is established between man and the world.

The Japanese love of nature is well known. Surely many visitors to Japan have been struck, upon entering a bank, by the sight of a flower arrangement on the counter, a sudden poetic message from brook and forest, reaching straight though dreamlike distances. Leaves, flowers, fruits, animals, clouds, waves appear in the decoration of *kimono*, lacquer boxes, pottery, hanging scrolls, or in the graphic neatness of a family crest. It has rightly been observed that if one were to ignore all the poems dealing with nature in the many Japanese anthologies produced down the centuries, very few pages would be left. "The Japanese esteem the sensible beauties of nature, in which they seek revelations of the absolute world."[21]

The essential unity of the phenomenal with the absolute planes is not generally explicit, and many Japanese might even deny it if it were presented to them in brutal, intellectual terms. It lies rather in the invisible quality of daily life as an element of all deeper emotions and becomes manifest in attitudes and choices; it is everywhere and nowhere at the same time.

[17] Donald L. Philippi, trans., *Kojiki* (Tokyo: University of Tokyo Press, 1968), p. 50.

[18] Jean Herbert, *Shinto: At the Fountainhead of Japan* (New York: Stein & Day, 1967), p. 21.

[19] Tsunetsugu Muraoka, *Studies in Shinto Thought*, translated by D. Brown and J. Araki (Tokyo: Government Printing Bureau, 1964), p. 36.

[20] Herbert, *Shinto*, p. 21.   [21] Nakamura, *Ways of Thinking of Eastern Peoples*, p. 359.

In this attitude to nature and to life, I think one can appreciate an extraordinarily favorable background to the acceptance and understanding not merely of the methods and application of science but of its very spirit. Men and women who for thousands of years have approached nature in trepidation and wonder and who have been inspired by it to extraordinary heights of artistic and poetic feeling are now admirably prepared to face this same nature in a framework of pure rationality. The language is different, but the relative positions have remained virtually unchanged: man, with all humility, expects nature to guide him; man, the disciple, looks to nature for inspiration and truth.

Such ideas may seem obvious today. It should be noted, however, that this attitude, achieved in the West by bitter victories over stake and proscription, springs in Japan from the most ancient frontiers of the collective mind, from myth, proverb, and folksong.

If all is sacred, then all is accepted.

Other consequences branch off from the principle of immanence. If all is accepted, then man is taken for what he is. Man is not a fallen angel but an ascending, living being. Man is accepted with his good and bad sides, with his luminous and darker parts. Society, too, is accepted for what it is, with its winners, who are greatly admired, and its stragglers, who are generally helped along. Japanese attitudes to work, gain, achievement, success, possessions, the body and its needs —attitudes that may often seem materialistic, or hedonistic, or brutal when viewed from outside— become entirely understandable. Here we have existentialism as folklore, vitalism as proverb and tale. Theories that have been put forward by philosophers as ultimate distillations of the intellect are mixed with the soil of farms, with wood gathered in the forest. Nature as a life-giving power is undisguisedly good. There can be no better world than this world.[22]

In this way, what we might call a spirit of realism (*genjitsu shugi*), or an overriding pragmatism becomes prevalent, though Western terminology is somewhat misleading. Realism in the West is marked by its opposition to idealism. Western pragmatism has something of the poor man's philosophy about it—let us keep to pennies and inches because the stars are too far away. Japanese realism and pragmatism are not goals reached after a critical journey through a philosophic night punctuated by renunciation; they have all the freshness of intuitions experienced at dawn, and they include the numinous roots that their Western counterparts have disdainfully cut off. Here is food for the whole man, not just for a small, cerebral portion of his being.

The coincidence between Japanese traditional values and the very essence of modern times is striking. If our world is ultimately a product of the Renaissance, it also stands in perennial opposition to the Middle Ages. Transcendence and contemplation are out; immanent values and action are in. The Japanese with their pragmatism, their achievement-oriented society, their elitism frankly accepted and squarely faced, and their aggressive belief in success are made for the modern world. They fit into it perhaps better than anyone else. A Christian or a Buddhist background engenders doubts. What is the use of it all? Why rush and conquer? *Cui bono*? A Shinto background cleaves no such rifts in the soul. Success is the obvious good; achievement, the natural

189

[22] Muraoka, *Shinto Thought*, p. 59.

goal of man; getting on in the world satisfies everybody, is recognized and rewarded on all sides.

The story of Daruma-san is instructive. The patriarch Bodhidharma is said to have spent eight years on Mount Chao-lin-ssu, with his face turned toward the wall of his cell. When at last he tried to stand up, he found that his legs had rotted away. This legend is the origin of the Daruma doll one sees everywhere in Japan, large and small, of wood, papier maché, or plastic. When you buy it, its eyes are blank, and you paint in a pupil when you embark upon some project; if all goes well, the second pupil is added so that Daruma is rewarded by gaining sight. The painting-in of the empty eye is now a gay ceremony for politicians after winning an election, for businessmen who have signed a promising contract or have completed a building, a merger, a fat deal. What was originally a spiritual achievement has become a symbol of worldly success.

If all is sacred, then all is accepted.

This principle applies not only to man and society but also to objects and their importance in daily life. The workers in the Matsushita factories, before starting their jobs each day, sing:

> For the building of a new Japan,
> Let's put our strength and mind together
> Doing our best to promote production,
> Sending our goods to the people of the world,
> Endlessly and continuously,
> Like water gushing from a fountain.
> Grow, industry, grow, grow, grow!
> Harmony and sincerity![23]

190

The spirit of this hymn to production is unmistakably similar to the spirit of the Norito liturgies, which are well over a thousand years old.

> There the divine treasures are presented:
>   Mirrors, swords, bows,
>   Spears and horses have been provided;
> Garments of colored cloth, radiant cloth,
>   Plain cloth, and coarse cloth have been presented;
> And the first fruits . . .
> As well as the fruits of the mountains and the plains . . .
> The wine—raising high the soaring necks
>   Of the countless wine vessels, filled up to the brim—
> And the various offerings are piled up
>   Like a long mountain range.[24]

Fertility, abundance! Mirrors, swords, bows! Radios, television sets, cars!

Superficially there is something very American, Fordian, Cecil B. de Millian, even Barnumesque

---

[23] Quoted from "Consider Japan," *The Economist* (London, 1963)
[24] Donald L. Philippi, trans., *Norito* (Tokyo: Kokugakuin University, 1959), p. 23.

in the air. Japanese foundations, however, are more solid; they rest on deeper layers of collective agreement. Americanism rises on foundations of ultimate dissent; Japan, on foundations of ultimate assent. Here, also, a Buddhist background is not very encouraging. Goods and material acquisitions are of doubtful value, and are seen rather as hindrances. Somewhere at the back of the mind, poverty is a virtue. Buddhism has waged a losing war in Japan; it has idealized the notions of *wabi*, *sabi*, and *shibui* (stressing asceticism, simplicity, and restraint), among others, and these have certainly had a deep and salutary effect on the arts, but in the final substance of life Shinto has won the day. Mirrors, swords, bows! Spears, horses, the fruits of the ocean, the fruits of mountains and plains! Wine! Saké! Suntory whiskey! The fruits of the steel mill and shipyard! The offerings of the department store and the supermarket!

Compared with Buddhism in Japan, Christianity in the West has gone much deeper in its affirmation of a jealously guarded sovereignty. Where, in European and American religions, are the Inari shrines, with their foxy gods of abundant harvests and thriving business? Or the Ebisu, Daikoku, and Kompira shrines, from which the Eastern brothers of Mercury are expected to grant fat dividends, spectacular catches at sea, miraculous strikes of gold, colossal sales, or felicitous tax exemptions to the faithful? Most Western religion tends finally to damn success that has nothing spiritual about it. Possibly this is the right way to look at things, but here we are not expressing judgements; we are merely observing a cultural scene that has certain definite characteristics—the modern world. In this particular scene, the Japanese are in a position of spiritual advantage. They are modern with their whole being, with their bodies and souls, with roots reaching back to myth and fable. Western man is modern only in the latest and topmost of his many layers; deep down his soul is cluttered with the remains of anti-modern beliefs. If he has to decide about birth control for instance, more often than not he still consults ancient books rather than statistics or the findings of biology. The Japanese have been modern since prehistory.

The Buddhist tradition, if taken literally and seriously, would have had a very sobering effect indeed on the joyous meeting of Japan with modernity. But Buddhism, since the Middle Ages, has become profoundly Japanized. It has ended by conforming with Japanese ways of thought and with the powerful ideas centered in the Shinto cultural cluster to such a degree that its antagonistic effect on modernism and modernization has been slight, one might say practically nil.

The modern age stresses communal life: ours are times of groups, crowds, collaboration, and social integration. The lone man—*in sacello cum libello* ("in his small room with his little book") —the independent operator, is gradually disappearing. In this, too, Japanese tradition has a great advantage. Western critics often point out that while a Japanese national entity may be worthy of close attention, a single Japanese, taken at random, will most probably be a rather miserable example of the human species; he lacks individuality, the recognizable traits of a character; he tends to be a number in a series, a small cog in a machine with a thousand wheels. This is perfectly true, and is acknowledged by the Japanese themselves. But, again, in taking the modern scene for what it is, the Japanese gregariousness and clubbishness turns out to have great advantages.

Upon entering a Japanese office, a factory, a bank, a school, where hundreds, sometimes thousands, of people are crowded together at work or study, one is generally struck by the atmosphere of relaxation and ease, sometimes of actual gaiety. The habit of living on top of one another since childhood, in a home without privacy, in a school where everything is done communally, has trained the Japanese not to be alienated by conditions that would drive most Westerners to neurosis. At present, the number of psychiatrists, even in large Japanese cities, is very small; mental cases may be increasing as life becomes more chaotic, but there is a fundamental sanity at large among the Japanese that makes their society formidable.

The final inner picture of Japan is one of near-complete harmony between tradition and modernity, of but slight alienation from the central axis of human progress. There is good reason to think that the grave spiritual crisis through which the West is now passing will barely touch the Japanese. The West is losing all faith in its traditional religions. Until very recently atheism and agnosticism were restricted to elites among the cultivated classes, who could tap other sources for ethical guidance. The decay of the old faiths is finally reaching the grass roots and becoming universal. Unfortunately ethical values in the West have been based entirely upon religious beliefs. Thus the decline of religion also signifies the weakening of ethical springs. If God is dead, who validates the Ten Commandments? If there is no hell, why behave? Violence and madness become the rule; society is diseased in its very marrow. Probably a long time will have to pass before a frankly post-Christian West finds some new inner structure. Communism offers a temporary solution but is too bleak to satisfy the entire human being; it lacks that cosmic dimension that is necessary for complete human balance, for some form of serenity and inner peace.

In contrast to the West, the Japanese position is enviable. The development of Japanese ethics has taken place predominantly under the auspices of secular philosophy, especially of Confucianism, and only to a limited extent under religion. A very competent Christian observer, J. J. Spae, notices that religion in Japanese means something that gives one "inner peace," that is not a guide to conduct. He also observes that "the more a religion appears as ethics, the more readily will it be seen as philosophy."[25] In Japan, ethics and morals have traditionally been anchored to rational springs, to reason. This puts the Japanese today in a position of psychological security. They can lose their religion (in fact they have practically lost it already) without being seriously deprived of solid inner moorings for ethical behavior.

The rich heritage of Confucianism affects Japan of the modern world on two other levels as well. The first is the traditional respect for authority, which gives corporate power to groups and ensures national cohesion. This may well be a by-product of emperor-worship, which has its roots in the oldest and most primitive layers of Shinto thought. Confucianism, however, rationalized this religious drive and turned it into bureaucracy. Marxists often speak disparagingly of Japanese state worship but, curiously, they then adopt the same mental habits. The Zengakuren leaders have often charged that the internal structure of the Communist party is "eroded by principles characteristic of the Emperor system."[26] The attractions of authority are absolutely irresistible!

———

Modernization, we are told by Nakane Chie, who is one of Japan's foremost women scholars, "has been carried out not by changing the traditional structure but by utilizing it."[27] Though the

[25] Spae, *Japanese Religiosity*, p. 162.
[26] Kazuko Tsurumi, *Social Change and the Individual: Japan before and after defeat in World War II* (Princeton: Princeton University Press, 1970), p. 342.
[27] Chie Nakane, *Japanese Society* (London: Weidenfeld and Nicholson, 1970), p. 115.

context of this quotation somewhat restricts it, I think that it is extremely important for Westerners to understand all the possible implications of this point. At the same time, a very great element of lucky coincidence must also be taken into account. Often in history, "it so happens" that the right man is born at the right moment; "it so happens" that Japan appeared on the world scene at the most convenient time, and that it was equipped with an ideal background for success. Among some minor lines along which the traditions of Japan happen to work in a consonant direction with some typical developments of the modern world, I would like to examine two in further detail, both in words and images.

The first concerns women. The position of Japanese women in modern Japanese society is difficult to evaluate. Conflicting opinions can be supported with good reasons. One often hears people (foreigners especially) state that the balance is heavily tipped in favor of men and against women. "This is definitely a man's world" conclude many women visitors after a brief stay in Japan, and one must agree that appearances do not encourage one to contradict them. There is very little polite opening of doors and offering of places; generally men enter first, sit first, are served first, drink first, and go to the bath first. Women are rarely molested but are more often completely ignored. "It is well known that Japanese women are nearly always ranked as inferiors; this is not because their sex is considered inferior, but because women seldom hold higher social status."[28] When I read this, I was emphatically reminded of an absolutely fundamental Japanese principle: status precedes sex.

Up to 1946, the position of women was made particularly hard by legislation that was definitely male-oriented, or rather *ie*-oriented (*ie*, 家, "the house," "the home," "the family"). Women were supposed to live always under the tutelage of a male; first the father, then the husband, later the eldest son, or some other male of the family, as custom dictated.[29] It is interesting to note that the Meiji era (1868–1912), which determined the course of Japanese life as it developed up until the end of World War II, in many ways represented the final maturation of ideas that had been developing since the beginning of the feudal era in the seventeenth century. There was a lot of modernization, some Westernization, but also much subtle and deep Easternization going on. A typical slogan of the times was *wakon-yōsai* (和魂洋才; "Japanese spirit and Western knowledge" or better still "Western technology"). During this period, Confucian philosophy spread through the entire country, down to the humblest workers and their families. The breaking down of class barriers, the introduction of universal education, the developing press and means of communication were all factors in what may be described as the supreme triumph of Confucius. The Duke of Lu may not have listened to him, but twenty-four centuries later the Meiji oligarchs certainly did, even though on the surface some homage was paid to Kant and to Compte, to British democracy and to German *Realpolitik*. Here we have another very illuminating example of how modernization may work independently from, or even against, Westernization.

The end of World War II, the new Constitution and the Occupation with its influences and initiatives brought about a real revolution in the legal position of Japanese women. Article 24 of the Constitution states explicitly: "Marriage shall be based only on the mutual consent of both sexes, and it shall be maintained through mutual cooperation, with the equal rights of husband

193

[28] Ibid., p. 32.
[29] See, for instance, Takashi Koyama, *The Changing Social Position of Women in Japan* (Paris: Unesco, 1961).

and wife as the basis." This seems, at least in theory, to do away with marriage as a family affair, and to put an end to the worst forms of subordination.

But what has happened in practice? The present situation is confused and difficult to assess. One can easily cite examples of complete female freedom next to others of total subjection. Women now take part in politics (39 were elected to the House of Representatives in 1946, though subsequently the number dropped); women hold important positions in civil administration, in education, in business, and in the professions; there are women judges, university professors, and women seem to take legal initiatives in cases of divorce more often than men. On the other hand, customs and mental attitudes change slowly and discontent is often expressed in private and in public about the discrepancy between legislation, the fine principles on paper, and the actual facts of life, the day-to-day relations with husbands, lovers, families, society in general.

One may say, however, that modern Japanese women, whatever the practical results, have seized with spirited eagerness most of the opportunities offered them. There are few countries in the world where the average husband hands over the entire monthly paypacket to his wife. The wife then takes care of household expenses, perhaps saves some, and doles out small sums for her husband's personal pleasures. Even in the strictly patriarchal times of feudal Japan, women became the virtual dictators inside the house, at least after they had passed a certain age. Confucian morality circumscribed their field of action, but it never dispossessed them completely.

Here we may look back over the long period of Japanese history during which the country was governed by a military class. All the available evidence shows that the further back we go towards the origins of the Japanese people, the more significant and important the position of women becomes. This situation is so pronounced in the remotest ages available for our inspection that some authors postulate the existence of a matrilineal family system in prehistory.

Japanese mythology clearly reflects a society in which women occupied an exalted position. The supreme presiding spirit of the pantheon, Amaterasu Ōmikami ("Heavenly Radiance Great Deity"), a symbol of the sun and its powers of life and fecundity, is female; moreover, "many male deities and heroes, even the powerful ones, are depicted as having a weak, tender, sensitive, emotional side."[30] Links with shamanism may have been important in remote times; the preeminent position of women may have been a social recognition of the magical powers wielded by female shamans who ensured contact between the world of men and the worlds above (Takamagahara) and below (Yomi) when they were possessed by the spirits of ancestors, gods, sacred animals.

Japanese society, as it appears with more definite delineation in the protohistoric and early historic periods, is no longer matrilineal, although women retain a position of high prestige. Despite the fact that marriage was by then patrilineal, it seems that only the eldest male in each family took a wife to live with him; younger brothers followed the so-called *mukoiri* or *tsumadoi* systems, and visited or lived in the home of their brides. Yanagida Kunio and others have found traces of *tsumadoi* marriage existing in outlying districts of Japan up to our own times. There is also evidence that women had special rights in naming children and that mothers supervised their daughters' marriages.

On another level, it is noteworthy that between A.D. 592 and 770, seven women became em-

---

[30] Shigeru Matsumoto, *Motoori Norinaga, 1730–1801* (Cambridge, Mass.: Harvard University Press, 1970), p. 184.

presses in their own right—out of a total of fifteen sovereigns. It was only the scandal of Empress Shōtoku's intrigues with the monk Dōkyo, who dreamed of becoming emperor himself, that stirred up a reaction against both the power of women and that of abbots. The capital was moved to Heian (now Kyoto), and from then on sovereigns of the empire were almost exclusively men. An exception occurred in the seventeenth century with the reign of Empress Meishō (1629–42).

Traces of female precedence over male are also embedded in the Japanese language. Formerly, one said *me-oto* (wife-husband), *imo-se* (sister-brother), *omo-chichi* (mother-father); *mi-oya* (honorable parent) in ancient literature was used only in reference to the mother. According to some Japanese scholars the transition from a society oriented in favor of women and with matrilocal marriage to one with a definitely male bias took place in the Nara period (eighth century A.D.).

This fact did not prevent many women from achieving distinction and enduring fame during the subsequent two or three centuries when culture flourished with great splendor in the Heian capital. Names such as Murasaki Shikibu (author of *The Tale of Genji*), or Sei Shōnagon (author of the *Pillow Book*) are widely known in the West, thanks to the superb translations of their works by Arthur Waley and to the clever presentation of their times by Ivan Morris. *The World of the Shining Prince*[31] is also in great part the world of the shining princess. Beyond the resounding names appearing in the literary chronicles of the time, one senses the presence of many other women of intelligence and wit, moving around unhindered by conventions, making decisions on their own, having love affairs, writing, painting, and traveling in an atmosphere of freedom.

The rise to power of the warrior class in the thirteenth century brought about a complete revolution; men were in the ascendant, women became more and more circumscribed in their activities. At first it may have been a simple question of necessity in hard and violent times, but later, especially during the long and peaceful Tokugawa epoch (1600–1867), the position of women became systematized and integrated into the frame of Confucian philosophy and was defined by the strictest rules of daily behavior. A famous document of the eighteenth century, the *Onna Daigaku* by Kaibara Ekiken, may be said to represent the most extreme position regarding women's subjugation to men. The actual spread of such ideas through the entire population of Japan was achieved, paradoxically, only in the nineteenth century.

As things stand today, it is amusing to see how Women's Lib., which is definitely revolutionary in the West because people speaking Indo-European languages have a past that shows few traces of matrilineal arrangments, in Japan becomes a reversion to conditions that date back to antiquity.

The second example of Japanese tradition working in the same direction as modern development is architecture.

The abundance of timber to be found in the Japanese archipelago, the fundamental links of the people with the sea, with skills developed in the construction of boats, and the constant threat of earthquakes are some of the factors that explain why Japanese architecture since its very beginning has been an art of building with wood. A long hut, in which walls support the roof, is a solution typical of northern people and well adapted for cold climates. The Japanese and other peoples of Pacific Asia usually built their houses as frames in which the walls were panels, movable at will, often replaced by sliding doors of light wood and (later) paper. The "Japanese sense

---

[31] Ivan Morris, *The World of the Shining Prince* (New York: Knopf, 1964).

of construction emerges in the process of fitting together many separate pieces of wood to outline space with a structural cage . . . ."[32] Japanese carpenters soon attained great sophistication in their art. Some buildings reached colossal dimensions. The *hondō* ("main hall") of the Tōdai-ji in Nara (rebuilt in 1708 after successive fires) is the largest wooden building in the world. Normal buildings—homes, temples, or shrines—were smaller but showed great refinement in detail.

Architecture in the West developed for thousands of years on a different foundation—stone. With certain exceptions (late Romanesque and Gothic), edifices were conceived as boxes not as frames, and walls were structural, built to sustain most of the weight. When metal and concrete appeared, offering new materials with which to build, a complete break with the past occurred. From Sullivan onwards, modern architecture had to be revolutionary. Everything changed. The atoms of architecture were no longer separate blocks (stones, bricks) but beams. Stresses could be distributed according to entirely new plans. Buildings tended to become frames on stilts, cages to be filled in with walls and partitions according to necessity and fashion.

But this was exactly what the Japanese had been doing for thousands of years! Unfortunately a first wave of modernization brought to Japan the eclecticism of Viollet-le-duc and encouraged the construction of the false and pathetic châteaus, chalets, and small *Trianons* that were so popular during the Meiji era. When a second wave arrived with the strong influence of Le Corbusier, links with the past finally became significant. Modern Japanese architects have to deal with new materials in terms of unprecedented size and sophistication, although the fundamental principles of their trade are as old as the hills: beams, a cage, stilts, partitions. "Skeleton structures of steel or concrete, sheathed with blank stucco surfaces, offered the purity required by Japanese taste," says Drexler, and he adds a few pages later, "To maintain continuity with the past would seem, to the Western architect, easier for his Japanese colleague than for himself."[33] Much of what is best in modern Japanese architecture is due rather to these roots that carry vital fluids from folklore, from the crafts of carpenters than to the cold, abstract researches of academicians in the stream of an international style.

―――――

Japan's modern century is often seen as progress induced by many foreign elements, representing modernization, against a background of obstinate resistance put up by the forces of tradition. In some cases this may be true, but the overall picture appears completely different. If Japan's past had been an obstruction to its future, the country would possibly still be something of a laudable and promising disciple of its Western mentors, not a potent rival who has picked up the ball and is playing with competence and gusto, threatening one day to beat the teachers at their own game.

This extraordinary situation needs to be explained by a bolder reappraisal of reality. If the tables are turned completely around, everything becomes much clearer. If Japan's past and traditions are seen not as hindrances but as powerful motors giving the craft that extra thrust, then the picture makes sense.

The ultimate secret of Japan may be the future of its past.

[32] Arthur Drexler, *The Architecture of Japan* (New York: Museum of Modern Art, 1955), p. 43.
[33] Ibid., pp. 247, 255.

▲ 237

▲ 238

239 ▶

Maiko girls will become full-fledged geisha after years of training. They are thought to have originated back in the twelfth century when ladies of the vanquished Taira clan were obliged to serve the Minamoto victors. Bar hostesses of today are a simplified, streamlined, and barbarized version of such highly accomplished traditional entertainers.

240 ▲

◀ 241

Japanese women very often, though by no means explicitly, act as a living and precious link with the Japanese past. A long-haired beauty in a red kimono may feel deeply attracted by the arts of her ancestors and wish to live as an exquisite heiress to the perfection of Heian times (244); in contrast, a working girl, seen in the country near Mount Yoshino (with its typical walls of large riverbed stones), may express her feeling of rebellion against old, useless constraints with a friendly grin and a casual shirt (242). One young woman may prefer to avoid possible problems and meekly follow an established family custom of serving for some years as a *miko* ("shrine maiden") in the Izumo Taisha (243), another may work in the Tokyo office of a large international organization that requires of her a superior capacity, linguistic ability, and a university degree (241). When the right moment comes, all will probably don the *uchikake* kimono, cover their heads with a *tsuno-kakushi* band, and hold a *sensu* fan in their hands—just as the young bride observed one day against a latticed wall of the Heian shrine in Kyoto (240).

THE FUTURE OF THE PAST

▲ 245

◄ 246

Every year the farming population of Japan decreases
a little; the percentage of workers engaged in agriculture now stands at roughly twenty-five percent of the
total labor force. For centuries women with their
menfolk have worked desperately hard in the mud of
the paddy fields. Rice is an exacting, unrelenting,
sometimes brutal master! In early summer the seedlings are transplanted, often with great pomp and ceremony, as in the Inari Shinto shrine, south of Kyoto, and
for the occasion women wear a costume patterned in
vivid colors (249). With autumn comes the harvest, and
in the bitter cold of Tōhoku (245) and the sultry heat
of Kansai (246) there are weeks of hard work that is
performed always with patience, often with a smile.
Summer and winter offer some periods of respite, but
there are other jobs to be done around the fields. A
farmer's wife rests for a moment in front of her family's
cottage near Kyoto (248), and two housewives clean
vegetables in the cold air of a mountain village (247).

▼ 249   247 ▲   ▲ 248

JAPAN'

▲ 252

253 ▶

To the new jobs of a modern world, Japanese women often apply ancient skills, habits of exceptional endurance, patience, and courage, and, in many cases, even a special schooling in refinement. Would the industry of cultivated pearls have been possible without the help of the *ama* fisher girls, who for centuries (they are mentioned in the *Manyōshū* poems, over one thousand two hundred years ago) have dived into the sea searching for abalone and for edible seaweed? Here four *ama* on Hekura Island, carrying their work equipment, are walking down to their boat (*252*); two are under water looking for the prized molluscs among bunches of seaweed on the rocky seabed around the island (*253*). At the other extreme, a long and exacting training in many traditional arts—flower arrangement (*250*), tea ceremony, calligraphy—has prepared hands and eyes for the less creative but highly responsible jobs of modern industry, where precision and a perfect understanding of intricate patterns and movements become invaluable advantages (*251*).

THE FUTURE OF THE PAST

▲ 254

▲ 256

◄ 255

JAPAN

▲ 257

258 ▶

The young orange seller on an icy New Year's morning in front of the Ise shrine keeps her child on her back, warmly ensconced under a specially large coat called *nenneko* (256). The same is done by a farmer woman of the north, near Hachinohe, as she feeds her baby with a bottle of milk (255). Children are coddled with great love and tenderness when small, and they are allowed a lot of freedom. Often, as we see in a remote village of the Izu peninsula, dolls are carried on the backs of little girls as little girls are carried on the backs of their mothers (254). When children start school, they are made to feel the first pressures of responsibility. An elder brother (*nī-san*) on a farm at the foot of Mount Fuji (258) looks after his little sister (*imōto*) with an air of manly concern. The boy dressed as a samurai for the Sōma-oi Noma-oi Festival at Haranomachi seems much impressed at being allowed to accompany his father to the competitions and ceremonies of the day (257).

JAPAN

▲ 261

262 ▶

For over twenty years, since World War II, Japanese schooling has tried to confine itself to imparting knowledge without ideology, as a reaction against the excessive, nationalistic indoctrination of former times. Results are much debated, and the system is slowly changing. But one may feel sure that a profound sense of identification with Japan's impressive heritage has been constantly absorbed through the widespread habit of school excursions to famous places and through open-air drawing classes. At certain periods of the year (mainly spring and autumn) it becomes a desperate enterprise to attempt a visit to any famous historical or religious site in Japan; schoolboys and girls of all ages noisily and happily take the place over. The usually silent Ryōan-ji garden in Kyoto is likely to be packed with inquisitive, staring eyes and to resound with childish voices (*259*). The cherry blossom season (*262*) and autumn, when the *momiji* maples are "on fire," become great occasions for classes in the open air (*260*, *261*).

263 ▲

◀ 264

Young couples were rarely seen in public before World War II. Confucian morals permitted prostitution but frowned on mixed company in the open street. Manjirō, the early nineteenth century castaway, expressed a typically Japanese judgement when he said "Americans are licentious by nature; they kiss in public." Westerners, on the other hand, thought the Japanese licentious because of mixed naked bathing! Now couples are seen everywhere in Japan, often happy, always unembarrassed. Visits to temples (263), shrines (265), and sacred mountains, such as Hiei (266), seem a favorite occasion to combine the pleasures of company with the enjoyment of beauty. The mild scandal of male and female shoes in front of a door (264) may create less stir than in the West—or more, according to the circumstances. It has been said that Japanese society is governed by *haji* ("shame"), the West by the sense of sin—surely an oversimplification, but perhaps useful to understand behavior.

JAPAN

▲ 265

266 ▶

THE FUTURE OF THE PAST

267 ▲

268 ▲

These young gallants of Tokyo's *shita machi* ("lower quarters") were seen standing by proudly naked, showing off entire mythologies on their tattoed skins (*268*) during the Sanja Festival that commemorates three fishermen who, some fifteen centuries ago, are said to have miraculously caught a small gold statue of Kannon in their nets. In a succeeding generation, the gallants may easily become transformed into the leather-jacketed motorbike fiends visiting a distant shrine on a winter's afternoon (*267*). Both groups manifest a similar cocky assurance, the same instinct to move and act in gangs, the same showy spirit of bravado, described in Japanese, when excessive, by the verb *ibaru* (威; "to swagger"). Curious patterns of continuity may suddenly become apparent when a portable microphone is held by a policeman in the precincts of the Imperial Palace in Tokyo (*269*), exactly like an archaic *horagai* shell in the hands of a wandering *yamabushi* (*271*), or in those of farmers who are taking part in a Shinto festival (*270*).

269 ▲   ▲ 270   271 ▼

THE FUTURE OF THE PAST

Continuity in everything pertaining to work is the real basis of Japan's outstanding modern achievement: continuity in skills, in a high level of education, in ambition, organization, group solidarity, in a pragmatic approach to problems both large and small. This theme, formidable as it is, has been developed to a certain extent in the text, following the author's idea that Japan at present, of all the countries in the world, is the most suited to embody the spirit of modernity with total commitment. Here tangential hints may be suggested. Lumbermen in Hokkaido (272) move with rhythm and gestures similar to those of an Izumo *kagura* folk dancer acting out the myth of Ōkuninushi (273). The similarity shows an inner dynamism that may well be considered something primary that cannot be broken into more basic components. A welder in a Kobe shipyard (274) handles fire with the same familiarity as *yamabushi* hermits in their nocturnal exorcisms (275), possibly expressing an ancestral relationship with matter that goes back to Shinto beliefs embedded in the very substance of Japanese culture.

JAPAN

THE FUTURE OF THE PAST

277▲ ▲ 279

280 ▶

Modernization may flow successfully in Japan because of a deep spiritual continuity sustaining it from within, but at the same time there are eddies and whirlpools at all levels; there is often confusion and bewilderment, or just amusing juxtaposition. Seemingly insignificant scenes that catch a visitor's eyes for their humor may really be symbolic of deeper, more serious contradictions. A fireman belonging to the fifth platoon (it is written on his back) keeps a small camera ready to record the festival in which he is taking part (276); a conscientious little nun, with her head carefully shaven, likes to have a personal souvenir of the Ryōan-ji garden in Kyoto (277). Probably her results will not be as good as the ones obtained by the professional photographer, with his large camera and tripod, dressed in a costume of the Heian period during the Aoi Festival so as not to spoil the aesthetic unity of the event (278). The smiling *maiko* running along a street in Kyoto (279) was noticed just a few minutes after the well-nourished person declaring herself LOVE BEAT (280).

▲ 281

◀ 282

To Western eyes, Japanese cities often seem, ugly, brutally utilitarian, immense, grey machines with bodies of cement. This is easy to understand. Japanese ideals of beauty are deeply interwoven with a cult for nature. The city, as anti-nature, is fundamentally incompatible with beauty. The ideogram for city (市; *SHI*) is the same as the one for market (*ichi*). A city is essentially a mart, a place for the production and exchange of goods, the locus of industry and commerce, with facilities for satisfying the more earthy human pleasures—food, drink, bath, sex. On the other hand, if a mart is naturally vulgar, it is just as naturally gay. The paper lanterns that must have been such colorful ornaments in the past and that can still be seen in temples or shrines on festival days (*281*) have their multimillion electronic descendants on the roofs of ferroconcrete buildings in the Ginza (*282*); the talent once used in designing banners hoisted by fishermen to celebrate bounteous catches (*283*) is now employed to plan neon displays (*284*).

▲ 283

284 ▶

285 ▲

◀ 286

One of the finest pagodas in Japan (288) has stood at Daigo, south of Kyoto, since A.D. 951. A pagoda is essentially an ornamented reliquary and a schematic symbol of the Buddhist universe with its various parts. From the architectural and functional points of view, it is a sublime exercise in fantasy and design, a much less utilitarian object than the bell towers that accompany Christian churches; it has all the semantic richness and the structural delicacy of a gigantic ideogram written into the landscape with wood, plaster, and metal. A "pagodic" line running through Japanese aesthetics, from buildings to writing, from lanterns to lintels, has been discussed previously (Ch. 3), but there are further and perhaps subtler developments. Anybody observing the skyline of a modern Japanese city will be struck by the luxuriant imagination displayed in crowning buildings with turrets, pinnacles, kinky skittles of iron, cement, or wood, often to be used as props for publicity signs (286, 290). Is this due to the long education of eyes accustomed to the pagoda, of minds used to the concept

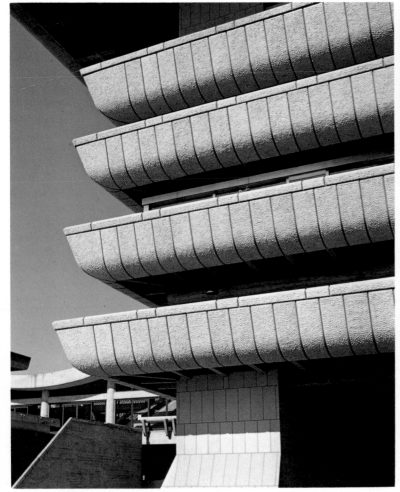

287 ▲

288 ▶

of a purely ornamental vertical structure? Already in the sixteenth century, castles were conceived "pagodically," as one can see in the fairy-tale-like outline of Himeji's White Heron Castle (285). Once the "pagodic eye" has become disengaged from its metaphysical and ritualistic trammels, it is free to play in space with all the new materials a modern builder can employ. At Expo '70, most Western pavilions were comparatively sedate: Americans, French, Germans favored varieties of domes; the British and the Dutch, boxlike structures; the Soviets and Italians, pyramids. On the other hand, the transmogrified pagodics of the Japanese were tremendous, pure exercises in vertical fantasy and design—minus the relics of ancient saints. Unfortunately, architecture directly inspired by the pagoda design, such as the imposing ferroconcrete Sōka Gakkai temple of Taiseki-ji, near Mount Fuji (287), seems somehow out of touch with our times. As usual, continuity is most effective when it represents a secret, inner guiding principle, not a purely external imitation of models.

289 ▲   ▲ 291

◄ 290

In the West, the discovery of iron, cement, and steel as construction materials produced a break with millenia of tradition. All of a sudden buildings were seen as frames, and walls became mere partitions. This was revolutionary and required new thinking in design; links with the architecture of the past were severed. This was not so in Japan where buildings had always been wooden frames with partitions of lighter wood and paper. Japanese architects, confronted with problems of modernization, merely substituted ferroconcrete or steel for wood, and extended their conceptions to larger and more complex blocks of space. In most other respects they were blessed by the advantages of a substantial continuity. In structure and design, ancient Japanese buildings often anticipate familiar sights in cities of our own days. The small *azekura* godown of Tōshōdai-ji in Nara (*289*), probably built in the eighth century, is superbly modern in design, though it is one of the few edifices with walls supporting the structure. The linear rhythm of Himeji Castle (*292, 293*) makes the well-known Okura Hotel (*291*) look benignly familiar.

JAPAN

THE FUTURE OF THE PAST

▲ 294

295 ▲ ▲ 296

▲ 297

Western modernization, in many aspects, is academic, cerebral, and revolutionary because, by chance, Western traditions do not simply and naturally harmonize with the new world created by the scientific revolution. The Japanese, on the contrary, and also by chance, can often look back to their folklore, to the artistic and spiritual traditions most solidly rooted in the soil, for inspiration and guidance in modernization. These felicitous coincidences are a major reason for spiritual balance in times of bewildering change. Signs of essential continuity strike one at the most unexpected moments and places. The obsessive rectangles of a gigantic building in steel and glass, the New Otani Hotel in Tokyo (295), seem to repeat in a different dimension the facade of a cottage near Hachinohe (294), where wooden beams have been turned into a decorative motif—perhaps ultimately leading back to the obsessive lines of newly planted rice seedlings (296). Tange's famous stadium at Yoyogi in Tokyo (297), built for the 1964 Olympics, on closer inspection turns out to be a glorious pagodic statement rooted in the most genuine traditions of cottage architecture, as seen for instance in two huts near Izumo (298, 299), on one of which a group of men is replacing the thatch.

298 ▼ ▼ 299

THE FUTURE OF THE PAST

▲ *300*

301 ▶

If the West is a civilization of stone, bread, and meat, Japan is one of wood, rice, and fish. This implies a deep primal relationship with the sea. In the heart of the Japanese mountains one is more often regaled with *sashimi* ("raw fish") and seaweed than with venison or fowl. Among the many ancient names of Japan is *Urayasu no Kuni*, "The Land of the Peaceful Bays." Floats in Kyoto's Gion Festival often have the form of ceremonial vessels (*301*), such as were also beloved of the Venetians. Building colossal ships of steel (*302*) comes naturally to a people who for millenia have been used to going to sea at all seasons in small, wooden vessels like the fishing boat entering Wakkanai port in Hokkaido on a bleak wintry day, forging a path to the pier through the floating ice (*300*).

JAPAN

302 ▶

▲ *304*

◀ *303*

The many-tiered scaffolding on the prow of a ship being built in the Ishikawajima docks near Kobe (*303*) suggests the terraced roofs of Himeji Castle (*304*). Both ship and castle represent impressive works of construction requiring the collaboration of men and the pooling of resources. Japanese group solidarity has been one of the major assets in confronting the challenge of modernization successfully. United into a nation of over twenty million in the early seventeenth century, mainly through the genius of Tokugawa Ieyasu, welded into a uniform though stratified society closed to the outside world till 1854, the Japanese people managed to pass from feudalism to partial democracy, from agriculture to industry, from a hermit curiosity to a world power without breaking apart, without losing identity or soul. On the contrary, as the trials of sport are for a healthy body, every blow seemed to be a stimulation, the last and worst—the surrender of 1945—being the most effective. Japanese national solidarity, often defined by

▲ 305

native critics as *shimaguni-konjō* "the spirit of an island country," and by alarmed foreigners as what lies behind "Japan Inc.," is an enviable but dangerous asset. It can easily become exclusive, jingoistic, but hopefully with extended foreign contacts and exchanges, it will become less provincial. Workers putting up a traditional wooden house in Kyoto (306), not far from a gigantic steel frame (305), may be symbolic of the innumerable and complex smaller groups into which the national entity is divided, creating a complicated web of allegiances, from the country *dōzoku* to the great modern *kaisha* with resounding names (Mitsui, Sumitomo, Matsushita, Sony, Honda), each in many ways a descendant of the feudal *han* (藩; "clan"). An X-ray picture of Japanese society would probably resemble a maze of those strange helicoidal models of complex organic molecules observed by chemists, rather than the clean-cut network of steel frames shown in the photograph above.

▲ 306

307 ▲   308 ▼

JAPAN

▲ 309

310 ▶

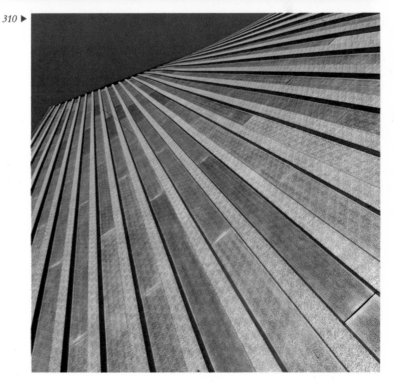

Simply two pages of images taken in joy! The Kōfuku-ji pagoda in Nara, which dates back to 1426, appears vaguely through the blossoms of cherry trees on a sunny April day (*308*); the tight steel skeleton of a new building towers above trees in snow blossom on a winter's morning in Sapporo (*307*). The precipitous facade of Tange's Catholic cathedral in Tokyo (*310*) takes up in soaring metal the linear motif of winter fields near an old thatched cottage among the mountains of Nikkō (*309*).

311 ▲

312 ▶

The lonely, silent valley among the temples of Chūson-ji at Hiraizumi in north Japan (*312*) may offer a suggestive image of the paths and roads that covered most of old Japan. Communications were considered important and were highly developed, but strangely the wheel was never much employed. Official communications were carried by messengers running or riding; travelers moved about on foot, on horseback, or, if enjoying exalted status, by *kago* ("palanquin"). The old Tōkaidō road (*311*), made famous by Hiroshige, along which processions of *daimyō* ("feudal lords"), imperial messengers, merchants, pilgrims, prostitutes, poets, hilarious jokers, such as Yaji and Kita of Jippensha Ikku's eighteenth-century novel (*Tokaidōchū Hizakurige*), could once be seen, is now a normal macadam highway. The recent opening of a parallel expressway between Tokyo and Osaka has returned the hallowed thoroughfare to local traffic—to trucks of vegetables and school buses.

313 ▲

◀ 314

During the eighteenth century, Edo is said to have been the largest city in the world: it is thought to have boasted nearly one and a half million inhabitants. The city developed around the castle of the shogun. The White Heron Castle of Himeji (285) may perhaps give us an idea of what it looked like at the peak of its glory. Since 1868, Edo has been called Tokyo ("Eastern Capital"), and the shogun's residence has become the Kōkyo (皇居), "the Imperial Palace." Few turrets and gateways remain intact as historical mementos. However, if we manage to isolate ourselves from the surrounding thunderous traffic, or if we take advantage of the rare stillness of a snowy morning (313), we can still conjure up visions of the veiled *kago* palanquins making their dignified entry into the hallowed grounds.

Tokyo, ever more a megalopolis and beautiful only in rare and fleeting inspirations of light and atmosphere (314), has kept its awesome position as the largest city in the world. Latest count: 11,398,801 inhabitants.

315 ▲

◀ 316

317 ▲

"The Thing" (315) stands some fifty feet high next to the New Imperial Palace in Tokyo. It is claimed to be a representation of a pine tree, but it looks more like the cubist interpretation of a tropical flower by an aggressive artist chopping up the sky with relentless fury into slices of blue. Somehow vague memories are conjured up—wooden window gratings in Kyoto (316), the scanned percussion of roofs of the Hōryū-ji pagoda (317) —the oldest in Japan—against the clouds of Nara, and "The Thing" suddenly looks more tame and plausible. One may even wonder if the artist was not unconsciously thinking in terms of a sōrin, the metal pinnacle that pagodas thrust up against the sky, their most quintessential part and the richest in metaphysical symbolism.

JAPAN

318 ▲

◄ 319

Ge-ba (下馬), "Dismount from your horse!" says an ancient sign near the entrance gate of Ise Shrine (319). Since those distant and spacious days, signs have multiplied with frightening abandon. Drivers are now confronted with a veritable phalanx of prohibitions, limitations, and injuctions (318) as they approach a crossing in downtown Tokyo. Sidewalks are overcrowded with people, streets clogged with vehicles. Japan's rush into modernization, taking place in a limited land area, has brought about wondrous gains in economy and prestige, but also terrifying pollution and, to some people in some districts, misery and illness. Two conflicting principles in the basic Japanese philosophy of life seem here to be at loggerheads. On the one hand there is the cult and love of nature and the instinctive recoil from *kegare* ("contamination"); on the other the drive towards achievement and production. Will *kōgai* ("pollution") be felt in the future as *kegare* ("contamination") and be cleaned away by some new version of the ancient *harai* ("purification")?

THE FUTURE OF THE PAST

金剛峯寺　高野山

◀ 320　　　　　　　321 ▲

Every year in December, a decidedly non-Christian country is invaded by a host of Christian symbols: Japan is flooded with angels and organs, mistletoe and holly, fir trees covered with false snow and silver stars; there is Santa Claus, the infant Jesus, the Madonna; there are jingle bells, candles, crackers. People give parties, go to dinners, exchange gifts. Carols and *O Tannen Baum* are sung to exasperation. At first it seems disconcerting, and one is tempted to dismiss it as a commercial stunt of the department stores to increase sales. In part it is so, but there is also a genuine popular response. Christmas is a solar and positive festivity; it harmonizes with the genuine Shinto spirit and its cult of life; it can also be seen as a great international *matsuri*. Christmas means food, presents, children, families, homes, the return of the sun on its upward swing—all definitely good things. On top of it, Santa Claus— here seen on a shop sign in Shikoku (*321*)—happens to look like a modernized Hollywood version of Daikoku (*320*), Ebisu, Hotei, or any one of the many jovial ancestral deities who carry bags of good things on their shoulders for the benefit of mankind.

JAPAN

▲ 322

323 ▶

Foreigners traveling around Japan by car are often struck by the presence of plastic policemen standing rigidly where traffic is supposed to be dangerous. The authorities claim that the dummies have a decidedly positive effect: "People slow down before they discover the trick!" If a stone god, Fudō, with his flaming sword can halt invisible enemies of the Buddhist faith (323), how could a plastic representative of the law (322) fail to ease toes from overly depressed accelerators? The magic is possible, perhaps, because of subtle differences between East and West in attitudes concerning personality. A Western person is like a little castle; he stands in defiant opposition to nature. In Japan, personality is fluid; it easily fades into groups, backgrounds, larger realities, and subjects mix disconcertingly with objects. Language is often hazy. Who does what to whom, why, when? In Western grammars the verb "to be" is unique, sovereign, and admits no dilution. In Japanese, the verb "to be" is generally left in a corner, or can ride on half a dozen ideograms, on all of them precariously. Be assured: the plastic policeman has his structural place in the monistic traffic.

324 ▲　▲ 325

◄ 326

Newest meets oldest.　Okamoto Tarō's great sun face at Expo '70 (324) grins to its remote ancestor, the mysterious sculpture of unknown origin, unknown date, unknown meaning, on a rock at Asuka, near the Tachibana temple (325).　In between stands what resembles a queer, egglike mask, seen along the road in the mountains of Okayama (326).　The face is really a Sanskrit monogram that is said to symbolize the North Star constellation (北斗七星).　Someone has offered a lone tangerine on a piece of paper to the stars.　May the stars bring good luck to him, to the reader, to us all.

INDEX

237

240

Louisiana State University Press, Baton Rouge

Photographs by Harri Peccinotti

Essays by Drs. Morsi Saad El-Din, Gamal Mokhtar, Gawdat Gabra & Soad Maher

CAIRO
the Site & the History

Consulting editor: Dr. Morsi Saad El-Din
Photographs by Harri Peccinotti
Editor: Gregory Vitiello
Designed by Derek Birdsall
Produced by Omnific Studios
Typeset in 12/14pt Van Dijck series 203
& printed in Great Britain by Balding + Mansell International Limited
Copyright © Mobil Oil Egypt (S.A.E.)

First published in the United States, 1988,
by Louisiana State University Press,
Baton Rouge, Louisiana 70893
Library of Congress Catalog Card Number LC 87-082873
ISBN 0-8071-1472-3

*Cover: Under the floodlights, and surrounded by darkness,
the Giza Sphinx and Pyramids are among history's most mysterious
and majestic sights.*

CONTENTS

PREFACE

Cairo, like any great city, is more than the sum of its parts. Over 5,000 years, many civilizations have asserted themselves; some have left mere traces in the sand, while others have left their indelible marks. It is these marks – these pyramids, obelisks, churches, mosques and palaces – that remind us of Cairo's past and that animate its present.

Fortunately, the past – of Cairo and of all of Egypt – is being restored to us through the herculean efforts of the Egyptian Government. We applaud the Government for all it is doing, and we urge the international community to support this effort since Egypt's heritage is a legacy to the world.

In the same spirit, through this book on Cairo, we celebrate the city's past. We also celebrate what Cairo has *become* – the complex living city of today.

It is a city we know and appreciate. Ever since Mobil came to Egypt 85 years ago, we have been based in Cairo. We have been involved in the nation's cultural life as sponsors of such projects as the Pegasus Prize for Egyptian Literature and *The Genius of Arab Civilization*. With this book on *Cairo, the Site and the History*, we are proud to continue our appreciation of this rich culture – and specifically the culture of Cairo.

We are especially fortunate in having assembled such a distinguished creative team: consulting editor Dr. Morsi Saad El-Din, art director Derek Birdsall, photographer Harri Peccinotti, and our outstanding group of authors – all Egyptians, and all leading scholars in their fields – Dr. Gamal Mokhtar, Dr. Gawdat Gabra and Dr. Soad Maher. I thank them all.

A special dedication must go to Mr. Oreste de Gaspari, former Chairman of Mobil Oil Egypt, who initiated this book.

Leslie B. Rogers III
Chairman
Mobil Oil Egypt (S.A.E.)

Mathematician to learn astronomy, and here Strabo was shown the houses where famous Greeks had lived."

Of this seat of learning and focus of religion nothing remains but an obelisk. Beside the obelisk is an ancient sycamore, riven with age and hacked with numberless names beneath which, tradition has it, the Holy Family rested in their flight into Egypt, and which is now known as The Virgin Tree. Nearby is a spring of fresh water, which it is said became sweet because the child Jesus was bathed there. From the spots where the drops fell from His swaddling clothes, after they too had been washed in this sacred spring, sprang up balsam trees, which it was believed, flourished nowhere else.

There is no evidence for those fancies. But as Lane-Poole puts it: "The tradition is no more than a legend, yet there is no place in Egypt to which the visit of the Holy Family would be more fit, than to the almost deserted seat of learning."

القَـاهِـرَة

Lawrence Durrell, the author of the *Alexandria Quartet*, often wrote about what he called the genius of the place, or the spirit of the place. What he meant was that the place is the main manipulator of character, and that the geographical features of a country reflect on its people.

Before dealing with the geography of Cairo, we should know something about the geography of Egypt, and its regional personality. This personality is not the work of geography alone, but of history as well as geology, archaeology and even anthropology.

Egypt is often called the land of paradoxes, the land of anomalies. It is at the same time a river land and a desert land. It is an example of a perfect river environment, or to be more specific, a flood environment. The river constitutes Egypt's very life; without it, there would be no Egypt. Herodotus said that Egypt was the token of the Nile. Indeed, Egypt *is* the Nile.

Egypt is a hydrological society, and it has one of the most complicated networks of irrigation canals. But it is also the largest desert country in the world. It is a land of agriculture, but no plants. It has no natural flora, no grass, no savanna, no forests. Its topography is a mixture of the natural and the artificial.

Egypt is a central country. It lies almost exactly in the center of the world. It is the only country where the Red Sea and the Mediterranean meet, where the River Nile meets the Mediterranean. It is in two continents, Africa and Asia, and is the gateway to the Far East. It is an example of the reaction between the site and the situation. The site is the environment with all its perspective, while the situation is geographical. The size of Egypt's site is not always in ratio with its situation, lying, as it were, at the hub of the world.

The Valley is another feature of Egypt. Looking down from an airplane, one would see a green strip on both sides of the river, then abruptly the green ends and the spatial expanse of desert takes over. Life is concentrated in this green strip, and this led to the creation of political unity, to the centralization of power that gave Cairo, the capital, a concentration of power and to the establishment of the first bureaucracy in the world.

At first, the desert led to the isolation of Egypt, but it was also a defensive belt that allowed the country to live, during the first centuries, in a state of independence. This allowed Egypt to develop its civilization unhampered by outside invasion. Egypt's situation made it a meeting place of east and west, north and south, and one of the first countries to develop trade. The first empire in the world was formed in Egypt, but it was a peaceful, not an aggressive empire. It is often said that the River Nile made Egypt a land power, while its extended shores made it a sea power.

Egypt is part of what geographers call the Arab-Nubian mass, and as such, part of the great Sahara Shield or the African Shield. Egypt was formed gradually and continually as a result of a chain of long and complicated eras of sea flooding the land from the north, then receding again. This process continued over many centuries. The resulting deposits formed the land of Egypt.

But the Nile has always played an important role in the formation of the country. Geographic and geological maps show that the Nile does not run in the middle of the desert, but veers to the east. It is often said that had the Nile run more to the west the course of history would have changed.

The Nile in its long and difficult course from its source to its mouth covers varied geological areas. It is a typical example of what is termed differential erosion with a succession of ridges and valleys. Egypt's limestone soil was able to resist the erosion of the river. We have an example in the Muqattam hills, which have survived this erosion. Basalt is also a feature of Egypt's land and it is found in the mountainous woods east of Cairo.

There have been many theories about the formation of the

Nile, and questions have always been asked about the time and the nature of its emergence. A geologist named Blankenhorn claimed that a large river originating in ancient times used to flow into the sea. Over the ages that river eventually dried up. At the same time, the sea inundated the land and formed the present course of the river. He called it the Libyan Nile and regarded it as the grandfather of the present river.

A theory put forward by a geologist named Cailliand was that a dried-up course of a river west of the Nile – often referred to as "a river without water" – in the Western Desert was the origin of the Nile and it ran parallel to the present course.

If Egypt is the meeting place of east and west, north and south, Cairo is the meeting place of the Nile Valley and the Delta, the thin strip of green and the fan-shaped fertile land. Cairo can be regarded as the waist of the Valley, a hydrological knot where the Nile begins to branch out into two arms embracing the Delta between them.

To the east of Cairo we can see the Muqattam heights with their broken line of beige and khaki, their weather-beaten, eroded cliffs that once overlooked the Mediterranean before the Delta had begun to form. They are 550 feet above the Nile. This is the protective shield of Cairo. Desmond Stewart compares the Delta to an open hand, and where Cairo stands is the pulse, the wrist. Whoever controls this pulse can control both the Valley and the Delta.

But the Nile was not the only route. To the northwest of Cairo, around the Muqattam hills, one can see a broad waterless valley, Wadi Tumilat, which leads to the Isthmus of Suez. This was supposed to be the route taken by caravans and it linked Europe with the Red Sea across Egypt.

The Western Hills, the Libyan plateau, are the start of the Sahara.

Desmond Stewart compares the strategic position of Cairo to that of Troy. Cairo dominates the Nile, which is a waterway easy to navigate. With the development of Cairo, standing at the top of the Delta, its needs expanded and its central position was exploited further. Waterways were dug, making it possible to ship goods from the Nile to the Red Sea.

If we follow the development of Egypt's capitals from Pharaonic times, we can clearly see the importance of Cairo as a site.

Egyptian capitals began with Memphis, after the unification of the country by Menes. Right from the start, the builders of

Memphis showed strategic sense. They built the city on the West Bank of the Nile. At that time, the Delta started to fan out a short distance north of where Memphis now is.

The city was then called Mit Rahira. After moving to Abydos (*Al Araba*), it returned to Memphis with the 3rd dynasty, where it continued as capital until the 8th dynasty when it moved to Aknasiu, then to Thebes where it lasted for 800 years.

The capital of Egypt continued to move, to Alexandria where it lasted for 1,000 years, and when the Arabs entered Egypt, Cairo became their capital, but under different names. This means that the first Egyptian capital was established in the Cairo area, and came full circle, ending there. The full life of Memphis/Cairo as a capital is over 2,500 years, of Alexandria, 1,000, and of Thebes 800. During Pharaonic times, the capital changed often, which means that the Pharaonic times were experimental. By the time the Arabs came, the importance of Cairo's site was well established, and its strategic value was recognized.

The movement of the seat of government from Alexandria, a coastal city, to an inland city like Cairo can be regarded as a manifestation of nationalism. The neck of the Delta, whether known as Memphis, Heliopolis, Fustat, Qatai or Cairo, was the natural site for a capital. As one writer puts it: "It was as if the site was chosen by the Gods." The site was like a magnet drawing to it all rulers. This also emphasizes the strong geographical centralization that would facilitate the administration of the whole country.

Cairo is an ancient, deeply rooted and noble city. It has a unique landscape, lying between two hanging curves of ancient history: the Pharaonic to the west and the Islamic to the east. In the Pyramids plateau at Giza, we find the remains of Pharaonic times, while at the Muqattam hills and at their feet we find Islamic Cairo, which still lives today. The city stretches in the lower part between the two curves, a point where the greater part of the history of Egypt is concentrated.

From the morphological point of view, Egypt is what geographers call "amphitheatral." It is, in fact, the last basin of the east and Upper Egypt, open from the north, to connect with the Delta gushing into it. In this sense it is similar to the morphology of the eastern part of Upper Egypt, as far as the elevation of the contours to the east are concerned. The area was always subjected to torrents from the desert and in many ways Cairo is a miniature of the whole valley.

Greater Cairo today is fan-shaped, narrow in the south, with its handle there and the wide parts of the fan to the north. This is the general shape of the fertile land of Egypt as well as of its capital.

From a purely geometrical point of view, Cairo is the center of gravity, the seat of government and administration. Cairo's position may not be at the exact middle between Upper and Lower Egypt as far as distance is concerned. But from the point of view of life, it is.

Egypt's population profile is like a pyramid whose top is the Cairo area. If we draw a circle with a radius of 75 kilometers with Cairo in its center, it will have one quarter of Egypt's population living in only one eighth of its size. This means that the human center of gravity is in Cairo.

Its population is a mix of people from all parts of Egypt, presenting a real and comprehensive sample of the population. It is estimated that one-third of Cairo's present population is from other governorates. This move toward urbanization, at one time a blessing, has now become a curse, creating for the Egyptian capital problems that are almost insurmountable.

With a flood environment and a hydrological society, centralization is essential. It is related to the functioning of the government. Irrigation means organization, which, in turn, led to political unity and was instrumental in teaching the people the fundamentals of civilization. It also created officialdom and central bureaucracy, which have become the stamp of Egyptian civilization. Bureaucracy is as old as Egyptian history. It began with the Pyramids, and the murals in the monuments show clearly the importance and esteem given to high officials and scribes. It played a serious role in Egypt and was, at that time, an organizing force. It was a blessing, and Egypt owed its prosperity to its bureaucracy. Without it, canals could not have been dug, and dams could not have been built.

Cairo was also the center of culture, the giver of life. It is often said that the whole of Egypt, indeed of the Arab world, dances to the tunes that are played in Cairo. Cairo is the very heart of Egypt, politically, economically and socially. This is why the fall of Cairo at the hands of invaders meant the fall of Egypt. This is why invaders always headed for Cairo. It is sometimes said that because of its situation, its size and its political importance, Cairo is the capital of the world.

The reader will notice that this book stops after Mohammad Ali, the founder of modern Egypt and consequently the founder of modern Cairo. Yet although he was a great innovator, Cairo still kept its original character and political traditions. The seat of government was still the Citadel where Mohammad Ali lived and carried out the affairs of state.

With the advent of Ismail the process of modernization became a process of Europeanization. He always declared that he wanted Egypt to be part of Europe, and he embarked on a process of construction unknown before: new palaces, boulevards, parks, and of course, the Opera House. But the country had to pay dearly for this, as a result of the loans Ismail obtained from European countries. One of his innovations was to move the seat of Government from the Citadel to Abdin palace.

We stopped with Mohammad Ali, but Cairo has been changing since then. With every positive new development have come new problems. In fact, Cairo's problems have drawn the attention of UNESCO and other organizations. Recently, a seminar pondered "The Expanding Metropolis Coping with the Urban Growth of Cairo."

Dozens of Cairo lovers and experts attended the seminar and delivered a multitude of papers dealing with the complex issues facing Cairo. But, as I said, there are many faces of Cairo; indeed, many Cairos. Ours is different from theirs.

القـاهـرة

Below: The desert at Dahshour, south of Saqqara, with Snefru's pyramids in the background. Right: A fertile stretch of the Nile Valley at the edge of the desert and its enduring landmark, the Step Pyramid of Zoser at Saqqara.

THE PHARAONIC ERA *Dr. Gamal Mokhtar*

Cairo is the political, economic, administrative and cultural capital of Egypt, the largest city in Africa, the gateway to the Middle East, the heart of the Arab world, the entrance to, and at the same time the mouth of, the Nile – the world's most famous river . . . the city marked by the Giza Pyramids and guarded by the Great Sphinx. Yet until 40 years ago, it was scarcely visited by people for its glorious past and its fabulous treasures. But since World War II, the city has overflowed with visitors from every part of the world, and they have returned to their homes inspired beyond words.

Cairo, in addition to its 600 or more Islamic monuments, is flanked by two mother cities with their own ancient and glorious past: Memphis in the south and Heliopolis in the north. Memphis was founded by Menes, the first pharaoh of Egypt, and after becoming the capital, it continued for tens of centuries to be the center of administration and power. Heliopolis, on the other hand, gained its importance much earlier, in the predynastic period and then became the center of Egyptian culture, faith and inspiration for not less than 3,000 years.

Cairo itself includes thousands of Pharaonic monuments, brought from archaeological sites all over Egypt to be exhibited in the Cairo Museum, one of the most celebrated in the world. In the center of the city, in Ramses Square, stands a magnificent colossus of Ramses II, which was transferred from Memphis to be an ambassador representing the old capital in the modern one. Two fine obelisks, originally erected in the temple of Ramses II at Tanis in the Nile Delta, were restored and brought to Cairo, to be resurrected there. Moreover, the major historical sites of the Giza and Saqqara necropolises are within the limits of Greater Cairo or Metropolitan Cairo.

القاهرة

Ancient Egyptian monuments were nearly forgotten and completely neglected after the spread of Christianity and the entry of Islam into Egypt. But suddenly Ancient Egypt was resurrected, much interest began to arise, and a new branch of study called Egyptology was established. This study followed the appearance of the landmark publication *Description de l'Egypte* written by the French savants who had accompanied Bonaparte's military expedition to Egypt, and by the deciphering of hieroglyphics by Jean Francois Champollion at the beginning of the 19th century.

The Ancient Egyptian treasures were then collected and stored for the first time in a small building in Azbaakiah garden in Cairo, and were subsequently transferred to the Citadel of Cairo. However, the entire collection was given to Austria by Abbas Pasha I, the ruler of Egypt when the Austrian Archduke Maximilian visited Egypt in 1855.

Three years later, after the French archaeologist Auguste Mariette was appointed general director of the Egyptian Department of Antiquities, he eventually succeeded in inducing the Egyptian authorities to construct a real museum to exhibit the Pharaonic artifacts. The dream was realized, first in 1863 in a museum in the suburb of Boulak, and then when the whole treasure was moved to Ismail Pasha Palace at Giza in 1890.

After some of Boulak's museum treasures had been shown in Paris in 1867, the Empress Eugènie, the wife of Napoleon III, sought them as a present from Khedive Ismail Pasha, the ruler of Egypt and a friend of the French royal family. But Mariette courageously and firmly refused her demand. It is therefore fitting that the garden of the Cairo Museum includes an elegant bronze statue of Mariette resting on his marble tomb, and bearing an inscription written in French citing *"L'Egypte Reconnaissant."*

The present neoclassical Cairo Museum, designed by the French architect Marcel Dourgnon, was inaugurated in 1902. It is located at the northern end of Tahrir (Liberation) Square in the heart of the main touristic area.

The Cairo Museum exhibits the world's largest collection of Pharaonic treasures, covering all of Ancient Egyptian history from prehistoric times until the Ptolemaic period. Although it is widely criticized as an overcrowded, inefficient museum, I believe that it succeeds in pointing out the richness of Ancient Egyptian civilization. At the same time, it reflects the peculiar mentality of the Ancient Egyptians, who left to us such crowded temples and tombs. In any case, current renovation and development work, including the addition of a new annex, will make for more suitable displays.

Among the masterpieces belonging to the Archaic Period and Old Kingdom are these artifacts from the Greater Cairo area:

King Zoser Statue, of painted limestone, found at Saqqara (3rd dynasty);

Seated statue of Khefren (Khafre), of diorite, found at Giza (4th dynasty);

Three triads of Mycerinus (Menkaure), of schist, found at Giza (4th dynasty);

Seated scribe, of painted limestone, found at Saqqara (5th dynasty);

Standing statue of Ka-Aper (known as the statue of Sheikh el Balad), from sycamore wood, found at Saqqara (5th dynasty);

Niche of Dwarf Seneb and his family, of painted limestone, found at Giza (5th dynasty);

Two statues of Re Nefer, of painted limestone, found at Saqqara (5th dynasty).

The museum also contains some famous collections from the same period, such as the collection of Hemaka, an important official who lived in the time of King Den of the 1st dynasty, and whose tomb was discovered in Saqqara between the years 1931 and 1936. A splendid collection belonging to Queen Hetep Heres, the mother of King Cheops, was found in 1925 by chance in a well beside the pyramid of her son.

The Cairo Museum houses many masterpieces belonging to the Middle and New Kingdoms.

Among the wonderful collections from the Middle Kingdom is the jewelry of the royal princesses of the 12th dynasty, which was found at Dahshur and El Lisht. There are unique scenes, models of quotidian life, mostly made of wood; and also models of Egyptian and Nubian soldiers from the tomb of Mesehti at Asyuit (11th dynasty). Also included are maids bearing offerings, weavers' workshops, cattle-counting, fishermen at work, a carpentry shop and other expressions of everyday life more than 4,000 years ago.

The New Kingdom treasures exhibited in the Cairo Museum are the most fascinating and celebrated, especially those of King Tutankhamon, which were discovered in 1922 in his tomb in the Valley of the Kings in Western Thebes. It contains about 3,000 pieces – of which only 1,700 are exhibited, including such masterpieces as the golden coffin, the golden mask, the throne, his unique beds, chairs, boxes, statues and statuettes, jewels, chariots, canopies, alabaster vases and models.

القَـاهِـرَة

Until recently, Cairo – unlike many other big cities such as Rome, Paris, London, New York and Istanbul – had neither an obelisk nor any Pharaonic monument adorning its parks or squares. In 1958, however, the Egyptian Government decided to bring an obelisk to Cairo to be erected there. Since the archaeological site of Tanis (now called San El Hagar, in the northeast Delta) has more than 20 broken obelisks among the ruins of the Ramses II temple, the parts of one of those obelisks were collected, restored, reassembled and transferred to Cairo. This obelisk now stands on a modern pedestal in a small garden on Zamalek Island, on the western bank of the River Nile, facing central Cairo, and surrounded by some monuments that were brought from Tanis. The Zamalek obelisk, which dates back to 3,300 years ago, is nicely inscribed with hieroglyphics praising King Ramses II. Although it is more than 40 feet high, it looks rather short because of its proximity to a high minaret and to the Cairo Tower.

In 1984, the Egyptian Antiquities Department brought another obelisk from Tanis to the capital, to be re-erected on an artificial pedestal in the wide square facing Cairo International Airport – thus welcoming visitors and bidding farewell to those departing from Egypt. After it was reassembled, the obelisk proved to be well preserved. It is nearly 54 feet high and weighs about 120 tons. Each side of its pyramidion has a scene showing the king kneeling in front of a divinity; below the scene is a column of hieroglyphic inscriptions with one of the titles and names of Ramses II and words about his strength and his victories. The Egyptian Antiquities Department capped the obelisk with an artificial gilded brass pyramidion, imitating the Ancient Egyptian tradition of covering the top of the obelisk with a pyramidion of gold or electrum to reflect the light of the sun.

Assembled in the Museum or on public display, these artifacts offer a mere glimpse of the civilizations that once thrived in this area. Through our readings, and by visiting the sites themselves, we can learn more, not only of what these civilizations built but often of how they lived.

القَـاهِـرَة

The capital of the 13th nome (province) of lower Egypt was an ancient city named Iwn (the tower), called by the Greeks Heliopolis (the city of the sun) and mentioned biblically as "ON." It stood on a slightly raised ground to the east of the apex of Cairo. The only visible remnants are the standing obelisk of Senusert I (12th dynasty) and a few tombs hidden beneath a modern suburb of Cairo called Ein Shams, and a neighboring village named Kom El-Hisn. There must have been a spring of

Left : The standing obelisk of Senusert I from the 12th dynasty marks the site of ancient Heliopolis at Ein Shams, a modern suburb of Cairo.

Below : One of the few remnants of Memphis' greatness, this alabaster sphinx from the 18th or 19th dynasty was excavated in 1912 by the British archaeologist Flinders Petrie.

fresh water in the center of the city known as Ein Shams (the spring of the sun). The sun was believed in Pharaonic Egypt to bathe himself there everyday, morning and night.

Heliopolis played a great role in the social and intellectual life of Ancient Egypt. It also represents the most remote and glorious spiritual center in the history of mankind. Its traditions were mentioned in the Pyramid Texts, the most ancient religious texts of Ancient Egypt.

The sun was worshipped there under different names. One of them was Atum (the creator), who was the original god. He was later absorbed by Re, the Sun God of excellence. Re proclaimed for himself other aspects of the sun, such as Kheper (the god of creation) and Re Hor-m-Akhty (the god of the horizon), and he amalgamated the most important gods, Amon Khnum and Sobek, with himself. Akhenaton's heresy and philosophy were derived from the Heliopolitan doctrines.

Heliopolis Ennead, the first of the doctrines, encompassed the nine universal deities headed by Re, the sole creator. Among his offshoots were two couples: Geb (the earth) and Nut (the sky), and Shu (the atmosphere) and Tefnut (the moisture). Geb and Nut gave birth to Osiris, who married his sister Isis and was appointed as the first king of the fertile land (Egypt), and Seth, who married his sister Nephthys and became the king of the deserts surrounding Egypt.

Originally, the Egyptians – like most of the people of antiquity – used a lunar calendar. Some Egyptologists believe that the priests of Heliopolis perfected a solar calendar that was also connected with the Nile and the agricultural stages. Other scholars attribute the development of that calendar to the famous architect and astronomer Imhotep of the 3rd dynasty. According to that calendar, the year contained 365 days divided into 12 months, each 30 days long, plus five additional days at the end of the year. The months, in turn, were divided into three periods. The year had three seasons, each of which was four months long. The first season was called Akhet (inundation), which begins with the arrival of the flood water. The second season was called Perret (the going out of the water), equivalent to our winter. The third season was called Shmsu, during which the harvest began.

Later, the 12 months were given names, which are still kept in what we call "the Coptic Calendar," and is used by the farmers for agricultural purposes. This calendar, with some alterations by Julius Caesar, is the origin of the current Gregorian calendar.

The priests of Heliopolis were highly respected, and they were frequently visited by cultured Greeks searching for more knowledge, wisdom and science. Even Solon, the famous Greek lawmaker, and Pythagoras, the great scientist, probably stayed in Heliopolis sometime around the 6th century B.C. The priests had worshipped the Sun God since very ancient times, when the city already had its privilege and spiritual importance. The temples of the Sun God, who was worshipped under several names, were very influential in ideological, religious and even political affairs. The obelisks were first placed in sun temples of Heliopolis and were strongly linked to the sun cult.

Although the Heliopolis obelisk goes back to the Middle Kingdom, it is considered the oldest surviving one in the world. It is one of the pair of obelisks that stood in front of the Temple of the Sun God in Heliopolis. Its mate, which was reported on by Arab writers in the 12th and 13th centuries, has completely disappeared.

The surviving one is about 67 feet in height and 121 tons in weight. A single red granite block, it was brought from the quarries of Aswan. Each of its four sides has a column of inscription including the titles and names of the king, and some laudatory sentences. Much patience, genius and faith must have gone into its creation.

Two obelisks erected by Thutmoses III (18th dynasty) were removed from their original site and transferred during the Roman period to Alexandria, where they stayed until they left Egypt in modern times. One of them, now known as Cleopatra's Needle, was given to England and re-erected in London on the bank of the River Thames, while the other one stands beside the Metropolitan Museum in New York City's Central Park.

And so the Heliopolis obelisk is the only landmark of that important and influential ancient city, which at one time had many standing obelisks. But many were destroyed, others were taken abroad, and some may still be buried under the modern buildings that cover the entire area of ancient Heliopolis.

القاهرة

In the Paleolithic period, stone-age men inhabited the site of what is now Cairo. We have found a great number of flint implements, particularly from the Atarian culture of the late Paleolithic, mainly in the Abassia desert and the Gebel El-Asfar (yellow mountain) on the outskirts of Cairo.

The only predynastic settlements in the area were found on the eastern bank of the Nile facing Memphis. These settlements, dating to the era between 3700 and 3100 B.C., are El-Omari near Helwan, and Maadi, located eight miles northwest of it.

Memphis, one of the oldest capitals in the world and the first capital of United Egypt, lay about 15 miles to the south of Giza and covered an enormous expanse, which is now limited to the area around a modern village called Mit Rahina.

Its original name in the time of Menes was *Inb hd*, which means The White Wall. Several centuries later, it became known as *Mn Nefer* – after the name of the Pyramid of Pepi I, the second pharaoh of the 6th dynasty – which is the origin of the Greek name Memphis and the Arabic name *Menf*. Its location, between Lower and Upper Egypt and near the branching of the Nile, made it ideal for establishing a capital of Egypt. The Ancient Egyptians seem to have recognized the importance of such central positions, as is clear from the names given to Memphis – *Ankh Tawy*, meaning "The Life of the Two Lands," and *Mkhat Tawy*, meaning "The Balance of the Two Lands."

Herodotus claimed that Menes, the first unifier of Egypt, had reclaimed from the Nile the ground on which he built The White Wall and its temple dedicated to the god Ptah.

It seems that before Memphis was built, the course of the Nile had to be changed, and there are two theories about this. The first is that the Nile's course at Memphis was static and that the city was reached by river by one or more lateral canals. Yet no traces of such canals were found to give credibility to this theory.

The second theory claimed by the team of the Egypt Exploration Society, when it carried out a survey of Memphis in 1982, is that "the river once flowed directly past the ruined field and has since receded eastwards by approximately 2.5 kilometers."

Whether Herodotus' story about the foundation of Memphis is true or not, there is no doubt that Menes created the town later known as Memphis. What we don't know is if Menes established it as a capital of the United Kingdom or just as a fortress to secure unity; nor do we know if it was Zoser, the first king of the 3rd dynasty, who took it as a capital. It remained the capital of Egypt during the Old Kingdom and was an important administrative and strategic city throughout the whole Pharaonic period, as is reflected in the splendor of the cemetery of Saqqara. Since Memphis was later known as *Hikuptah*, referring to the main god Ptah, the Greeks may have taken the name "Aegyptos" from it, and extended the name of that important city to cover all of Egypt.

By the end of the Old Kingdom, Memphis suffered from political and social upheaval, and its importance decreased steadily, until the Hyksos were driven from the area at the end of the Second Intermediate Period. From the beginning of the New Kingdom until the end of Pharaonic history, Memphis was again one of the foremost cities in Egypt. It was the center of military activities, the main army base, and site of the military school and the manufacture of weapons and arms. It was also considered to be one of the royal residences, and many pharaohs built palaces there and constructed chapels that enlarged the area of the temple of the god Ptah. It was also the first and main city occupied by all the conquerors of Egypt in its late period – the Nubians, Assyrians, Persians and Macedonians.

The recent survey by the Egyptian Exploration Society led to a number of startling results, including the discovery of traces of the famous Memphis harbor.

The port of Memphis had been the chief center of shipbuilding, especially in the middle of the 18th dynasty. The ships built there were for military campaigns in Syro-Palestine. During Ptolemaic times, the port collected tax on all traffic passing through the city. Excavations revealed that Memphis was also a craftsmen's center, especially for carpentry and preparation of pigments.

Memphis maintained much of its importance even after the foundation of the city of Alexandria, which was chosen to be the capital of Egypt by Alexander the Great while he was on his way from Memphis to Siwa Oasis in about 330 B.C. With its splendid harbors, Alexandria became the greatest marketplace of the contemporary world and the most important city in the Hellenistic empire. Memphis, meanwhile, was finally deserted and entirely destroyed after the beginning of the Islamic era.

A small special museum houses the most important monument still preserved on the site: a magnificent colossus of Ramses II lying on its back. It is made out of one block of limestone and shows excellent workmanship. Its original height is estimated at about 45 feet, but it is now shorter, since a large part of the statue's legs, as well as one arm, are missing now. The royal cartouches are engraved on its shoulders, hand and girdle.

It is one of two huge colossi of Ramses II that adorned the main temple of Ptah. The second colossus has stood for more than 30 years in Ramses Square in the center of Cairo. It was brought from Memphis in 1954, when the Egyptian Government decided to erect in Cairo a colossal statue that would symbolize Ancient

Right: The upper part of the colossal limestone figure of Ramses II, representing the king in his youth, which now occupies its own museum in Memphis. Below: The right hand of the statue, inscribed with cartouches of Ramses II.

Egypt. The statue, more than 30 feet high, wears the double crown of Egypt. A third one was discovered in 1962 in very bad condition, broken into three large pieces and about 40 smaller fragments. Early in 1986, in preparation for the exhibition of Ramses the Great in Memphis, Tennessee, in the United States, it was agreed that the colossus would be included. About 30 Egyptian restorers reassembled the colossus that now weighs 48 tons and is 28 feet high. The statue stands as the focal point of the exhibition of Ramses II, after passing thousands of years and crossing thousands of miles, as a testament to the power of international cultural relations.

Near the recumbent colossus in Memphis are scattered several statues and pieces of monuments, notably a fine alabaster sphinx, about 27 feet long, 13 feet high and weighing about 28 tons. Although it is uninscribed, its style suggests that it may belong to Amenophis III of the 18th dynasty.

Beside the ruins of the Great Temple of Ptah, which was excavated by the English archaeologist Flinders Petrie, are scattered fragments of monuments belonging to the New Kingdom and Late Periods. These include the palace of King Apris, from the 26th dynasty, and the embalming place of the Apis bull, which contains a fine alabaster embalming bed. Excavations and research are being conducted into King Sity I Chapel, the temple of Ramses II and the palace of King Merenptah, as well as other ruins that confirm the importance and vastness of the ancient city of Memphis.

The necropolis of Memphis extended more than 50 miles from Abu Roash on the north to Meidum on the south. Although most of the burials were in the two main cemeteries at Giza and Saqqara, the kings of the 5th dynasty usually built their pyramids and temple in Abu Sir and Abu Ghurab, nearly halfway between Giza and Saqqara. King Snefru, the founder of the 4th dynasty, built his two pyramids in Dahshur, a few miles south of Saqqara. Jedef Re, son of Cheops and the third king of the 4th dynasty, built his pyramid in Abu Roash, north of Giza, while Hwny, the last king of the 3rd dynasty, built his pyramid at Meidum to the south of Dahshur.

القـاهـرة

Saqqara is an extensive stretch of land at the edge of the Western Desert, overlooking the city of Memphis. It occupies an area almost four miles long and not more than one mile wide. Its name possibly derives from Sokar (Sokaris in Greek), a hawk-headed god of the dead who dwelt in the desert west of Memphis. Another possibility is that the name is taken from a Bedouin tribe that lived in the area during the Middle Ages.

Saqqara cemetery includes tombs and architectural buildings ranging from the 1st dynasty to the Graeco-Roman Period, a span of more than 3,000 years. It is the largest cemetery in Egypt, housing about 20 pyramids and royal tombs, and hundreds of *mastabas* and private tombs, scattered around the Step Pyramid that dominates the site. (The *mastaba* is an Arabic word for the rectangular bench on which the Egyptian farmer used to sit with his friends in front of his house.) One of the richest archaeological sites in Egypt, it has frequently been explored and excavated over the past 140 years.

Excavations before World War II by Walter Emery led to the discovery of a group of large tombs – all plundered – belonging to the 1st dynasty. Some may have been actual tombs or even cenotaphs of kings, while others were built for the nobles and high-ranking officials.

Of all the monuments of Saqqara, none is more impressive or interesting than the Step Pyramid of Zoser, the founder of the 3rd dynasty. The pyramid marks an architectural evolution in the advanced planning and design of every element in the pyramid's complex. In its construction, nothing like it had been seen before and it is a true pioneer among the architectural miracles of antiquity.

The Step Pyramid complex reflects the impressive change from the mud-and-brick to rock-and-stone construction, and from the style of a simple flat rectangular *mastaba* to a design of a high, intricate pyramid with a complex of buildings. This striking development represents a great architectural evolution and a transition in belief concepts.

This enormous complex was constructed for King Zoser under the direction of his great architect Imhotep, who succeeded in building the first step pyramid anywhere on earth. His genius later became legendary and convinced people to come from every part of Egypt to Saqqara thousands of years after his death, making pilgrimages to his tomb, which the great archaeologist Emery had sought in vain. The Ancient Egyptians even made his name the third element in the Memphite triad in place of the god

Nefertum, composing the triad of Ptah with his wife Shmet and their son Imhotep. He was also identified by the Greeks with their god Aesculapius, god of medicine.

The Step Pyramid is a huge limestone structure, formed of six enormous *mastabas*, narrowing gradually on all four sides. The steps rise, like stairs to the sky, to a height of about 200 feet. The lowest "stage," a rectangle of 410 by 344 feet, anticipates Imhotep's development of the Egyptian tomb from a rectangular *mastaba* to a square pyramid.

The original entrance of the pyramid is at ground level on the north but another entrance was opened on the southern side during the 26th dynasty. However, because of the danger of falling blocks, it is forbidden to visit the inside through either entrance or to climb the pyramid. A large vertical shaft hewn in the subterranean rock beneath the pyramid leads to the burial chamber. It is surrounded by other chambers and corridors carved in the rock. Some of the elements are adorned with blue faience tiles imitating reed mats and with limestone reliefs representing Zoser performing religious ceremonies. More than 30,000 fine alabaster vases are stored inside the pyramid, but most of them were found to be broken.

The Step Pyramid is just one of the elements in Zoser's funerary complex, which is surrounded on every side by a rectangular limestone wall. The periphery of the wall extends for more than a mile at an approximate height of 33 feet and is decorated with recessed panels.

The entrance to the complex is located in the southeastern corner of the enclosure. It leads to a long colonnade composed of 40 columns in the shape of bundles of reeds. Each column is joined to the wall by another connecting wall.

Past the colonnade is the Heb Sed building. It consists of a court and an adjacent building in which Zoser might repeat in his second life the Jubilee ceremony, which the Egyptians called the Heb Sed. This ceremony was supposed to renew the king's strength. To the north of the Heb Sed are two large rectangular buildings, called the southern and northern houses. The facade of the southern one has lotus columns, representing the land of the south, while the northern building has papyri columns, representing the land of the north.

At the northern side of the Step Pyramid, in the middle of the complex court, is the Serdab, a very small building that remains virtually intact. It once contained a seated limestone statue of Zoser, which is now housed in Cairo Museum, while a copy has been put in the Serdab. To the west of the Serdab are the ruins of the mortal temple that is traditionally located to the north of a pyramid.

The complex also includes a tomb with underground rooms that resemble those of the pyramid. They have similar carved reliefs of the king and blue faience tiles on the walls. The function of this southern tomb – and of the southern and northern houses – is still under debate.

The Antiquities authorities have done an extensive job of restoring the subsidiary buildings of the complex, with the help of the French architect F. Lauer, who is still doing a job he began more than 60 years ago.

القَاهِرَة

In 1954, Zakaria Ghoneim discovered a huge unfinished pyramid to the southeast of Zoser's complex, belonging to Skhem Khet, the reputed successor of Zoser. This second Step Pyramid gained wide interest since it helped us to know more about the methods the Egyptians used to build their pyramids. Although none of the kings of the 3rd dynasty constructed a pyramid complex to compare with Zoser's it is clear that they had abandoned the *mastaba* style of tombs for this new style. An interesting example is the huge Step Pyramid constructed in Meidum, to the south of Saqqara, by Hwny, the last king of the 3rd dynasty.

Snefru, the first king of the 4th dynasty, built two pyramids in Dahshur, a short distance from Saqqara, from which they are visible because of their size and well-defined shape. Although the southern one was surely designed to be a true pyramid, with a square base and four sloping sides toward a point at the summit, its incline suddenly changes midway up the pyramid, a sure sign that the architects did not succeed in fulfilling their plans. Accordingly, this pyramid is called the bent, the rhomboidal, or the false pyramid. Its northern neighbor, which is larger and about 343 feet high, is considered the first true pyramid in Egypt.

During the 12th dynasty, 400 years later, kings Amenemhat II, Senusert II and Amenemhat III built their pyramid complexes in Dahshur to the east of Snefru's. They are smaller and not as well preserved.

In Saqqara, there is a limestone tomb in the form of a sarcophagus known as the *mastaba* of Pharaon. It was built by Shepseskaf, the sixth king of the 4th dynasty, on the western side

27

of the Saqqara plateau. It, like the tomb of his reputed sister Khentkaus at Giza, has gone back to the *mastaba* form.

In the 5th dynasty, the pharaohs chose a new burial place at Abu Sir and Abu Ghurab, halfway between Saqqara and Giza. Their pyramid complexes are distinguished by their rather high pyramids and uncovered sun temples, which were nicely decorated. Although they are in bad condition, they are still worth seeing. King User Kaf, the first king of the 5th dynasty, built his pyramid directly at the northeastern edge of Zoser's complex, but it is badly damaged because it was used as a quarry in the Late Period.

To the southwest of the Step Pyramid stands the Pyramid of Unas, the last king of the 5th dynasty. It is a small pyramid, about 55 feet high, whose core is composed of rubble and pieces of stones cased with limestone. Among several chambers in its interior is the funeral chamber with its granite sarcophagus still in place. It was the first pyramid ever decorated on the inside, and the walls of its chambers are covered with texts arranged in columns and painted in blue, called the Pyramid Texts. They are considered the oldest collection of religious and funerary texts, containing more than 750 spells to protect the deceased king. The ceilings are decorated with stars in imitation of the night sky. More than 1,000 years later, Prince Khamunese, son of Ramses II, inscribed on the bottom of the southern hall a record of his restorations on that pyramid. Similar inscriptions found in monuments at Abu Sir register his interest in preserving monuments of the Old Kingdom.

Most of the kings of the 6th dynasty – Teti, its founder; Pepi I; Merener; and Pepi II, the last king – built their pyramids in both northern and southern Saqqara. Some of them are decorated with the Pyramid Texts. Through the Saqqara tombs, belonging to kings from the 1st through the 6th dynasties, we can gain a clearer idea about the development of funeral and religious conceptions in the first 1,000 years of the Egyptian civilization.

Among the most interesting and celebrated monuments of Saqqara are the *mastabas* belonging to members of the royal family and high officials who were buried, usually with their families, in the vicinity of their kings. The *mastabas* were equipped with supporting pillars, false doors, offertory tables, statues and other amenities. They contain brilliant painted bas reliefs in a classical style from a period regarded as the golden age of Pharaonic art. The paintings symbolize activities, responsibilities and joys of the Egyptians' everyday lives: agricultural scenes, professions,

the feeding of animals, leisure-time amusements, fishing, and hunting for birds, hippopotami and crocodiles. Some of these scenes are full of charm, humor and other human feelings. Among a score of interesting tombs, the most famous of them is that of Moreruka (Mera), constructed for this important official, his wife and their son. It is the largest tomb and is composed of 31 rooms and passages. Other tombs, especially those of Ti, Ptah Hotep, Nefer, Kagemni Khnumhotep and Ankh Mahor, are also splendid. Among the later tombs of importance are those of General Horemheb, the last king of the 18th dynasty, and Tef Nakht from the 26th dynasty.

Mariette discovered in 1851 the serapeum to the northeast of the Step Pyramid, which contains the subterranean galleries where the sacred Apis bull was buried. Inside that rock-hewn sepulcher were found 24 granite and basalt sarcophagi, some of them weighing as much as 70 tons. The bull Apis was worshiped in Memphis and was associated with the main god Ptah.

Nearby is an open space that was adorned in the Ptolemaic period with statues of Greek philosophers. The ruins of a Coptic monastery lie at the edge of the desert to the southeast of the Step Pyramid. It is the monastery of St. Germeah, dating from the 5th century A.D.

القَــاهِــرَة

Of all Egypt's heritage, the deepest impressions and greatest admiration are reserved for those three massive triangular-faced monuments, which the Greeks called "The Pyramids," and for that huge leonine statue with a human face, which they called "The Sphinx." All four rise from an expanse of sand on the Giza Plateau.

No doubt those three pyramids and the great Sphinx are the most famous, glorious and renowned of all Egyptian monuments. Giza, which began as a medieval town to the west of Cairo, is now a large modern city and an important part of Metropolitan Cairo, but its fame is linked with its magnificent monuments.

The three pyramids at Giza are arranged from northeast to southwest in chronological order and in a descending volume, size and standard of perfection. Their owners – Cheops (Khufu), his son Khefren (Khafra) and his grandson Mycerinus (Menkaure) – represent three successive generations of the 4th Pharaonic dynasty. Those pyramids were built mostly of local limestone, but also contain fine limestone from Tura and Aswan, as well as granite. The use of granite must have caused serious problems owing to its hardness, heaviness and need to be transported from Aswan quarries more than 500 miles from Giza.

Egyptian civilization was nearly 3,000 years old when Greek travelers like Herodotus visited Egypt and saw the huge pyramids standing on the edge of the desert and looking toward the River Nile. It was a sight unlike any ever seen or dreamt of in Greece. When Napoleon made his military expedition to Egypt, he calculated that the stones of the Giza pyramids would have been sufficient to build a wall 10 feet high and one foot wide, running around the whole of France. It has been calculated that the volume of the Great Pyramid could house London's Westminster Abbey, Paris' Notre Dame Cathedral and Rome's St. Peter Cathedral altogether. It has also been said that if the 2.3 million stones of the Great Pyramid were cut in smaller pieces, they might be used to build a city for 100,000 inhabitants. Yet another speculation is that if the stones of the Great Pyramid were divided into one foot cubes and extended in a straight line, they would reach two-thirds of the way around the Equator.

The site of the Giza necropolis is certainly one of the best preserved, excavated, registered and studied of all pyramid sites, and it has had a vital role in clarifying the different aspects of royal funerary establishments of the Old Kingdom. Nevertheless, there are still some isolated areas that ought to be excavated, and a great deal of significant research that is still needed to provide us with important new scientific data.

The largest and oldest of the three is the Great Pyramid of Cheops, built about 4,500 years ago; it is one of the seven wonders of antiquity, and a monument that made the name of Cheops famous all over the world. Its base covers an area of 13 hectares, its original height was 481 feet before it lost its summit (which was about 31 feet high), and it is estimated to contain 2.3 million limestone blocks averaging 2.5 tons, although some stones may weigh as much as 15 tons.

The original entrance in the northern face of the pyramid is 55 feet above the ground. Since it is blocked, the pyramid is now entered through a hole that was made during the 9th century in the false hope of finding treasures hidden inside.

The monument's interior is almost as impressive as its exterior. Here are corridors, passageways, rooms, apertures for ventilation; here too is a grand gallery, 153 feet long and 28 feet high with a braced ceiling and a burial room, called "the King's

Room," with a ceiling of nine blocks of granite weighing about 400 tons, supported by five pillars to reduce the pressure on the ceiling. It is not only an extraordinary work, but a miracle seemingly beyond human capacity at such a remote time.

We now believe that Cheops originally planned a smaller tomb with an underground burial chamber, but it was not completed. As his ambitions for it grew, he altered the tomb's plan twice, each time deciding to raise the burial chamber higher and to increase the size of his pyramid. His second project needed an upward sloping corridor, and another smaller horizontal one leading to the burial room, which was later mistakenly called "the Queen's Room." The third project called for enlarging and extending the main corridor, which is now called "the Grand Gallery" and leads to the new burial room (the King's Chamber), where the lidless granite sarcophagus of the king is still housed.

To the east of the pyramid lie the ruins of the funerary temple, which was a rectangular building of limestone connected by a long causeway to a second lower temple, the Valley Temple, on the edge of the desert. It is presently covered by the houses of the village of Nazlet El Seman. Three small pyramids, now in bad condition, are the tombs of his queens and are situated to the east of the pyramid. Rows of stone *mastabas*, running parallel on the western and southern sides, belonged to nobles, high priests and members of the royal family during that period.

More than 60 years ago, the American archaeologist Reisner excavated three huge pits in the shape of big boats on the east side of the pyramid, but he found nothing inside those pits and his work was unrewarded. But in 1954, Kamal El Malakh, chief architect of Giza, was working on the southeastern side of Cheops' Pyramid when he discovered two pits covered with 41 limestone slabs. After opening the eastern pit, which was 103 feet long and 17 feet deep, he found at its bottom 1,224 wooden pieces. These pieces, mostly of Lebanese cedar, ranged in length between 75 feet and less than four inches and were arranged in 13 orderly layers. It clearly constituted the largest archaeological boat ever discovered, and it became known as the Solar Barque of Cheops. This discovery added to Cheops' fame, and raised questions in scientific circles about its construction, dismantling, burial, and religious and funeral significance.

The wooden pieces were fitted, restored, chemically treated, assembled and bound with their old cords by restorer Haj Ahmed Yousef, in a difficult, complicated and long operation that lasted for 15 years. The result was a gigantic boat, almost in perfect

condition, 139 feet long and weighing about 15 tons. It is considered the oldest "big ship" ever discovered. The boat now stands in a magnificent museum in the form of a ship, located on the top of the pit that housed the dismantled parts of the boat. The second pit, neighboring the first one on the west, has not yet been opened.

القــاهـِـرة

Egyptian records shed no light on the construction of the three pyramids at Giza. Herodotus, the father of history, reported that 100,000 men shared in the task of building the Great Pyramid, working three months every year during flood time for 20 years. Even so, the debate continues over the method of building the pyramids. It is clear, however, that the stones were raised from ground level by means of artificial ramps – as determined by the fact that the remains of such ramps have been discovered in the pyramid sites of El Lisht, Meidum and Amon Temple at Karnak. Before being raised up, the blocks of stone must have been dragged by human hands and carried on sleds drawn by oxen.

The Great Pyramid is amazing for the genius of its planning, its survival over the past 5,000 years with very little damage, and its inner design. Equally amazing is the volume of the task and the perfect administration needed to raise the pyramid, its complex and the pyramid city, using the simplest implements and elementary technology available during Cheops' reign of no more than 25 years. The architects showed great cleverness in choosing the most appropriate site in the desert to bear 2.3 million blocks of stone – a site near the Nile and not far from local quarries. What is also astonishing was their ability to level the site and flatten a surface of 13 acres to an equal level, differing by no more than half an inch from one corner to another; their ability to orient the four sides of the pyramid to the four cardinal points; and their capacity in casing the enormous surfaces of the pyramid with the limestone from Tura and pink granite from Aswan.

Not surprisingly, many attempts have been made to prove that Cheops' Pyramid was not only a burial place, and many reasons have been given for building such a mountain of stone. Nor is it surprising that a number of books dealing with the secrets and hidden powers of that pyramid have been written in recent years. There is, however, no evidence to support such ideas and suppositions. At the same time, many scientists became interested in solving the mysteries of the pyramids through modern science and technology. Cosmic rays and geophysical methods were used to discover the inside of the second pyramid, but they did not succeed in adding to our knowledge. Investigations using microgravimetric readings and electromagnetic soundings are now being conducted in the Great Pyramid under the auspices of the Egyptian Antiquities Department. We hope that these tests will help us to know more about the Cheops Pyramid and to reveal some of its secrets.

Of all the pharaohs who followed Cheops, only his son Khefren dared to build a pyramid and its complex competing in volume, magnitude and perfection with that of his father.

The Pyramid of Khefren, the second of the Giza group, is situated on the southwest side of Cheops' Pyramid. It gives the impression of being taller than Cheops, because it is built on slightly higher ground, but in reality it is eight feet shorter than the Great Pyramid. Most of its casing has disappeared, but a granite casing can still be seen on its summit. It has two entrances facing the north, one about 50 feet high and another below it.

The funerary temple of Khefren's Pyramid is virtually destroyed, while the causeway has disappeared except for the portion near the Valley Temple, which is built of granite and thus is called the Granite Temple. It stands near the Sphinx and attracts the eye with its simplicity and perfection. Flanking the funerary temple are what appear to be six boat pits, but no boats were found in them.

The third pyramid of Giza, built by Mycerinus, occupies less than half of the area covered by the Great Pyramid, and is only about 230 feet high. Its lower 16 courses are still cased in granite. The mortuary temple lies to the east of the pyramid, which is fronted on its southern side by three subsidiary pyramids for the queens, each not more than 30 feet high. All three are badly damaged. Khent Kaus, the last queen of the 4th dynasty, built her *mastaba* in the shape of a sarcophagus, beside the third pyramid. Many *mastabas* and rock-cut tombs are spread over the area. Their walls are covered with scenes from everyday life and drawings of the deceased and his family. They include the well-known tomb of Queen Meres Ankh III, wife of Khefren; the tomb of Kar, overseer of the pyramids; and the *mastaba* of Idu, a high priest.

In the early evening, after sunset, the pyramids of Giza come to life through the spectacle of sound and light. The colored floodlights, the playful shadows, the attractive narration and the fitting music give the monuments new dimensions.

Southeast of the Great Pyramid, near the village of Nazlet El Seman, lies a gigantic Sphinx (called in Arabic *Abou El Hawl*). It has the body of a lion and a human head and face, and is believed to be the portrait of Khefren. Most likely, when the architects and sculptors were preparing the causeway of Khefren's complex, they came to a knoll. Instead of flattening it, they transformed it into a Sphinx. Later in the New Kingdom, they identified the statue with the Sun God Hor-m-akhty. The Sphinx is 240 feet long and 66 feet high, and faces the east, probably to greet the rising sun.

A great granite stela, found beneath the sand in 1916 and lying between the paws of the Sphinx, was erected by King Thutmoses IV (18th dynasty), 1,000 years after the Sphinx was sculpted. The inscription on the stela relates that when Thutmoses was a prince, he went hunting in the desert near the pyramids. Becoming tired, he lay down to have a nap in the shade of the Sphinx. While he was sleeping, he dreamt that the Sun God promised him that if he removed the sand around the monument, he would be entitled to ascend the Egyptian throne.

The Giza Sphinx is not only the oldest one in Egypt, but also the largest and most mysterious of all the sphinxes. Beyond it stands a limestone temple that is related to it and is called the "Sphinx Temple."

According to legend from Middle Ages, an emir who hated the Sphinx's pagan smile destroyed its nose and mouth with his cannon. Another story is that this destruction was caused by Napoleon's cannons in the Pyramids Battle with the Mamelukes. I believe that decay is the real cause of this destruction, since the Sphinx is sculpted in soft limestone, and has suffered considerably from erosion and from the rising of the underground water table.

القاهرة

Although more than 80 Egyptian pyramids still survive in Egypt and Sudan, most of them are little more than mounds of loose stone and sand. The most important and well-known ones are from the Pyramid Age (the Old Kingdom). All were built on the edge of the Western Desert, from Abu Roash in the north to Meidum in the South, in what we can call the Necropolis of Memphis, the capital during that period.

القاهرة

Today, the grand city of Cairo, with its museum, its transferred obelisks and statues, the Heliopolis ruins, as well as Memphis and Saqqara, symbolizes and represents Pharaonic Egypt and its remote civilization, although the actual city was established 10 centuries ago – nearly 14 centuries after the disappearance of the pharaohs.

THE COPTIC LEGACY   *Dr. Gawdat Gabra*

Our knowledge about Egypt during the Roman, Byzantine and early Islamic periods is based mainly on the written material preserved on papyri, parchment and ostraca (potsherds or stone chips bearing inscriptions). Many Greek, Roman and Arabic historians left detailed reports covering all aspects of life in Egypt.

When Octavius, later Emperor Augustus, defeated Antonius in the sea battle of Actium in 31 B.C., he was able to occupy Alexandria and to put an end to the Ptolemaic dynasty in Egypt under its famous queen Cleopatra. Egypt became a Roman province under the personal authority of the emperor. The new rulers had to introduce different administrative and agricultural reforms to stop the instability that had prevailed in the last decade of the Ptolemaic period. Egypt was for Rome the most important supplier of corn. In addition to transporting corn to Rome, Egyptians were subjected to other forms of forced labor. At the same time, they faced a heavy burden from the poll tax and other taxes.

In order to defend the country and to crush any rebellion, the Romans placed legions at Pelusium to control the eastern Delta, at Alexandria to control the western Delta, and at Babylon to control the rest of Egypt. Emperors presented themselves as pharaohs and erected Egyptian-style temples in honor of Egyptian gods. The Greeks, though no longer rulers, remained among the elite of society, especially in the self-governing cities. The Greek language continued to be the official language, while Latin was used mainly in the army. The Egyptians kept their own ancient language, as seen on the walls of the temples and especially in the demotic and Coptic writings.

During the Roman occupation of Egypt, resistance sometimes flared up, especially among the people of Thebes. In 172 A.D., in the Delta there was even an uprising of herdsmen. The Roman army also had to interfere to stop fights between Greeks and Jews, especially in Alexandria. The Blemmyes, a Nubian tribe, often attacked Upper Egypt and threatened the flow of commerce between the Red Sea and the Nile Valley. Meanwhile, severe economic conditions throughout Egypt prompted the Emperor Diocletian to introduce administrative reforms in 297.

At the same time, Alexandria developed into one of the most important and cosmopolitan cities of the civilized world and its population represented different currents of cultures, religions and philosophies. There, and elsewhere in Egypt, feelings of nationalism increased among the oppressed people. A catalyst for these feelings was the spread of Christianity in the area.

The Christians became subjected to such persecution under Diocletian that the Coptic church begins its calendar with the Era of Diocletian, known also as the Era of the Martyrs. The official persecution of Christians by the Romans finally ceased between the years 311 and 313 through the Edict of Toleration and the Edict of Milan.

The final years of the Byzantine rule of Egypt were characterized by large estates. Strong land-owning families even usurped governmental functions. Under this feudal system, most native Egyptians were relegated to serfdom.

In the first decades of the 7th century the Persian army attacked Syria and Egypt. Despite the efforts of Emperor Heraclius, Egypt was soon lost to the Byzantine Empire. The emergence of Islam brought a new power to the Arabian Peninsula. In 643 the Arabian army general Amr Ibn el-As extended the complete authority of the Islamic state of Egypt. A new era began in the long history of this country.

القَاهِرَة

The Coptic Church is one of the oldest in the world. According to tradition, it was founded by St. Mark the Evangelist. We are told that he preached the Gospel in Alexandria as early as 50 or 60 A.D. Gradually Christianity began to spread in the Nile Valley — as evidenced by the appointment of several Egyptian bishops by Demetrius, the Patriarch of Alexandria (188–230). The Catechetical school of Alexandria was the most important theological school of the time, led by great scholars of the 2nd and 3rd centuries such as Pantaenus, Clement and Origen.

The Egyptian Christians were first persecuted in the year 201 during the reign of the Emperor Septimius Severus. The Copts suffered another persecution during the reign of Decus (249–251). Each citizen had to prove that he made offerings to the gods. Thousands of Egyptians preferred death rather than to deny their Christian faith. Many escaped into the desert and others were captured and tortured. The most severe wave of persecution began during the reign of the Emperor Diocletian (284–305) and continued under Maximinus Daia (305–313). Church sources speak of hundreds of thousands of martyrs enduring a long, systematic persecution. The Patriarch Peter I was described as the "Seal of the Martyrs." The commemoration of martyrs as saints is an important feature of the Coptic church.

The Patriarchs of Alexandria played a remarkable role in religious policy and had a leading position in universal theological controversies, especially in the 4th and 5th centuries. The Patriarch Alexander and his young deacon Athanasius, later the most distinguished Patriarch of Alexandria, fought against the heresy of Arius, who was condemned during the Council of Nicaea in 325. The Creed of Faith, which survives to this day, was a result of that Council. It is said that 318 bishops from around the civilized world assembled there.

With the career of Patriarch Athanasius (328–373), who was exiled five times by the Roman authorities as a hero of orthodoxy and defender of the faith, national feeling increased among the Egyptians. Athanasius' struggles and exiles were a glorious part of the history of the Coptic Church and a spur to Egyptian nationalism.

The "unity or duality of Christ" was a matter of controversy among theologians for many years. An irresolvable schism resulted in the church after the Council of Chalcedon (451). At the same time, the Coptic Church became a national church, united behind the Patriarch of Alexandria.

The emperors of the Byzantine Empire wanted to fill the see of Alexandria with men loyal to Constantinople who would provide them with imperial political and military support. The Copts recognized only their patriarch, who often had to leave Alexandria to lead his church far from the Byzantine authorities. In 631 Emperor Heraclius sent Cyrus – known also as al-Muqauqas – to Alexandria as an imperial prefect to control Egypt and to continue as a loyal patriarch to the Empire. Cyrus forced the Patriarch Benjamin to flee from Alexandria to Upper Egypt in the years 631–644, and even attacked monasteries to hunt out the heads of the Coptic Church.

The last ten years of the Byzantine rule in Egypt were among the fullest in Egyptian history.

The Arab conquest of Egypt, which put an end to the Byzantine rule there, had immeasurable consequences for the history of the Coptic Church. It is a wonder that the Church survived the many waves of persecution. Still, it had a direct influence on other churches in Africa. Cyrenaica, the Pentapolis of the five towns (between Tripolis and Alexandria), appear to this day in the title of the Coptic Patriarch. The Nubian Church was also influenced by the Coptic Church. We know that a bishop was in Philae as early as 362 A.D. Recent excavations in Nubia show

the good relations between the two churches continuing as late as the time of Patriarch Gabriel IV (1370–8) who consecrated a bishop for the people of Nubia. For many centuries the Coptic Patriarchs sent a monk from Egypt to be the head of the Ethiopian Church. This tradition remained in effect from the 4th century until 1948.

القَهـِرَة

Monasticism is, perhaps, the Copts' most important contribution to civilization. It had a special character in Egypt where one could stand with one foot on fertile agricultural land and the other on the desert. During the Decian persecution (251 A.D.) many Christians fled into the desert, and some discovered that life there was more suitable for religious practice and meditation.

We know nothing of the first monks other than the absence of rules by which they had to live. We do know, however, about St. Antony, considered to be the father of monasticism. Antony was born around the year 251 and died when he was 105 years old after living 70 years as an anchorite. Patriarch Athanasius the Great compiled the biography of that eminent hermit, which was soon known in Europe.

In about 320, St. Pachom established the first community of monks at Tabennisi, in the district of Nag' Hammadi, in Upper Egypt. His form of monasticism, known as cenobitic, was based on precise rules. These rules cover all aspects of monastic life such as prayers, masses, calls, meals and work. Cenobitic monasticism proved highly popular, and monasteries spread throughout the country, especially in Middle and Upper Egypt. Many fathers of the Church from different parts of the world desired to learn about monasticism and spent time in Egypt, especially in the 4th and 5th centuries; they included St. John Chrysostom, bishop of Constantinople; Rufinus, the ecclesiastical historian; and St. Basil, the author of the liturgy. The monastic rules of Pachom were translated from Coptic into Latin and this directly influenced monasticism in Europe.

Another great figure of monasticism is Shenoute, who accompanied the Patriarch Cyril to the Council of Ephesus in 431. His monastery, known as Deir al-Abiad, or the White Monastery, received thousands of refugees in hard times. Shenoute was also a great preacher, administrator and nationalist who struggled against heathenism and Hellenism.

Left: A remnant of the Babylon Fortress, an interesting example of Roman and Byzantine military construction. Below: A fresco in a niche from Bawit (7th century). The lower part represents the Holy Virgin Mary with the Christ Child and apostles. The upper part represents God in the Chariot of Fire with the four symbolic creatures.

Following pages: Two views of the Church of the Holy Virgin Mary, called the "Suspended" or "Hanging" church because it was built on the ruins of the Babylon Fortress.

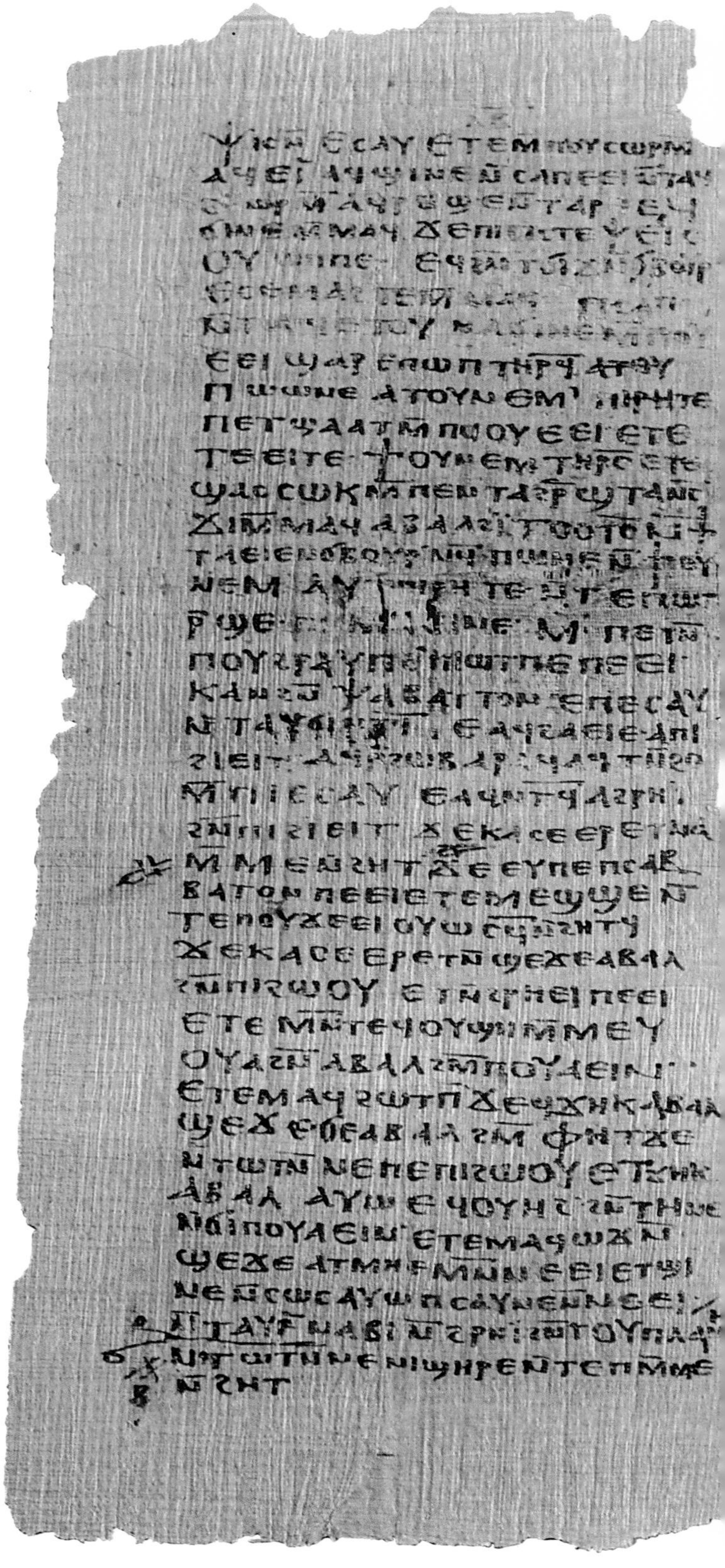

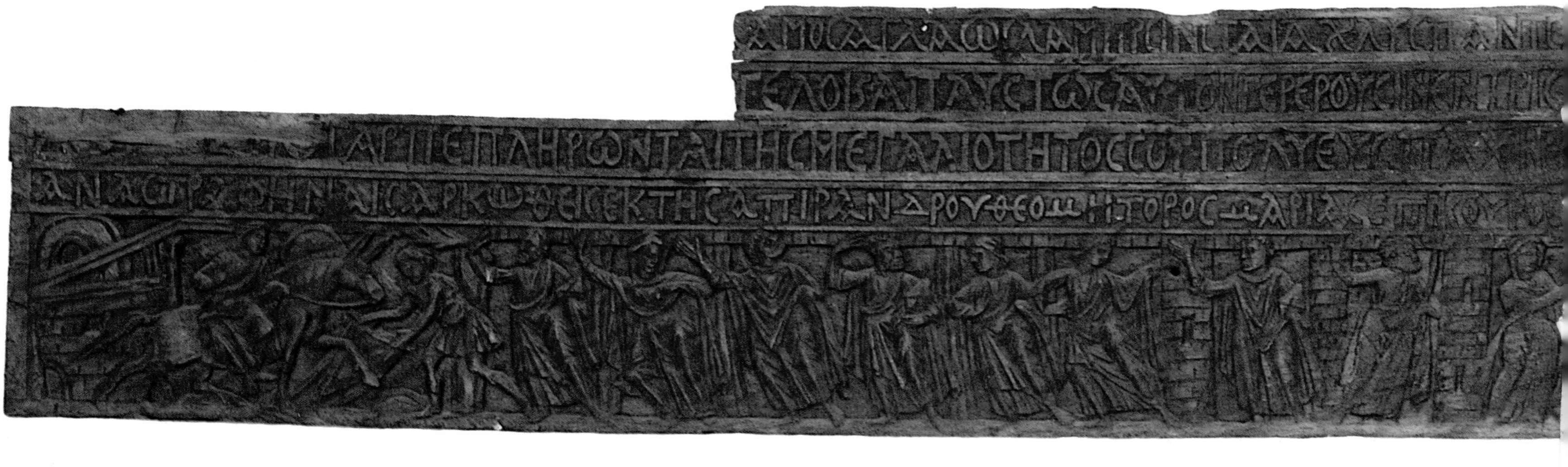

Left: A 4th-century Coptic Gnostic papyrus. Below: A carved wooden frieze written in Greek and depicting the triumphant entry of Christ into Jerusalem; 4th/5th century, from al-Mo-allaqa, now in the Coptic Museum.

To the west of the Delta (*Wadi al-Natrun*) many colonies of monks were founded in the desert during the 4th century. Literary sources inform us about the hermits in Scetis and about the famous Macarius, the founder of monasticism in this district. Hundreds of monks' cells with interesting architecture and fine wall paintings have recently been discovered in Kellia. The earliest date back to the 4th/5th centuries.

The monks played a considerable role throughout the history of the Coptic Church. The great Athanasius was the first Patriarch who encouraged monks to become bishops. Since the 8th century most of the patriarchs of the Alexandria see have been elected from the monasteries in Wadi al-Natrun. The Coptic monasteries received Greeks, Romans, Nubians, Ethiopians, Syrians, Libyans and others.

القَـاهِـرَة

Cairo can be proud of its Coptic legacy. The most significant group of Christian monuments lies within the Roman and Byzantine Fortress of Babylon with its ancient churches and the Coptic Museum. Another group is to be seen in old Cairo outside the Babylon Fortress. A third group is represented by some important churches scattered about different parts of Cairo. Some monuments are associated with the flight of the Holy Family.

The Fortress of Babylon lies on the east bank of the River Nile in the district known today as Old Cairo. The site has been a bishop's residence since the middle of the 5th century or earlier. The Fortress dates from early Roman times, when a Roman legion resided in this strategic point between Upper and Lower Egypt. Apparently it was enlarged and fortified by the emperors Trajan (98–117 A.D.) and Arcadius (395–408). The Coptic historian John of Nikou tells us that the Arabs were able to spread their authority over Egypt after holding this well-fortified fortress. The Babylon Fortress had 10 bastions, of which four are partly preserved. One of its two towers and the southern gateway can be seen from the gardens of the Coptic Museum. Most of the walls are built of three regular layers of red bricks alternating with five stone layers. The remains of this fortress provide an interesting example of Roman and Byzantine military buildings.

The ancient churches within the Fortress of Babylon – known also as *Qasr el-Sham* – are almost certainly the oldest in Cairo.

Pieces of woodwork dating from the 4th and 5th centuries were found in the churches of al-Mo-allaqa, St. Barbara and St. Sergius. These masterpieces are now displayed in the Coptic Museum. While it seems incongruous that these churches existed inside a Roman and Byzantine military fortress, it is not unlikely that the churches were built sometime after the end of the persecution of the Christians.

The Church of the Holy Virgin Mary (*al-Mo-allaqa*) is called the "Suspended" or "Hanging" Church because it was erected upon the ruins of two southern bastions of the Babylon Fortress. Its famous wooden lintel with the scene of Christ's entry into Jerusalem, now in the Coptic Museum, dates to the 4th/5th centuries. The church was partly demolished in the time of the Patriarch Joseph (831–850) and was rebuilt by the Patriarch Abraham (976–979). When the patriarchal seat of Alexandria was transferred to Cairo in the 11th century, it was located in Mo-allaqa in view of the church's importance.

In 1672 the Frenchman Venselb referred to Mo-allaqa as the most ancient and beautiful church in Egypt. This church, like many ancient churches of Egypt, is of a basilican type adopted from ancient Egyptian temples. It has a front vestibule or a narthex leading to the main church with its nave, columns, ambos and sanctuaries. The columns that separate the aisles are executed in marble, except for one that is of black basalt. Some of the capitals of these columns are Corinthian, presumably taken from older Graeco-Roman buildings. The attractive ambo or pulpit is attributed to the 13th century. It rests upon 15 marble pillars inlaid with mosaics. In the eastern part of the church stand three sanctuaries. The one in the center is dedicated to the Holy Virgin, the right-hand one to John the Baptist, and the left-hand one to St. George. The splendid screen or iconostasis of the middle sanctuary dates to the 12th/13th centuries and is of ebony inlaid with ivory. The altar inside the sanctuary is surmounted by a canopy and supported by four columns. Behind the altar is a marble tribune, where the clergy usually sat. As in many Coptic churches, the Church of Mo-allaqa is decorated by very interesting icons.

A small door of fine pine wood in the southern aisle of the main church leads into the "little church." This church was built on the floor of one of the bastions of the Fortress. To the left is the sanctuary of Teckle Haimanout, the famous saint of Ethiopia. Traces of fine wall paintings are still visible on its eastern wall. One of the scenes, in what is most likely the oldest preserved part of the church, apparently represents Jesus Christ flanked by Apostles. Coptic frescoes have recently been discovered there, showing a wonderful scene of the Nativity.

To the south of the sanctuary is the baptistery, which contains a granite basin and a niche ornamented with mosaics. Although this church has been restored at several different times – most recently in 1983 – it still preserves the atmosphere of a medieval Coptic church.

The Church of Saints Sergius and Bacchus (*Abu-Sarga*) can be reached through a door in the garden of the Coptic Museum. It is probably the oldest church in Cairo, having been built over a traditional site blessed by the Holy Family. The Church of Abu-Sarga also has historical importance. The 55th Patriarch, Shenoute I (858–869), was the first to be consecrated in this church. After him, patriarchs of the Coptic Church continued to be elected there up to the beginning of the 12th century.

The church is of a basilican type. Its front vestibule or narthex has a Mandatum Tank that was used for the service of the blessing of water on the Feast of Epiphany, though today a portable basin is used. Two rows of six columns each separate the aisles from the church's nave. Eleven of these monolithic columns are of marble, and one is of red granite. The columns still preserve traces of painted figures, which appear to represent apostles or saints. Some panels of the old wooden church's pulpit are in the Coptic Museum; others are in the British Museum. The pulpit has been replaced by a copy of the marble ambo of the Church of St. Barbara, which is nearby. The screen or iconostasis of the main sanctuary is a wonderful piece of art. It is attributed to the 12th/13th centuries. Its fine panels are inlaid with ivory and ebony, carved in a very attractive relief with arabesques. Some wooden panels are of special importance, being of older origin. They represent three warrior saints, the Nativity and the Last Supper. The altar stands inside the sanctuary, surmounted by a lofty canopy supported by four pillars. A semi-circular tribune with seven steps was built around the walls of the apse. It is decorated with strips of red, black and white marble. The bishop's throne with the niche that lies behind it is in the center of the apse. The icons of the Church of Abu-Sarga are of special interest. Some of them are relatively old and could be assigned to the 16th/17th centuries. They represent the life history of Christ, the Holy Virgin and some of the Saints.

The Church of Abu-Sarga also boasts the Crypt of the Chapel of the Holy Family.

Many other Coptic monuments were erected in the same enclosure of the Roman and Byzantine Fortress of Babylon. Although they are not famous like the churches of al-Mo-allaqa and Abu-Sarga, they show the great importance of this site for the patriarchs of the Coptic Church. These are the Church of St. Barbara, the Church of St. George, the Church of the Virgin known as *Qasriat al-Rihan*, and the convent of the nuns of St. George. It is noteworthy that a Jewish synagogue is also located in the enclosure.

القَاهِرَة

The Coptic Museum is the one institution in Cairo that best conveys the Coptic legacy. Its status as a monument reflects its unique position within the Fortress of Babylon, surrounded by Cairo's oldest churches, as well as its attractive *mashrabias*, windows, wooden arabesque ceilings and arches.

Marcus Simaika founded the museum in 1908, but portions of it are actually much older. Some *mashrabias* and parts of the ceilings were brought to the museum from other older buildings. In 1931 the museum was put under government control and a new wing was subsequently established in 1947.

With its 14,000 pieces, the Coptic Museum boasts the largest collection of Coptic art in the world. A significant number of the exhibited objects originate from Cairo and its environs, such as Saqqara and Memphis. Many fine pieces – such as wooden panels and doors, icons, metal censers and bible caskets, pottery, sculptures and manuscripts – once belonged to edifices within the Babylon Fortress.

In 1983 the greater part of the museum was renovated and the objects were displayed according to material, consistent with modern methods of exhibition. Most of the exhibited monuments go back to the periods between the 3rd and 13th centuries. The abundance of precious objects demonstrates the development of Coptic art as a popular, individual and national art. These monuments represent the different aspects of Coptic civilization.

The section of woodwork in the old wing contains carved and painted panels, friezes, doors, combs and musical instruments that reflect the skill of Coptic carpenters. A special section is dedicated to Coptic pottery, which is famous for its different techniques, variety of forms, fine designs and decoration in lovely colors.

Below: A bronze lamp representing the cross amid the crescent; 14th/15th century, Coptic Museum. Right: A 15th-century silver casket for the Gospel; from the Church of Abu-Sarga, now in the Coptic Museum.

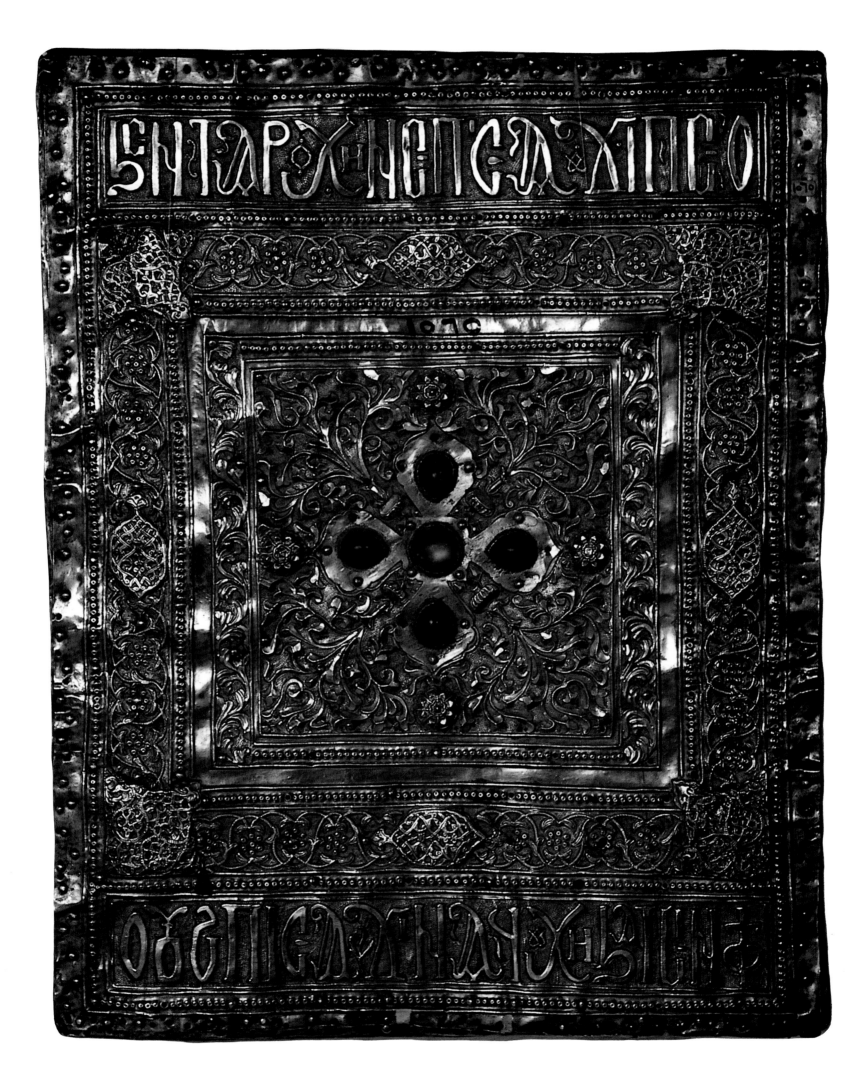

On the first floor of the new wing is exhibited the collection of Coptic stonework, the most important of which are the architectural carvings: niches, columns, capitals, lintels and friezes. They illustrate the development of Coptic sculpture. The masterpieces of stonework of such high quality bear witness to the splendid churches and monasteries that once existed in Egypt.

Textiles are the most characteristic products of Coptic art. Coptic textiles were exported all over the world during Roman, Byzantine and Islamic times. The Coptic Museum possesses a rich collection of textiles. The collection is on the upper floor of the new wing and contains tunics, curtains, parts of shrouds and various fragments.

On the same floor are the icons, metalwork and manuscripts. Most of the icons were brought from Cairo's old churches. Although the bulk of them are not more than three centuries old, they are very interesting for their themes. Some of them bear features of old Coptic art. The names of some artists are immortalized on icons. The metalwork section is remarkable for its different materials such as gold, silver, copper, bronze and iron. It contains objects from everyday life: jewels, medical instruments, keys and lamps. Many churches' liturgical vessels, crosses and Bible caskets reflect the skill of Coptic craftsmen. Of great importance is the museum's collection of manuscripts on papyrus, parchment and paper. The texts are written in Old Greek, Coptic, Syriac, Arabic and Ethiopian. Coptic Gnostic codices could be considered one of the most valuable collections of papyri in the world. Both wings of the museum also contain wonderful frescoes. These masterpieces tell us how the monasteries and churches once were decorated.

The Coptic Museum also possesses fine collections of glass, ivory and ostraca.

القَاهِرَة

Old Cairo boasts of more Christian monuments than any other district of the city. To the south of the Fortress lie some minor churches. The Church of the Holy Virgin belongs to a small convent of Babylon known as the Cloister of Babylon al-Darag. In the same spot stands the convent of Theodore with the Church of Saints Cyrus and John and the Church of Theodore the Eastern. To the north of the Fortress lies an important group of churches,

not far from the mosque of Amr at Al-Fustat. These are the Church of Mercurius (*Abu-Saifain*), the Church of Shenoute (*Shenouda*), and the Church of the Virgin Mary, known as al-Damshiria. A nunnery is also located there. North of Al-Fustat are the Church of St. Minas (*Mena*) and the Church of St. Behnam at Fom al-Khalig.

This group of churches provide evidence of the expansion of Christian buildings north of the Babylon Fortress and of Al-Fustat long before the foundation of Fatimid Cairo. So we know, for example, that the Patriarch Michael I was elected in the Church of Shenoute in the year 743 A.D. The famous historian Al-Maqreezi tells us that the Church of St. Minas in Fom al-Khalig was restored in 724 A.D.

The most significant church of this group is St. Mercurius. According to tradition, this church was restored around 927 A.D. – and in the year 1080, 47 bishops assembled there. The nave of the church is separated from its narthex or front vestibule by a screen. Its beautiful ambo is decorated with mosaics and is supported by 15 marble columns. The central sanctuary of the church is dedicated to St. Mercurius. Its screen is a wonderful piece of art of ebony inlaid with fine engraved plaques of ivory. The doorway is flanked with two Corinthian columns of marble.

The church is famous for its interesting icons. Over the doorway of the screen or iconostasis are two icons, one of Christ, the other of the Holy Virgin Mary. The lower row has icons of Christ in the center; the Holy Virgin, the Archangel Michael and three apostles on His right; and St. John the Baptist, the Archangel Gabriel and three apostles on His left. The church's sanctuary is imposing. Its altar is surmounted by an attractive canopy decorated with wonderful paintings. The most important scene shows Christ surrounded by the Four Creatures, symbolizing the four Evangelists, and by the seraphim. A fine tribune of red and white marble is behind the altar. The east wall of the niche has frescoes with Christ and the seraphim; the walls around are ornamented with paintings representing the 12 apostles.

Many historians, among them al-Maqreezi and Abu Saleh, have stated that Fatimid Cairo and its later extensions had many old churches. But most were destroyed in times of disorder and anarchy, especially during the reign of the Mameluke Sultan el-Naser Mohammad Ibn Qalawoon. Of those that still exist, the churches of Haret al-Rum and Haret Zuwaila are considered among the most important.

The Church of the Holy Virgin Mary at Haret al-Rum is

situated in the quarter of al-Ghoria. It was probably founded in the 10th century and was restored in 1086. It was a patriarchal seat during the years 1660–1799. In the years 1460, 1703 and 1785 Holy Chrism was consecrated there. The church has a narthex, nave and three sanctuaries. Five piers separate its choir from the nave. Seven icons adorn the wooden pulpit of the church, representing Christ, the four Evangelists, St. John Chrysostom and St. George. The iconostasis of the central sanctuary is in wood inlaid with ivory. Its top is decorated by an icon of the Holy Virgin flanked on each side by six icons of apostles. The ceiling of the church consists of 120 domes, three of which are over its three sanctuaries. A little church of St. Theodore with one sanctuary and a baptistery is attached to its northern aisle. In the upper floor of the Church of the Holy Virgin is the Church of St. George. The same group also includes the convent of nuns of St. Theodore.

Another important complex of Coptic monuments is to be found in Haret Zuwaila, near al-Muski in the district known as al-Khurinfish. We are told that the Holy Family blessed the place. This complex includes the Church of the Holy Virgin, the Church of Mercurius (*Abu-Saifain*) and the Church of St. George. A convent of nuns is attached to the Church of the Holy Virgin. The oldest of the three, the Church of the Holy Virgin was probably founded in the 10th/11th century and later, for three centuries – until the year 1660 – was a patriarchal seat. The church has a narthex, nave, choir, two aisles and three sanctuaries. Most of the church's marble columns have Corinthian capitals. Of special attraction is the screen before the sanctuaries, the dome of the altar in the central sanctuary and the tribune in its apse. The church contains many interesting icons, including one that represents the Annunciation and dates from 1355 A.D.

The district of Abbasia, where the new Cathedral stands, is known for its attractive, but relatively new churches. One of them, the Church of Anba Ruwais, was mentioned by al-Maqreezi. The most important part of this church is the crypt where Anba Ruwais is buried, as are some patriarchs of the 14th and 15th centuries. The Patriarch Marcus VIII (1796–1809) transferred his seat from Haret al-Rum to the district of al-Esbakia. A church was erected there around the year 1800. The church was rebuilt into a cathedral during the 19th century and is known as the Cathedral of St. Mark, though its style resembles that of a modern Greek Orthodox church.

The Holy Family found refuge in Egypt from the persecution of Herod. The Coptic Church celebrates the memory of the flight of the Holy Family to Egypt on the 24th day of the Coptic month Bashons, corresponding to the first day of June.

The Holy Family crossed the Sinai Peninsula through Rafia, al-Arish and al-Farama. After crossing the narrow isthmus at al-Kantara, the Holy Family passed by Bubastis on Their way to Belbeis in the eastern Delta. Many sources have preserved wonderful details of this flight including the different places blessed by Their presence. Four sites in Cairo claim to be among these places. The best-known site visited by medieval pilgrims and modern tourists is al-Matarya, now a suburb in northern greater Cairo. According to tradition, the Holy Family rested beneath a sycamore tree that is still standing.

The second site is in the district of Babylon where the Holy Family took refuge in a cave. This crypt is beneath the center choir and a part of the central sanctuary of the Church of Abu-Sarga. The crypt chapel has nine columns in two rows, four on the north and five on the south, separating the nave from the two aisles. On the eastern wall is an altar and on the southern a baptistery. This chapel is one of the most ancient Christian monuments in Cairo. The third site in Cairo blessed by the Holy Family can be seen in Haret Zuwaila.

In the floor before the southern sanctuary of the Church of the Virgin is a well. We are told that Christ blessed the water of this well and the Holy Virgin drank from it. The district of Maadi, some kilometers to the south of the Fortress of Babylon, has a church built according to tradition on a site honored by the presence of the Holy Family.

القاهرة

Right: A detail of the painted ceiling in the old wing of the Coptic Museum. Below: An icon with unique iconography showing the flight of the Holy Family into Egypt; 18th/19th century, Coptic Museum, Cairo.

ISLAMIC CAIRO *Dr. Soad Maher*

Cairo has occupied – and still occupies – a prominent position among cities of the world. Since its birth in the Middle Ages, it has never lagged behind the march of civilization. Cairo has evolved as the capital of Egypt and remains so today. Throughout all its successive periods it has been a jewel, and still is, on the forefront of the Orient.

Those who want to write about Cairo should start by studying the history of the three Islamic capitals of Egypt that preceded the establishment of Cairo. It is necessary, not only chronologically and historically, but also because the topography of the new city contained these three capitals.

القاهرة

Throughout their conquests, Arabs established new capitals in the conquered lands. The sites for these new Arab towns were chosen to suit the public and private interests of the new rulers.

After the Arab conquest of Egypt, a new capital was built by Amr Ibn el-As in the Year 21 A.H. (After Hejira) – 641 A.D. – north of the Babylon Fortress, where the Muslim troops encamped for the first time. Amr called his new city Al-Fustat. The site of Al-Fustat was well chosen geographically and militarily. It was located at the head of the Nile Delta, where it was protected from enemy attacks. It was also close to Arab lands, which facilitated food provisions. To the east of Al-Fustat was the Muqattam Plateau, its protective shield against enemies. Amr Ibn el-As proved his foresight when he planned his new city so that it could later be extended at its northeastern side.

Having established Al-Fustat, Amr built Al-Atique (the old) mosque in its center. It was the foremost mosque in Africa, "the source of lights; blessed is the man who keeps praying in it and persistently looks after it," wrote Ibn Duqmaq. The mosque was expanded to its present size during the Umayyad period. In the middle of the mosque there is a *sahn* (courtyard) surrounded with arcades on four sides. Its famous minarets are erected above the western arcade (*riwaq*). The stucco decorations of the windows are considered the most beautiful made during the 3rd century of the Hejira.

The mosque was rebuilt in the 7th century A.H. (13th century A.D.). However, the *riwaq* of the prayer niche (the *qibla*) was not rebuilt in its original site; its arches were rebuilt vertically on the *qibla* wall instead of parallel to it as in the original construction.

Within these colonnades the first Islamic university was founded. By the 4th century A.H. there were more than 40 active educational institutions, as well as educational and guidance circles for women. During the Fatimid period, women's circles were led by the esteemed lady, Um el-Khair Al-Hijaziya.

The treasury building (*Bayt el-Mal*) where the orphans' money was kept was located in the middle of the courtyard. In Amr's mosque were also courts where both religious and civil disputes were settled. In the area around the mosque, the Arab tribes designed their living quarters.

Historians and travelers in the Middle Ages gave elaborate descriptions of Al-Fustat. For instance, Al Kudai reported that Fustat had 3,600 mosques, 800 roads and 170 public baths. Though these figures may have been exaggerated, other travelers' books indicated the degree of progress and civilization that had been reached in Al-Fustat, particularly during the Umayyad caliphate when the city was the seat of its rulers.

Unfortunately, only a few ruins remain from the oldest Islamic capital. Al-Fustat was burned in the 6th century A.H. in anticipation of a European occupation. Although the fire burned for 54 days, the remaining relics clearly indicated the civilization and prosperity the city had once enjoyed. Its streets were paved and passable; its houses were well designed and spacious, with five to seven stories each.

The city had sanitary public facilities, including numerous public baths. On a given Friday, the revenue from one bath might have reached 500 dirhams.

Amr has described Egypt as "a dark earth with a green tree within which a blessed river is running with increase or with decrease." Arabs paid a great deal of attention to the Nile. A Nilometer was built in the Island of Roda during the Umayyad period and was rebuilt during the reign of the Abbasid Caliph Al Mutawakkil. It still stands in the southern corner of Roda Island; repaired several times, it is a stone-lined pit that goes well below the level of the Nile. Three tunnels lead into it at different depths. In the center of the pit is a marble column graduated into cubits. When the water rose during flood time, it was possible to tell by the highest point it reached on the column whether the year would be one of too much, too little or just enough water. On wooden panels, Quranic verses are engraved. Running around the pit is a frieze of stone incised with Kufic inscriptions from the 3rd century of Hejira, representing the oldest inscription in the Islamic monuments of Egypt.

Amr's mosque was built by Amr Ibn el-As; hence it was named for him. When Amr made a *minbar* (a pulpit) for his new mosque, he received a message from Caliph Omar Ibn el-Khattab ordering him to remove the *minbar*. Omar wrote: "Is it not enough for you to stand while Muslims are sitting at your feet?" Amr removed the *minbar*, but it was said he brought it back after the death of Omar.

The first addition to the mosque of Amr was carried out in 53 A.H. by Mussallamah Ibn Makhled Al-Ansari, the Wali (the governor) of Egypt during the reign of the Umayyad Caliph Moawiya Ibn Abi Sufiyan. The caliph instructed him to expand the mosque at both its eastern and northern sides. Mussallamah made a courtyard, painted the mosque, and decorated its walls and ceilings.

Moreover, Moawiya ordered that a minaret should be built for the mosque in Fustat, and Mussallamah built four cells, one in each of its four corners. He also was the first one to furnish the mosque with mats instead of gravel.

The second addition took place in the reign of Abdel Aziz Ibn Marwan (79 A.H.), the Umayyad prince of Egypt during the era of the Caliph Abdel Malek Ibn Marwan. Abdel Aziz pulled down the mosque to make room for a new extension toward the west, and the northern yard was included in this addition.

In 175 A.H., during the reign of Haroun el Rasheed, Mousa Ibn Issa added the Abu Ayyoub yard at the back of the mosque. He also widened the road around the mosque.

The mosque reached its present size in 212 A.H. when Abdullah Ibn Taher, prince of Egypt during the rule of the Abbasid Caliph Al Ma'moun, doubled the mosque's area, erected a green panel, restored the roof, built a drinking fountain and constructed the courtyard next to the minting house.

During the Tulunid dynasty most of Ibn Taher's addition as well as the *riwaq* of the green panel were destroyed in a fire. As instructed by Khumarawaih Ibn Ahmad Ibn Tulun, the mosque was restored at the cost of 6,400 dinars. The name of Khumarawaih was recorded in the *riwaq*.

In the Ikhshidid period, most columns were decorated, carved and encircled with silver collars.

In 564 A.H., Al-Fustat was destroyed by fire, and the mosque of Amr was also severely damaged. After Salah el-Din came to power, he ordered the restoration of the mosque. In 568 A.H., the facade was reconstructed, and the large *mihrab* (prayer niche) was covered with marble and his name carved on it.

Throughout the Mameluke period, the mosque was repeatedly renovated. The latest additions were made in 703 A.H. on the western side of the mosque. These are the stucco windows and the exterior stucco *mihrab* with its beautiful inscription band and a highly precise masterpiece of floral decoration. The main restoration was done by Burhan el-Din Ibrahim Ibn Omar Ibn el-Mahalli, the chief of merchants in Egypt at that time. Al-Maqreezi wrote "the Mosque has become new again after it was about to fall down. God sent this man (Burhan), in spite of what was known about his greed, who restored the mosque. May God thank his endeavor and make his face white. Restoration works were completed in 804 A.H. However, no Friday prayer was performed in the mosque during the course of restoration."

The Arab historian Ibn Iyass described the last renovation carried out in the mosque during the Mameluke era: "The Sultan rode down from the Citadel toward the Mosque of Amr Ibn el-As. He inspected the collapsing walls and roofs and gave his instruction to rebuild them at his own expense. The work was immediately started."

As the oldest and the first mosque in Islamic Egypt, the mosque of Amr naturally was a subject of many stories and legends. For instance, people used to tell about certain places inside the mosque in which their prayers are accepted. They also spoke of two adjacent columns on the left of the great northern gate (which is closed now), through which no one could pass unless he was pure. Those who were heavy with sins and faults would try to pass through the two columns in the hope that they might be forgiven. It is usual to see people crowding around these columns after the prayer of the last Friday of Ramadan.

القَاهِرَة

When the Abbasids took over the caliphate, they established a new capital in Egypt. The new city was situated in the northeast of Al-Fustat in a region known as Al-Hamra Al-Kuswa; extending up to the Yashkur hills, it is near the place where Ahmad Ibn Tulun later built his famous mosque. There, the Abbasid army built their houses and lived. Ali Ibn Salih established the governor's headquarters (*Dar al-Emarah*) and soldiers' barracks. Al-Fadl Ibn Salih then built the mosque of Al-Askar in the center of the town.

Eventually, Al-Askar and Al-Fustat became linked to form one

Left: The iwan (prayer place) *for the saying of prayers in Amr's mosque, the first to be built in Egypt. Below: The courtyard of the mosque of Ibn Tulun. In its center is a dome mounted on four arches and surrounded by a band of Quranic writing. At the far left is a minaret with three discretely shaped stories: square, circular and octagonal.*

large city. Princes of Egypt continued to live in Dar al Emarah in Al-Askar until the establishment of Fatimid Cairo (*Al-Kahira*).

Though there is no evidence of the works that had been carried out or the buildings that had been founded, Al-Maqreezi has elaborately described Al-Askar and its houses, gardens, mosques, markets and public baths. And we do know that Al-Askar was the political capital of Egypt for more than one century (133–256 A.H.).

القَاهِرَة

When Al-Fustat became overpopulated, Ahmad Ibn Tulun founded the new town of Al-Qatai. In its center, he had built a large mosque (*Masjid Jami*) that was completed in the middle of the 3rd century of Hejira. Ibn Tulun's mosque is actually one of the largest in the Islamic world: more than $6\frac{1}{2}$ acres, including its surrounding sanctuary. It is one of the hanging mosques whose doors can be reached by circular staircases. In the center of the mosque is a square courtyard surrounded by two arcades on each of its three sides. The arcades are erected on brick piers with engaged columns. The capitals of the columns are decorated with arabesques.

In the *qibla* wall (which points to Mecca), there are five arcades and five *mihrabs* beside the main central *mihrab*. All *mihrabs* are adorned with beautiful floral, geometrical and calligraphic decorations. The mosque's *mihrabs* date to different ages. One goes back to the Fatimid Caliph al-Mustanser; another *mihrab* belongs to Sultan Lajin. Two other *mihrabs* are situated on the side of the seat of the prayer caller. The one on the right belongs to the Tulunids, while the one on the left dates back to the Fatimids. On the left side of the big *mihrab* is situated a 7th-century *mihrab* belonging to al-Sayyda Nafiesah. Around the upper walls of the mosque is an inscription written in simple Kufic style.

The niche of the main *mihrab* is ornamented with gilded mosaic and Kufic inscriptions.

On the left side of the main *mihrab* is located a wooden *minbar* ornamented with star-like units.

The mosque has 128 stucco window grilles, four of which are original. Arches are crowned with decorated stucco friezes, above which is a wooden band carved with Kufic inscriptions.

In the middle of the courtyard is a large dome mounted on the walls of four arches and surrounded with a band of Quranic

writing. The minaret in the western arcade is the only one in Egypt with a spiral staircase from the outside. The lower story is square, the second circular in plan, the third is octagonal and the upper story is covered with an incense-burner-like *mabkhara*.

Al-Qatai was the first royal city founded in the Nile Valley during the Islamic era. It was the center of an independent ruler whose connection with the Abbasid caliph in Baghdad was purely religious.

The inspiration for Al-Qatai was Samarra in Iraq, where Ibn Tulun had lived before coming to Egypt. Both cities were divided into *qatai* (quarters) in each of which lived a community of people related to each other.

Samarra's style of architecture and decoration seems to have had a great influence on Ibn Tulun — as was quite obvious in the remaining stucco decorations of the Tulunid monuments.

القَاهِرَة

The city of Al-Kahira (Cairo) was founded in 359 A.H. by Gawhar Al-Sikkeli, commander of the Fatimid troops, one year after the Fatimid conquest of Egypt. A wall of clay bricks was built around the city whose sides were each 1,200 yards long. The area enclosed inside the wall was 340 acres. In the center a large palace was constructed on 70 acres. An additional 70 acres were given over to gardens, thoroughfares and squares. The remaining 200 acres were divided into 20 districts and distributed among the army brigades. And a mosque was constructed near the caliph's palace.

The city of Al-Mu'izz li-Din Allah – the first Fatimid caliph in Egypt – was bordered on the east by the Muqattam hills and the gulf of al-Khalig (an irrigating canal that branched off the Nile), now Port-Said Street. Its southern end can be defined by a line drawn from Bab el-Khalq square moving eastward through Bab Zuwila (one of Cairo's old gates).

Cairo began as a modest capital of the Fatimid state and remained for some time a royal city where the caliph's palaces, princes' houses and governmental departments were located.

Since Cairo was the royal city, Egyptians were not allowed to enter it without permission. Cairo's high walls and guarded gates were real barriers between the caliph and his people. During official occasions, commissioners of foreign countries had to get off their horses and walk to the palace between two rows of soldiers.

However, as the emerging city expanded, it soon occupied a remarkable position under the Fatimid caliphs. Its buildings gradually overlapped its walls and reached Al-Fustat. Hence, the two cities became one great city – the largest in the Islamic world during the Middle Ages.

The most important remaining Fatimid monument in Cairo today is the mosque of Al-Azhar, which is considered the first artistic and architectural work built by the Fatimids in Egypt. Al-Azhar lies in the southeast of Al-Mu'izz near the Big Palace, between the Dylam district and the Turkish district to the south.

Al-Azhar has long occupied an esteemed position throughout the Islamic world. It was a lighthouse of science and scholarship until the arrival of the Ayyubids – the orthodox followers of the Sunna. Thus, Friday prayers were abolished in Al-Azhar, but it was continued in el-Hakim mosque in accordance with the Shafei rite. This discrepancy endured for a century until the Mamelukes came to power.

The idea of using Al-Azhar as an educational institution came about as a result of the religious propaganda activities. In time, Al-Azhar evolved into a famous Islamic university. It also had a special official significance as the seat of *Kadhi al-Kudhah* (chief of judges) and the center of *Al-Muhtaseb* (the public auditor), and it was a forum for judicial meetings and debates. Although the Friday prayer was canceled in Al-Azhar during the Ayyubid rule, the mosque continued playing its educational part.

The Mameluke period was the golden age of Al-Azhar, highlighted by its leading position among Islamic scientific centers.

The Ottoman Turkish invasion of Egypt represented the severest blow to Al-Azhar. After the Abbasid caliphate in Baghdad was defeated by the Mongols in the 7th century of Hejira, all intellectual institutions – including Al-Azhar itself – underwent deterioration and even collapse. Nevertheless, the mosque soon became a last resort of theological and religious sciences and a stronghold of Arabic linguistics – a noble task during hard times for Egypt and the entire Islamic world.

As designed by Gawhar Al-Sikelli in 361 A.H. (972 A.D.), Al-Azhar contained only about one-half its present area.

The Fatimid caliphs made many additions to Al-Azhar and many portions have subsequently been renovated over the past few centuries. It is, therefore, difficult to recognize the original plan of the mosque. Nonetheless, there are some bands of Kufic decorations and inscriptions as well as the pointed arches that are characteristic of the Fatimid architecture.

In the northern facade, opposite Al-Azhar square, are the Barbers' Doors, built by Prince Abdul Rahman Katkhuda in 1176 A.H. (1752 A.D.). A passage from the two leads to two schools, the one on the left known as al-Madrassa al-Akbaghawiyah (or eastern); built by Prince Aqbugha Abdel Wahid (740 A.H.–1339 A.D.), it is now occupied by Al-Azhar Library. In this *madrassa* is a *mihrab* whose niche and arch were ornamented with gilded, multicolored mosaic. This *mihrab* is considered one of the most beautiful in Cairo. The second school is al-Madrassa al-Tybarsiyah, built by Tybars al-Ala'i (709 A.H.–1309 A.D.). It is presently an annex of the Library. It also has a beautiful *mihrab* decorated with marble mosaic and very handsome ceramic columns. The facade of this school was restored by Prince Abdul Rahman Katkhuda.

At the end of the passage on the southern side are another door and a minaret, which were established by Sultan Qaitbey in 873 A.H. (1458 A.D.). Stone decoration in both the door and the minaret is highly creative and beautiful (though the door may not be original).

This door leads to an unroofed courtyard surrounded on three sides by arcades. The facades of the arcades are mounted on arches with refracted angles. In the middle of the eastern arcade is a corridor leading vertically to the ancient *mihrab*. Over the entrance of the corridor is a dome mounted on pillars and shoulders. The arches of this corridor are the oldest ones in the arcade. Both the arches and the roof of the corridor are more elevated than the rest of the arcade. The keel arches are decorated with interlaced flowers and floral Kufic inscriptions. In the upper portion of the original wall are old windows distinguished by their circular arches and stucco decorations with geometrical motifs and colored glass. These windows are surrounded by a frieze of Kufic Quranic writings and border the original mosque on three sides. It is believed that the ends of the first arcade were once covered by two domes.

The elevated area behind the recess (or *iwan*) up to the present southern wall was also constructed by Abdul Rahman Katkhuda, whose mausoleum is located west of the palace inside Bab el-Sa'aiyda (Gate of Upper Egyptians).

In 725 A.H. (1324 A.D.) Al-Azhar was renovated by the judge Negm el-Din Mohammad Ibn Hussein Ibn Ali As'udi, the *muhtaseb* of Cairo.

In 740 A.H. the Agbaghawiyah school was built by Prince Ala'a

el-Din Aqbugha, chief of the Mamelukes under King el-Naser Mohammad Ibn Qalawoon.

In 761 A.H. (1359 A.D.) another restoration was carried out in Al-Azhar when Prince al-Tawashi Saad el-Din Bashir al-Gamdar al-Naseri removed the many chambers that had been introduced to the mosque. He then began to restore all of its walls and roofs. The mosque was painted and the floors were tiled. People were prevented from passing through the mosque. A Quran reader was appointed. At the south gate a *sabil* provided people with fresh drinking water. Above the *sabil*, a *kuttab* (a small Quranic school) was built to teach orphan children the reading of Holy Quran. Daily meals of cooked food were allocated for poor students of Al-Azhar. In addition, teaching circles were arranged at the big *mihrab*.

In 800 A.H. the old minaret of Al-Azhar was pulled down because it was too short to harmonize with the vast mosque. A new, taller minaret was erected by Sultan al-Zahir Barquq. The total expenses were at least 10,000 dirhams of pure silver. When construction was completed that year, a great celebration was held, and the new minaret was completely illuminated with lanterns and candles. Readers and preachers of the mosque held a gathering at which they read the whole Quran and prayed for the sake of the Sultan. This minaret was subsequently removed in 818 A.H. because of architectural defects and a new minaret was made out of stone.

In 884 A.H. (1440 A.D.) Prince Gawhar al-Qanqaba'i, treasurer of King al-Ashraf Bersbay, constructed a beautiful small school at the northern end of the eastern wall of the mosque near Bab el-Sirr. The school, though small, included all the details of the *madrassa*.

The main restoration in Al-Azhar during the period of Sharkasi Mamelukes was done by Sultan Qaitbey in 873 A.H. (1468 A.D.). He pulled down the big old western gate and built the present gate, to the right of which a beautiful new minaret was erected. In 881 A.H. (1476 A.D.) when Sultan Qaitbey visited the mosque, he gave orders to restore the collapsing parts and to remove all the hermitages from the roof.

Despite the cultural deterioration that Al-Azhar suffered during the Ottoman age, Turkish rulers maintained the mosque's physical condition. They also showed great care for Al-Azhar's students and staff. For instance, al-Sharif Mohammad Pasha, a governor in the service of the Ottoman regime, restored the ruined parts of the mosque in 1004 A.H. (1595 A.D.). He also allocated certain amounts of food for the poor, who then came to the mosque from far away.

In 1014 A.H. (1605 A.D.), Hassan Pasha al-Daftardar, another governor, renovated the school of the Hanafites (one of the four Islamic orthodox rites), and covered its floor with tiles.

A great expansion of Al-Azhar took place under the Ottoman Prince Abdul Rahman Katkhuda beginning in 1167 A.H. (1753 A.D.). The area added to the mosque included all the arcades behind the *mihrab*. These arcades now have 50 marble columns supporting 50 stone keel arches. The ceilings are made of wood. This section of the mosque contained a marble *mihrab* covered by a dome. A wooden *minbar* was added, with an octagonal marble panel to its left, carrying rectangular Kufi script of Allah, Mohammad, and the names of the 10 followers to whom paradise was promised. The panel was moved to its present place from the Katkhuda tomb in Al-Azhar. Beside this *mihrab* is a smaller one known as the *mihrab* of al-Dardir. Close by is a third *mihrab*, made by the Department of Preservation of Arabic Monuments to maintain the wooden linings that had covered the old *mihrab*.

Katkhuda also introduced the big gate now known as Bab al-Hallakin (or the Barbers' Door). A minaret was erected to the right of the gate. Above the entrance a *maktab* (or *kuttab*) was built. To the right of the entrance is an ablution fountain with a water wheel.

In 1306 A.H. (1888 A.D.), more restoration work was done on Al-Azhar. The *iwan* built by Katkhuda was renovated and the old eastern *iwan* was largely repaired, as were the al-Saiyda and al-Harmin arcades. Decorations of the arches surrounding the courtyard were restored though their original styles were kept untouched.

In 1890 A.D. portions of the western *iwan* as well as their Kufic inscription bands and stucco decorations were renovated. The Fatimid dome above the entrances was also renovated.

In 1315 A.H. (1898 A.D.) the western facade, including the western Barbers' Gate, was renovated and the Abbassi *ruwaq* was created.

القاهرة

Many Fatimid mosques still exist in present-day Cairo. Among them are al-Aqmar mosque in Al-Mu'izz li-Din Allah at al-Nahhasin, the mosque of Al-Salih Talai near Bab Zuwila, Al-Fakahani mosque at the entrance of Housh Qadam passage at al-

Ghouriya, the sanctuary of el-Guyushi on al-Muqattam hills, the mausoleum of Ekhwat Youssif (Youssif Brothers) at el-Khalifa district and the mausoleum of Sayyda Ruqayia in Khalifa Street.

The city was once surrounded by a wall, which Gawhar had built to protect it from enemy attacks. Though it no longer exists, its position can be approximated by historians' references and archaeologists' findings.

Gawhar opened eight gates in the wall of Cairo, two on each of the four sides. Those on the northern side, which no longer exist, were Bab el-Nasr (The Victory Gate) and Bab el-Futuh (The Conquest Gate).

Bab el-Nasr was located at the crossroads of Bain Al Sayarig and al-Mu'izz streets, 20 meters north of the mosque of el-Shohada (martyrs) known as Wekalat Qussun, in Bab el-Nasr Street near Zawiat al-Kassid.

On the eastern side of the wall were the Bab al-Barqiyah and Bab al-Qarratin gates. According to a map drawn at the time of Napoleon's French Expedition, Bab al-Barqiyah was located at the foot of al-Barqiyah hills opposite to al-Darrassa Street. This gate was named for a group of soldiers who came from Barqah (in Libya) with Gawhar's troops. Bab al-Qarratin was near the present Bab el-Mahrouq at the end of Dar el-Mahrouq in al-Gamaliyah.

Al-Maqreezi reported that al-Bab al-Mahrouq was given its name – the burned gate – because the Mamelukes set fire to it in 652 A.H. after learning that their leader, Prince Aqtai, had been murdered. It was said that they tried to leave the city through this gate one night. But after finding the gate closed, they burned it down and then left.

In the western wall, the two gates of Zuwila referred to a North African Berber tribe whose soldiers joined Gawhar's army while marching toward Egypt. The site of the two gates was said to be at the mosque of Ibn el-Banna.

On the site of these two gates now stands Bab Zuwila, a large gate built by Badr al-Gemali. People call it al-Metwali Gate, "Bawabet al-Metwali," because the Metwali – the man who was responsible for collecting taxes from those coming to Cairo – used to sit there.

On the western side of the walls, parallel to Khalig Amir el-Mu'menin were the two gates of Sa'ada and al-Qantara. Sa'ada gate was related to Sa'ada Ibn Hayyan, one of al-Mu'izz's officers. The gate was 10 meters to the north of the Court of Appeals (now the headquarters of the Ministry of Municipalities). Bab al-Qantara was located at the entrance of Amir el-Gu'yoush el-Guwani Street. It was so called because Gawhar built an arched bridge on the Khalig (or the gulf) on which the army could pass on its way to al-Maqs, a Nile harbor, to fight against al-Qramitah's incursions.

Added to the wall around Cairo and the mosque of Al-Azhar in its center, Gawhar built a great palace near Al-Azhar. It was said that the foundations of the Great Eastern Palace were laid on the same night as those of the wall. Work continued for four years until the palace was ready to receive the Caliph al-Mu'izz.

The palace reportedly had 4,000 rooms well furnished and rich in ornaments, jewels, draperies, receptacles and arms. The palace was virtually a complex of palaces brought together in one huge building. However, when al-Aziz came to power, he built the smaller Western Palace. Between the two palaces a vast yard was left; it was said that 10,000 soldiers were able to stand in it. Interior courtyards, roof gardens, galleries and other annexes of the two palaces covered 70 acres.

Medieval historians and travelers have given rich descriptions of the architecture of these palaces and their luxurious furnishings.

Unfortunately, these palaces were soon destroyed due to the political instability that prevailed because of the hostility between the Sunnite Ayyubids and Shia Fatimids. The Great Palace gave way to the el-Salihya and el-Zahiryah schools, the *sabil* of Mohammad Ali (al-Nahhasin School), Beshkat Palace, al-Gamaliya police station and its environs, most of which are now in al-Mu'izz Street. The Western Palace was replaced by the mosques of el-Mansour Qalawoon and his son el-Naser, the mosque of al-Zahir Barqouq and al-Kamaliyah School. Inside these Mameluke buildings, which still exist, is a good deal of woodwork that had been taken from Fatimid palaces. The woodwork contains relief carvings representing dancing and singing parties, hunting scenes, birds and animals. They tell us something about the social life in the Fatimid period.

When Naser Khisro, the traveler, arrived in Egypt during the reign of the Caliph al-Mustanser in 439 A.H., he noted that the wall built by Gawhar in 358 A.H. had crumbled, only 80 years after it had been established. Since Cairo had no walls at the beginning of al-Mustanser's rule, his vizier (or prime minister) Badr el-Gemali undertook the fortification of Cairo against foreign invasions and rioting soldiers. A new wall was built instead of the ruined wall of Gawhar.

Left: The entrance of El-Moaed mosque with its famous door taken from the madrassa of Sultan Hassan. Below: Bab el-Futuh (the Conquest Gate), located in the north wall of Old Cairo. The arched portal of the gate contains a hole from which liquids could be poured over an attacking enemy.

The site of el-Gemali's wall can still be identified from its remnants, the most important of which are the three gates: Bab el-Nasr and Bab el-Futuh to the north, and Bab Zuwila to the south. These gates are among the finest examples of medieval military fortifications.

Bab el-Futuh contains two cylindrical towers; the lower two-thirds of each is solid while the upper third had soldiers' chambers and slits from which arrows could be shot. Between the two towers is an arched portal with a hole above from which liquids could be poured over the attacking enemy.

Bab el-Nasr has two square towers whose stones are decorated with reliefs representing shields, armor and other weapons. In the middle, it has an elevated gate with an opening from which burning liquids could be poured. Both towers are solid in the lower two-thirds, and are encircled by a flowered Kufic band listing the founder's name and the date of construction.

Bab el-Nasr is connected to Bab el-Futuh by two vaulted galleries with domed chambers and arrow slits on its sides.

The most beautiful of the three gates is Bab Zuwila. It has two cylindrical towers similar to those of Bab el-Futuh. Yet, the upper third of each tower was removed in 818 A.H. by King al'Mu'ayad Abul Nasr Sheikh when he built his mosque beside the gate and built two minarets on the towers.

During the Fatimid period, social life in Cairo was said to be prosperous, lively and cheerful. The Fatimid luxury was beyond imagining. After 200 years, at the end of the Fatimid monarchy, Cairo became a large city full of houses, markets, entertainment, mosques, palaces, mausolea and parks. Surviving buildings and monuments are a good witness of that era.

القَاهِرَة

Egypt remained under the Ayyubids for only about 80 years, during which the city was rich with beautiful buildings and the most refined Islamic arts. Although most of these monuments no longer exist, the ones that remain provide evidence of the progress and prosperity of the arts at that time and their architectural influences on the buildings established in later eras. During that period the multi-rite religious schools (or *madrassa*), with their characteristic square architectural details, appeared in Egypt. Meanwhile, many military fortifications such as citadels and fortified walls as well as public works, like the barrages of

Giza, were also established by the Ayyubid sultans.

During this brief time in Cairo, Salah el-Din left several monuments that demonstrate his wisdom, political insight and military skill.

The most important of them is the Citadel – or the Mountain Citadel as it has been commonly known – built on a big rock split off the Muqattam hills, to the east of Cairo. The Citadel overlooked the capital of Salah el-Din's empire, protecting it from any expected invasion, and providing a headquarters for the sultan. The Citadel was built on the same spot where the Abbasids had once established el-Hawa dome (the dome of the air) in the 2nd century of Hejira. Salah el-Din ordered a residential palace to be built for him, and Yosif's well provided the Citadel with water in times of war or siege.

His vizier Baha'a el-Din Qaraqoush was given the responsibility for building both the Citadel and the wall. Though Salah el-Din died before completing his plans, they came to fruition during the rule of his brother, Sultan al-Adel.

Since that time, the Citadel has been the royal headquarters of all the successive rulers of Egypt until Khedive Ismail moved to Abdin Palace in 1850 A.D. Over the centuries, the Citadel has undergone additions.

The continuous wars in which Salah el-Din was involved had their obvious influence on the construction carried out during his lifetime. Having established the Citadel, he started to encircle all the previous Islamic capitals of Egypt as well as his Citadel with a single wall extending from Fatimid Cairo in the north up to the south of Al-Fustat. Many parts of this wall still exist today.

The present-day Citadel is practically a great town surrounded by huge walls and towers on all sides. The Citadel can be divided into two distinguishing parts, the northeastern and the southwestern. Each part has walls on all four sides. The two parts are connected by a joint wall.

The features of the southwestern section clearly indicate that it underwent many changes and much reconstruction from the time of Salah el-Din to that of Mohammad Ali. On the other hand, there is a great harmony in the walls of the northeastern section, and archaeologists have proved that this section was constructed during the Ayyubid dynasty itself.

The northeastern section is confined in a trapezoidal shape. Its length from east to west reaches 560 meters, and its width from north to south is 317 meters. The circumference is approximately 2,000 meters. The joint wall – between north and south – extends to 150 meters. It is huge, a thick wall culminating in two great towers with the Bab el-Kullah in the middle.

The southwestern section, which is slightly smaller than the first one, is irregular in shape, and is separated from the northern part by an acute angle. Its maximum length from north to south is 510 meters, and the maximum width from east to west is 240 meters. While the northern walls are supported by several circular and semi-circular towers, the southern walls are uninterrupted by any towers.

The interiors of the two sections are also different. While the northern section has the rough features of a military fortress, the southern section resembles a royal city with its mosques and palaces.

During the ages following the Ayyubids, expansions were made in the fortifications and in the civilian buildings, including houses and palaces.

During the Ottoman rule, the Citadel continued to be the headquarters of Egypt's rulers, and the Ottoman governors added many buildings.

When Mohammad Ali came to power, he restored the Citadel to its former glory. He founded several buildings inside the Citadel, the most important of which are the mosque of Mohammad Ali (1262 A.H.–1845 A.D.), the Mint, the Archives House (*Dar al-Mahfouzat*), the Gawhara Palace, the Palace of Justice (1262 A.H.–1811 A.D.) and the palaces of the Harem (among which is the palace presently occupied by the Military Museum).

The Citadel continued to be the focus of the rulers' attention as the center of power and authority. But after Khedive Ismail moved to his new headquarters, the Citadel began to deteriorate. This decline has recently intensified, due in part to environmental pollution and other modern encroachments.

Thanks to Salah el-Din, the religious schools – in which the four Islamic Sunnite rites were taught – were modeled after the schools built by Nour el-Din Zinki in Syria. The main point of these schools was to counter the Shiite thought that prevailed under the Fatimids. The architecture of the *madrassa* was completely different from that of the mosque. The *madrassa* consists of four *iwans* surrounding a small courtyard, often with a fountain in its center. In each *iwan* one of the four rites of Islam was taught. Parts of the *madrassa* were often used as residences by either the teachers or students. There were also libraries and lecture halls.

Among the religious buildings from the Ayyubid period is the dome of Imam al-Shafei, which includes significant architectural details, especially in the style of the interior decorations of the dome. The dome is distinguished by its *muqarnas* (squinches) with their characteristic floral and geometric decorative style.

القَاهِرَة

Egypt was ruled by sultans of Bahrite Mamelukes for about 100 years. In spite of the violent and arbitrary character of the Mameluke rule, their era was a prosperous one in the architectural history of Cairo. Their love of fine arts was obvious in their civil and religious buildings alike, as in their furniture and dress. Museums and private collections all over the world have examples of outstanding Egyptian monuments and masterpieces that clearly show the extent of the richness, prosperity and refinement that Cairo reached under their rule.

Cairo itself has many buildings that date from this era, including an outstanding collection of great mosques with their skyscraping minarets. Just as Pharaonic Egypt had the pyramids, Islamic Egypt can be proud of Sultan Hassan's *madrassa*, an incomparable building among all the countries of Islam.

Though the buildings of the Bahrite Mamelukes differ in their geometrical details and architectural decorations, they do have some common characteristics.

While mosques and other religious structures from former ages are characterized by their simplicity and lack of external decorations, the facades of Mameluke buildings are rich in friezes, cornices, crowns and other elements of architectural decorations. Minarets of Mameluke mosques are more elegant and finer than earlier ones. They are made out of carved stones, and their bases are octagonal, and later cylindrical, rather than squares. The waists of the minarets have been ornamented with fringes that make them more beautiful and charming. It might be said that the Mamelukes were dome builders. During their era, the horizons of Cairo were full of domes and cupolas erected over *mihrabs* and entrances of the mosques. The simple dome developed a more complicated shape, with a lobed cupola above the dome, or a dome made from carved stone, and decorated with accurately interlaced geometrical and structural forms.

Buildings of the era of Sultan el-Naser are distinguished by the stone facades in two colors, a style called *al-ablaq* (piebald). On

Bab el-Nasr (left) and Bab el-Futuh, two fine examples of medieval military fortifications. The gates are remnants of a wall built to fortify Cairo against invasions.

Below: The mosque of Gawhar El-Lallah, a minister of
Sultan Hassan who himself became sultan after Hassan's exile.
Right: The dome of ablution in the center of the courtyard of the
madrassa of Sultan Hassan. The courtyard is surrounded by the
four iwans where the Islamic Orthodox rites are conducted.

Overleaf: An exterior view of the madrassa of Sultan Hassan with
its dome and minaret built during the 7th century A.H.

Left: The mihrab of the madrassa of Sultan Hassan with its rare gilded inscriptions. Below: The mihrab of el-Hakim, one of the important Fatimid mosques, built in 401 A.H.

Below: The complex of Sultan Barqouq, which includes his mosque and khanqah, *a building used for religious instruction. Right: the mosque of Ibn Qalawoon with its beautiful astral designs and bands of calligraphy.*

certain occasions, black-and-white marble was used. Facades were decorated from the outside with ornamented Arabic calligraphy in comparison with earlier periods when decoration was only internal. Ceilings were now made of wood with the supporting beams gilded or oil-painted in a wonderfully harmonious and balanced frame. Buildings began to be illuminated at night by lanterns made of copper or bronze inlaid with silver and gold, or by enameled glass lamps (*mishkah*).

Construction during Mameluke times also included aqueducts, barrages and water wells. Among the most important of these works is the aqueduct established by el-Naser Mohammad Ibn Qalawoon to provide the Citadel with Nile water. This aqueduct, known as *Magra al-Iuoun*, is one of the most outstanding medieval monuments still existing in Cairo.

At the instructions of el-Naser Mohammad Ibn Qalawoon, a well was dug along the Nile and a new barrage was connected up to an existing aqueduct by the ancient barrages in Salah el-Din Wall. In that manner, water collected from the two wells supplied the Citadel. The aqueduct was restored twice: once by Prince Yalbugha al-Salemi in 812 A.H., and again in 911 A.H. by Sultan al-Ghouri. During the Ottoman era, the aqueduct was partially repaired by Abdi Pasha in 1140 A.H. Napoleon's troops later blocked most of the arches in the aqueduct and used it as a defensive wall. The present aqueduct, which extends from Fumm el-Khalig to Bab el-Sayyda Aisha, is about 3.1 km. long, and the cornice now separates the Nile from the head of the aqueduct. The aqueduct then runs eastward to Sabil al-Wassiyah near Qaitbey Gate, before turning to the northeast, past al-Zumor mosque, to the gate of al-Sayyda Aisha.

The aqueduct is mounted on bridges; of the 271 remaining arches, most are circular. The aqueduct has undergone several restorations as a result of deterioration and after being used as a military fortification during the French Expedition.

The head of the aqueduct is an unequal hexagon with an area of 625 square meters. Inside it is an equal-sided hexagon with a column in its center and six raised arches surrounding it. These arches are slightly wider than the hexagon and are uncovered. A sloping ramp leads to the roof where animals were brought to run the water wheels. The roof contains a basin in which water was gathered, before being poured into a ditch, and running from it to the rest of the barrages.

The *madrassa* of Sarghatmish, named for the chief of the Mamelukes during the reign of King al-Muzaffar Haji Ibn Mohammad Ibn Qalawoon, was founded in the year 757 A.H. as a teaching center for the Hanafi rite. Located adjacent to the western sanctuary of Ibn Tulun's mosque, the *madrassa* is noteworthy for its Persian-style architecture. It consists of an unroofed *sahn* surrounded by four *iwans*. In the center of the courtyard is a fountain surrounded by eight marble columns. In the eastern *iwan* are four doors, two of which lead to hermitages and the other two to the teaching halls. The *madrassa* is the only one in existence with a dome above the *mihrab*. It also has wooden stalactites. The minaret is built of stone, 40 meters high, with three levels. The lower two are octagonal while the third level consists of marble columns with beautiful and elegant *muqarnas* topped by a carved crown. On the second level, the white stones are inlaid with red stones in a beautiful decorative piebald pattern. The minaret has a balcony on one side of its lower base, unlike other minarets of the time that had four balconies.

The Mameluke age was responsible for one of Islam's architectural wonders, the mosque and *madrassa* of Sultan Hassan. The huge complex gathers into a whole structural excellence, artistry, the precision of its geometry, and the harmony of decorations in stone, marble, wood, copper, gold, silver, and stained and enameled glass.

The *madrassa* is located at the foot of the Citadel on a site formerly occupied by one of the most beautiful Mameluke palaces. This palace, founded by King el-Naser Mohammad Ibn Qalawoon for Prince Yulbugha al-Behyadi, was razed, and the new complex began construction in the year 757 A.H. Over the next 10 years, Sultan Hassan allocated tremendous amounts of money on the *madrassa*, nearly exhausting the treasury and leaving him in doubt over whether the work should continue.

The plan of the *madrassa* is cruciform, having four main sections with a central uncovered courtyard in the middle of which is an ablution fountain covered by a wooden dome. The original design allowed for four minarets but only two were finally erected. The *madrassa* is actually a polygon with an area of about two acres including the dome adjacent to the eastern facade. Around the courtyard, there are four schools for the four Islamic rites. Each school consists of an *iwan* (or teaching hall), a courtyard with a central fountain and a number of stories looking over the small courtyard from one side and over the facade of the great *madrassa* from the other side.

The discipline of study in these schools was similar to that followed in the 20th-century schools. For each school, a sheikh (or a headmaster) was appointed by the sultan; in addition, there were teachers of the Quran and the Hadith (the sayings of the Prophet), a reader of the Quran, and two tutors. Each school had a library and a librarian. One hundred students were admitted to the boarding school, including 25 advanced students. Thirty students acted as heads of students and others prayed for the sultan at the end of each day's lessons. Two *kuttabs* (small schools for teaching) were annexed to the *madrassa* to enable orphans to learn the Quran and Arabic calligraphy. The children were provided with food and clothing. When an orphan memorized the Quran, he and his teacher each received 50 dirhams. A physician, an opthalmologist and a surgeon were appointed to provide students with medical care. Sultan Hassan allocated suitable *wakfs* (or trusts) for the school's expenses, including the salaries of students, teachers and employees.

The *madrassa* of Sultan Hassan was used as a military fortress in times of political instability, strife and turmoil. In the year 791 A.H. cannons were installed on its roof, and from there the Citadel was shelled in the course of fighting between two conflicting Mameluke groups. The fighting was so frequent that Sultan Barqouq ordered the removal of the stairs leading to the roof. Combatants subsequently used minaret staircases to reach the roof. The *madrassa* of Sultan Hassan became a target of the Citadel's cannons, leading to much devastation and plunder.

القاهرة

Among the important religious buildings in Egypt during the Mameluke time were the *khanqahs* (or monasteries), which gained fame throughout the Islamic world, particularly in Iran, in the 4th century of Hejira. The *khanqah* is a house for the accommodation of Sufis or *al-Mutsawifa* (the devotees) who dedicated themselves to worship.

Concerning the emergence of Sufism, or Islamic mysticism, al-Qushairi stated that "following the death of the Prophet Mohammad, Muslims showed great respect to the Prophet's companions who were known as *al-sahaba*; the second generation of Muslims who followed the *sahaba* were known as *al-tabi'een*, or the followers. Those who expressed a great deal of attention towards the religion were called the devotees, because they voluntarily renounced the worldly pleasures and devoted their life to the service of Islam. They have become famous as *Sufis*."

According to another opinion, Sufism evolved in Islam among those who spent their days in worship and prayer in the Prophet's mosque. A third point of view refers the term Sufi to *al-Safaa*, which means clearness – specifically spiritual clearness.

Al-Gahez first used the term *Sufi* to describe many of the devotees who were famous for the purity of their Arabic. Later in the 2nd century of Hejira, the terms *Sufi* and *Mutasawif* became commonly used. This period marked a transition in the development of Sufism. At this time, Sufis only differed from other Muslims in their more pronounced devotion to certain Quranic rules. The most outstanding Sufi of this period was al-Hassan al-Basri, who used to hold study circles in the Friday mosque of al-Basra, at which he discussed various theological viewpoints and encouraged spiritual education.

During this second century, some hard-line Sufis began to show an extreme interest in spiritual exercises and renounced the pleasures of life as a trivial struggle for evanescent things.

By the 3rd and 4th centuries of Hejira, Sufism was no longer restricted to abstinence and devoutness, but had developed its intellectual and spiritual principles. A long-standing ideological dispute erupted between Sufis and many other religious thinkers. This conflict was not limited to books and theses, but escalated into repression against the Sufis. Their recourse was to create a symbolic language understood only by their partisans and scholars.

They also began to organize themselves into groups similar to political parties. Each group had its own principles, fundamentals, leader and followers. Each Sufi had to obey his sheikh.

As their numbers increased, they became a significant faction in Islamic society, with their own traditions, regulations and qualities. They then formed *khanqahs* or *khawanek* where they could gather.

The early fundamentals for regulating the *khanqahs* were laid down by Abu Saed Ibn Abi el-Khair, who became known as the "Father of Khanqahs" and "The Hawk of the Way."

By the 5th century of Hejira, there was a considerable body of Sufi literature, and its traditions and regulations provided models for education and public manners. Respect for Sufis was shown by rulers such as Sultan Mahmoud al-Ghaznawi, who used to pay visits to Sheikh Abdul Hassan al-Kharqanah in his own *khanqah* at al-Rayy.

The 6th century of Hejira was the springtime of prosperous Sufism. *Khanqahs* proliferated throughout the Islamic world.

Sufism was practiced by people in all classes of society. Its principles and foundations became well-known and became the subjects of poems and songs. Kings and sultans – such as Al-Khiushani and Salah el-Din – invited Sufi leaders to their intimate meetings and listened to their advice. Having gained widespread respect, the Sufis even tried to mediate between the different Muslim sects, especially between Sunna and Shia.

The *khanqah* of Saed el-Soada is considered the first to have been founded in Egypt. It was established in the 6th century of Hejira by Salah el-Din for poor Sufis from abroad, and it was known as "the little house of Sufis."

After the Mongols flooded Persia and Iraq during the 7th century of Hejira, Sufi immigrants fled to the western parts of the Islamic world in large numbers, and many settled in Egypt. At one time, Egypt had 21 *khanqahs*, and today eight from that period still exist: al-Bunduqdariyah, al-Gawliyah, al-Baybarsiyah, al-Shrabishiyah, al-Gibgha, al-Muzaffari, Khanqah Syriaqous and Khanqah of Arslan.

The Mameluke *khanqahs* in Egypt date from the 8th century. In addition to their original functions they were used for religious courses. For example, the rite of Imam al-Shafi was taught in the *khanqah* of al-Gawliyah; the al-Hanafi rite was learned in al-Gamaliyah Khanqah; and the four Islamic rites, the reading of the Quran and interpretations of the Prophet Hadith were all taught in Shikhuniah.

Other *khanqahs* remained loyal to their fundamentalist traditions such as the performance of Friday prayer in certain Friday mosques. For example, the Sufis of Beybars *khanqah* used to pray in the mosque of el-Hakim adjacent to their *khanqah*.

القَاهِرَة

The Egyptian Department of Antiquities has shown great interest in the restoration of houses and palaces from the time of the Bahrite Mamelukes.

Al-Ablaq Palace was founded by Sultan el-Naser Mohammad Ibn Qalawoon inside the Citadel of Salah el-Din, in the southern part of the Banner Yard. The palace contains a *durka'a* (a rectangular low-floored hall) with an octagonal fountain in the center. On two sides of the hall, the floor is raised. A door on the north corner leads to a spiral staircase and to an underground passage. The western door leads to a staircase and an uncovered

passage; both of them may connect up with the tunnel leading to the relics of the palaces located beneath the mosque of Mohammad Ali. West of the hall is the main *iwan* of al-Ablaq Palace with its floor 30 cm. higher than that of the hall.

Beshtak Palace was founded by Prince Seif el-Din Beshtak al-Naseri, a prince in the time of King el-Naser Mohammad Ibn Qalawoon. It was located in the vicinity of the Fatimid Eastern Big Palace and was accessible through Bab el-Bahr (The Gate of the Sea), later known as the Gate of Beshtak Palace. Historians considered the palace one of the greatest in Cairo. It had windows with iron grilles that looked out over Cairo. The marble work was wonderful. On the ground floor were stores for selling sweets and other things.

The construction of the palace was completed in the year 738 A.H. Despite its grandeur, Beshtak hated the palace, and so he sold it to the wife of Prince Buktomor al-Saqi. The palace's ownership moved among their heirs until Sultan el-Naser Hassan, son of Mohammad Ibn Qalawoon, came to power. The palace settled under the ownership of his sons. At last, Ustadar Gamal el-Din had it razed, but his family retained the property.

القَاهِرَة

At the time Sultan Barqouq came to power, rulers of Egypt were known as Circassian Mamelukes; they took their name from the homeland of Barqouq. Although Egypt was suffering from internal instability and the oppressive character of the Circassian Mamelukes, under their rule it reached unprecedented heights in the arts and civilization. This reflected the Mamelukes' interest in the arts, literature, science and religion. Their good taste was manifested in their style of life and their architecture. For instance, kings Barqouq, al-Muayyad and Qaitbey were all fond of taking part in the forums of thinkers and writers. King al-Zahir Tamarbugha was known for his wide knowledge of the origins of languages, history and Sufism. The kings also abided by the religious rules, which included abstaining from alcoholic beverages and making the pilgrimage to Mecca.

Cairo has retained many of its structures from that time, and they provide good examples of the development of religious and civil architecture. They also demonstrate the high level of applied arts and design during the 9th and 10th centuries of the Hejira in Egypt.

A distinctive new art was born in this period when engraved decorated stone replaced decorated plaster. The stone *minbar* of Qaitbey in the mausoleum of Barqouq is one of the outstanding examples of stone carving in the 15th century A.D. It is so intricate that it resembles a piece of lacework.

Circassians differ from Bahrites in both their origins and their system of succession. All Circassian sultans were Turks with the exception of two Greeks. Moreover, Circassians had no firmly established principle of hereditary succession like that of the Qalawoons. The sultan was considered as the chief of Mamelukes, or their leader rather than a "king." The Mamelukes, in fact, elected the sultan. The authority of the sultan totally depended on the strength of his army and his military skills. At the same time, his political experience, proficiency, self-dependence and ability to control the conflicting Mameluke groups all had great influence on his success or failure.

When the sultan died, his followers formed their own party, giving it the title of the late sultan. Hence the names: Ashrafiya, Naseriyah, Muaiadyah and Tahiriyah.

Of the 29 Circassian sultans, six ruled for a total of 103 out of the 134 years the Circassians were in power. Since the era was one of frequent and bloody struggles for power, a Mameluke leader had to be efficient and strong to reach the throne of Egypt. Once a Mameluke became a sultan, he had to leave his position in the army; the one exception was Sultan Farag, a famous general.

Circassian sultans left several monuments, including mosques, hospitals, schools and colleges. Nonetheless, Egypt suffered from the conflicts between Mameluke groups and their bloody competitions for the seat of sultan. As foreign rulers, the Mamelukes were indifferent to the Egyptian people.

The injustice and corruption of Mameluke soldiers were also so flagrant that women were not able to go out of their houses to shop, or to attend weddings or even funerals. Farmers lived in terror, unable to enter the markets of Cairo to buy their crops or their cattle for fear of being plundered by the Mamelukes or – at the very least – selling their goods at low prices to meet the huge requirements of the sultan's palaces. It was said that, for instance, 1,200 pounds of beef were consumed daily in the palace of Bersbay.

Government administration was corrupt, unjust and in-effectual. Judges were dishonest and unfair. On rare occasions, people were able to revenge themselves on their despotic governors. But in most cases they underwent terrible suffering.

Accordingly, social unrest and instability were frequent, especially during tax-collection season or when the country was preparing for war. These calamities were aggravated by plagues or by natural catastrophes such as floods and droughts. Under the reign of Sultan Farag, the population of Egypt was reportedly reduced by two-thirds. Another Circassian sultan, Muaiad Sheikh, was a good and modest man, a lover of music and poetry, builder of a mosque, a hospital and many schools; even so, he failed to protect the people from his followers' excesses.

Under Khushkadam, a Circassian king of Greek ancestry, corruption was at its worst. The government added to its revenues by selling official jobs. The governor of Tripoli paid 45,000 dinars to receive a better post as a governor of Damascus. Another prince paid 10,000 dinars to replace him in Tripoli. On another occasion, the sultan invited a rich prince for a royal banquet; before the night had ended, the guest was forced to pay a sum of money to his host as ransom.

Nevertheless, the Mamelukes did succeed in keeping Egypt free from foreign invaders, particularly against the Mongols who devastated Iraq and parts of Syria. Thanks to Sultan Barqouq and his son, Sultan Farag, their strong army stopped the march of Tamerlane toward Egypt in the year 1400 A.D.

During this period, however, a succession of civil wars and bloody struggles for power caused the decline of political authority and deterioration of the economy. This condition prevailed until the emergence of a strong prince, Sultan Qaitbey, who returned Egypt to stability.

The 29-year reign of Sultan Qaitbey was one of the longest of the Circassian Mameluke era. He stood out as the Circassians' most powerful and courageous ruler, and his political experience and military skills enabled him to impose discipline and order until the final years of his rule. By that time the state economy had been depleted by continual wars and the need for military fortifications, as well as a plague, which brought mass death to Egypt. While conflicts between the Mamelukes escalated once more, King Qaitbey died, a saddened man in his 80s. After four kings ruled for only five years of constant turmoil, a strong, experienced, 60-year old ruler, Al Ashraf Qansuwah al-Ghouri, came to power. His first tasks as ruler were to bring security and order to Cairo, and to refill the state coffers, though poverty was still widespread.

Al-Ghouri put a great deal of money into new buildings and public facilities; he established a *madrassa*, a dome and other

buildings in the area known now as Al-Ghouriyah. He reconstructed the road of pilgrimage to Mecca, built way-stations and cleaned the wells along the road. He fortified Alexandria and Rasheed with citadels and towers and restored Salah el-Din's Citadel. At that time, the royal court was very rich and luxurious.

The most remarkable feature of the religious structures from this period is their modest size – especially those built inside the walls of the old city of Cairo. Of course, a small *madrassa* or *khanqah* could only accommodate small *iwans*. Accordingly, the north and south *iwans* of contemporary mosques became known as the two niches. In addition, study in schools of the Circassian age was limited to two rites only, and so the new *madrassas* came to have two large *iwans*, the *iwan* of the *qibla* and another one opposite it, as well as two other small *iwans*.

Similarly, the area of the courtyard was reduced, and the new *sahn* was covered by a wooden roof that usually had a central octagonal skylight (or *shukhshekha*). The new wooden floor gave a special significance to the courtyard. Architects surrounded the roof with Mameluke-style inscription bands, usually beginning with Quranic verses and ending with memorial texts recording the name of the founder, his title and the date of its foundation. Since the floor of the courtyard is usually 25 cm. lower than those of the *iwans*, the new *sahn* acquired the term *durka'a*.

Since the northern and southern *iwans* were reduced in size, the *qibla iwan* became greater than it had been before, occupying its whole wall.

There was no longer a need for four doors in the courtyard, and doors could lead from one room to another. Niches became more frequent, especially in the western *iwan* opposite the *qibla's*. The western *iwan* had a large niche occupied by the platform (or *dekka*) of the messenger. The *dekka* was now usually made of marble or stone rather than wood, and was supported by piers of marble, usually in the shape of a palm-leaf fan; it was reached by an external staircase behind the *iwan*. The arches of the *iwans* were decorated with fine floral forms carved in stone, similar to those found in the metallic monuments and famous inlaid doors dating from the Mameluke age.

The late Mameluke period was distinguished by a new type of dome that was used as a resting place and for entertainment and sports. It was very similar to the domes built by the Fatimids in the suburbs of Cairo and in the rural areas; the best examples are the domes of Yashak Ibn Mahdi in Kubri al-Kobba, and al-Kubba al-Fedewiyyah in Abbassia Square.

The Circassian Mamelukes achieved architectural fame for the multi-crowned minarets, which were unique in Egypt. This type of minaret appeared for the first time in Egypt in the second half of the 8th century of Hejira, and became common in the 9th and early 10th centuries.

One of the earliest examples was the mosque of Junbulat adjacent to Bab el-Nasr, north of Fatimid Cairo. The minaret of Kany Bey al-Rammah's school near the citadel, which was built in 908 A.H., also had two crowns. This minaret was reconstructed according to its original design in the year 1278 A.H./1870 A.D. The same architect had another double-crowned minaret in his *madrassa* in al-Naseriyah, which is still in its original state.

The minaret of al-Ghouri's *madrassa* was the first one in Egypt with four crowns. It was cited in the document of its *wakf* that "in its western corner there is a minaret of three stories. The upper story has four semi-domes, each of which is independent, supported by four piers, and has three columns in the shape of a candlestick."

It is noteworthy that the Committee for the Preservation of Islamic Monuments has renovated the minaret of al-Ghouri and rebuilt its upper part with four crowns instead of two.

Al-Ghouri constructed another minaret in Al-Azhar mosque in the year 915 A.H. characterized by its double crown. It resembles the minaret of Azbak al-Yosofi, near Ibn Tulun, built in 900 A.H., as well as the minaret of Khayer Bek's mosque.

The only multi-crowned minaret from the Ottoman period is that of Mohammad Abdul Dahab's mosque in Al-Azhar square, which was built in the year 1188 A.H./1774 A.D.

القَـاهِـرَة

After the Mamelukes were defeated, Sultan Selim took over Egypt in the year 923 A.H. (1517 A.D.). Cairo then changed from the capital of a vast empire to the capital of a dependency ruled by Istanbul, and it remained under Ottoman rule until World War I three centuries later.

Having conquered the Mamelukes, Selim stayed in Cairo for eight months while he established a regime to keep Egypt under his firm control. Selim divided the power among three competitive authorities: Al-Wali, the governor who ruled Egypt in the name of the Ottoman sultan; Al-Diwan, an assembly formed of high officers of the Turkish occupation troops; and the

Mamelukes, the former rulers of Egypt. Al-Wali had the title of pasha, and was ensconced in the citadel. He was mainly responsible for implementing the sultan's orders.

Governors were assigned to Cairo for no more than three years, and they often dedicated themselves to accumulating as much wealth as they could during this short period of time. Since the money that was collected as taxes was supposed to be sent to Istanbul, there were frequent disputes between the Wali and Diwan or between the Wali and the king himself over money problems.

The Diwan consisted of leaders of the occupation army, who held their meetings in the Citadel. Their main task was to keep an eye on Al-Wali, while providing him with necessary assistance. The occupation troops had great influence in the early period of the Ottoman rule. The army frequently disobeyed the Wali and more than once drove him out of office – or even killed him. So, many Walis were mere puppets in the hands of the army commanders.

When Sultan Selim took over Egypt, he appointed a few of the surviving Mamelukes as provincial governors, and others were given high positions in the Government. Although there were at most 10,000 Mamelukes in Cairo at that time, they constituted an aristocracy, living in magnificent palaces and enjoying great luxury. They bought children to be slaves. The boys were trained to ride horses, fight, hunt and learn the principles of Islam. When a male slave grew up, his master would emancipate him, and he could adopt the title of Bek in a magnificent celebration. He then became a follower of his master.

The Mamelukes' influence increased as a result of the weakness of the Ottoman state after the end of the 17th century, the continually changing Walis, and the frequent conflicts between the Wali and the Diwan. Under such conditions, the chief of the Mamelukes – Sheikh el-Balad – became the real ruler of Egypt with power to dismiss the Wali if he saw fit.

Having set up a ruling regime for Egypt, Selim I transported from Cairo to Istanbul weapons, books, rare manuscripts and other precious things. He also sent 1800 skilled artisans to Istanbul, depriving Egypt of their workmanship. Therefore, the arts in Cairo suffered.

Selim also removed the last Abbasid caliph to Istanbul, forcing him to renounce his office and transferring the caliphate to the Ottomans.

In the early Ottoman period, while the country enjoyed economic prosperity, Cairo was full of bazaars, *wekalat*, inns, hotels and public baths. Although the Portuguese discovered the sea route via the Cape of Good Hope to India in the 16th century A.D., a great part of the transit trade to India and the Orient still passed through Egypt, and goods from Venice, Genoa and Marseilles continued to flow into Cairo's markets. And the merchants of Cairo constituted a strongly organized community.

Yet, in the year 1535 A.D., Cairo lost all it gained from the transit trade, when Sultan Selim II agreed to offer France the Decree of Foreign Concessions to protect its merchants and trading houses. Thus French merchants not only sought to protect their own interests, but they also began to impose their will over the Egyptian government and to control its public facilities. Immediately, England – followed by other European states – asked for the same trade agreement that France enjoyed, and these concessions eventually became an obstacle in the development of modern Egypt. This situation prevailed until the foreign concessions were abolished at the Conference of Montreux in the year 1937.

Since the Ottoman rulers made no effort to maintain the city's architectural monuments, the center of Cairo suffered without improvements until the middle of the 19th century. Most of Cairo's districts deteriorated with rare exceptions such as Bab el-Luk, which was isolated by beautiful parks and gardens on one side and a cemetery on the other.

During the 17th and 18th centuries the area of Kanater al-Sebaa (The Lions' Barrages) became overpopulated. It was bordered by the Khalig (the canal) on the west and Berket el-Feil (the elephant's pond) on the east. Between Berket el-Feil and the Citadel, the quarter of Ibn Tulun evolved, with the great mosque in its center. Wealthy residents left the areas close to the Citadel and Sultan Hassan's mosque as a result of repeated rebellions and civil wars. Many houses were destroyed, and others were taken over by vagabonds, while Berket el-Feil and al-Azbakiyah became Cairo's aristocratic sections.

During the 17th and 18th centuries wealthy people built many houses, elegant palaces and gardens on the Nile bank. Many of these palaces still exist, such as the house of el-Sehemi in el-Gamalia that dates from 1648 A.D., the palace of el-Messafer Khana (1789 A.D.), the house of Gamal el-Din el-Dahabi (1637 A.D.), the house of Zainab Khatun, the house of Ibrahim Katkhuda in al-Saiyda Zainab (in Haret Monge) and Bait al-Kredliyah near the mosque of Ibn Tulun.

Below and right: The mosque of Mohammad Ali, known as the Alabaster Mosque for the extensive use of this delicate stone on its interior walls. The mosque was built in 1845 A.D. in proximity to Salah el-Din's Citadel.

The Cairo of *MOHAMMAD ALI* Dr. Morsi Saad El-Din

The opening years of the 19th century found Egypt in a state of chaos and intrigue. A game of politics was in progress between England and France. The Supreme Porte, the name given to the Ottoman caliph, was the cat's paw.

On the other hand, the Mamelukes were working furiously for the possession of power; the Turkish Wali was trying his best to cling to his tottering seat, while Mohammad Ali affected the role of public servant and promoter of public interests. He championed the cause of the *felaheen* (farmers), and mobilized the backing of the *ulamas* of Al-Azhar, because his insight had enabled him to see a source of power – the people – previously untapped and moreover despised by both the Turks and the Mamelukes.

Because the people were convinced that the Mamelukes were the root of all their ills and under the stress of despair, both the people and the *ulamas* took up arms and a revolution ensued. The battles that were supposed to be fought by the French and English were instead fought by the Egyptians themselves.

Sheikhs, *felaheens* and soldiers believed that their salvation from the privation of the rule of the Turkish Wali and the Mamelukes could only be accomplished at the hands of Mohammad Ali. He was their choice, because he was their friend.

When finally in 1805, Mohammad Ali was confirmed by the Porte, the sheikhs retired to their ecclesiastical castle and resumed their teaching duties. The will of the people was asserted, a ruler of their choice was installed, and the foundation stone of Egypt's political structure had been laid. The story of his rise to the throne of Egypt is well known, but the principal feature of the adventure was his insight into the decisive factors of state-building. That insight made him temporarily align himself with the representatives of the Egyptian people to secure their support in his fight for the throne of Egypt; it also enabled him to see that the essence of modern government as represented by Napoleon's Expedition consists of good administration and of the supremacy of the scientific outlook in dealing with problems of policy. Mohammad Ali was a discoverer in a world blind to Western civilization. In putting into effect what he discovered, he achieved real greatness in the history of government.

The deplorable state of the Ottoman Empire made it clear to him that it needed a man of his caliber at its head, and if not at the head of all, at least the head of the Arabic-speaking lands of which Egypt was center. And Napoleon's Expedition to Egypt made it clear that the arts of peace must go side by side with the arts of war. His plan for the monopoly and development of Egypt's

agriculture, manufacture and commerce was closely interwoven with his ambitions for expansion.

Having come in on the heels of the French Expedition, he was quick to grasp the attitude of the French, and to pick up the threads of their stifled reforms. Whatever is said about Napoleon's invasion of Egypt and whatever political consequences that invasion had, there is no doubt that in the social and cultural spheres, Egypt benefited greatly.

Napoleon landed at Alexandria on July 1, 1798, and took Cairo within three weeks. The French occupation of Egypt lasted to September 1801, and can be regarded as a turning point in the history of Egypt, launching the country into the modern world.

Although Napoleon was a military man, and although the reasons behind his invasion were purely military and political, he was instrumental in the process of modernization that was later advanced by Mohammad Ali. For Napoleon arrived in Egypt not only at the head of an invading army, but also accompanied by a number of scholars with a view to making scientific research necessary for maintaining rule. It was through those French savants that Egypt for the first time came in touch with modern European thought.

Napoleon showed a real sense of history when he decided to fathom the depth of Egyptian history and civilization. He created a 165-member commission and set them the task of investigating all aspects of Egypt. He also founded "L'Institute de l'Egypte" in August 1798, and its job was twofold. First to discover Egypt, and second to introduce European science into Egypt. The commission produced the famous *La Description de l'Egypte*, which was published in 1822. In the same year, Jean-Francois Champollion published his discoveries about hieroglyphics by scrutinizing the Rosetta Stone, discovered in 1799.

When Mohammad Ali came on the heels of the French in 1801, he continued the process of modernization initiated by the French. This process changed the whole structure of Cairo from a typical Islamic capital to a modern city. In 1801, when the scientists and men of letters evacuated Egypt along with the French troops, they took with them all the documents and the research work they had brought with them. But before they left they were able to create in Egypt, indeed in all the Arab countries, an interest in Western civilization: Mohammad Ali, shrewd as he was, could not fail to realize the importance of diffusing such civilization into his.

His aim was to create from shattered medieval Egypt a

powerful and healthy country, a great, united and independent nation. And he lived to see his aim fulfilled. His first step was to plan a policy of vocational education based on the principle that the country's first need was for qualified candidates to fill up the posts of vital importance. The first two schools established were the Darskhanah to produce Government officials, and the military school at Aswan. These two were followed by a third to train clerks and translators.

القَـاهِـرَة

Prince Muskau, who found much to admire in Cairo, including the number of fortified castles of the old Mameluke chieftains, which gave the city a feudal appearance, and the "handsome, artificial fountains," said: "The most striking feature of all, however, is the numerous splendid mosques . . . with their high turrets, painted and round windows, their huge masses and the wonderful richness of their innumerable decorations . . . (they) brought to my mind stirring scenes and images of chivalrous valor." During the Prince's visit to Cairo in 1837, Mohammad Ali was building a new mosque, to which he gave his name, to the extreme south of the Citadel opposite the old mosque of Salah el-Din which had fallen into ruins. It was to be "one of the most costly edifices in the world" as its pillars were constructed of polished alabaster and the exterior and interior walls covered with the same material. From the unfinished walls of the mosque the whole of Cairo and beyond – to the distant pyramids of Giza, Dahshur and Saqqara – could be clearly seen. Almost directly below was the beautiful mosque of Sultan Hassan forming a splendid foreground.

One of the most surprising things to those travelers who had made journeys to other eastern cities like Constantinople, Damascus and Teheran was the lack of gardens in Cairo. Carne remarked, "this city is almost without gardens" – different, indeed from the Cairo of today – and Muskau complained that he had to go out to the Pasha's favorite palace at Shubra before he saw a garden worthy of the name. The long road from Cairo to Shubra, built by Mohammad Ali, was a fine avenue. It had been planted with sycamores, forming an arch impenetrable to the sun, and through which the Nile could continually be seen to the left and the desert with its undulating sand-hills to the right. The gardens of Shubra were laid out in the European and Oriental styles. The former consisted of long, graveled walks with little

formal borders and no welcoming shade, but as one writer said, so symmetrical "that George IV would have been delighted to have it at Virginia Water and his English gardens could not have been kept with more neatness and elegance." The Oriental gardens were thickly planted with "myrtles, jessamines, roses, and young orange trees cut to form graceful arcades and festoons." The walks were mosaics of small colored stones, and there was a lake "with splendid marble baths, which are filled by water issuing from crocodiles' mouths." Inside the palace – and most travelers were received by Mohammad Ali who was insatiably curious about all that was going on in the outside world – it was pleasant to sit in the divaned and gilded apartments on rich sofas placed around the windows that looked on to the garden. "The cool rooms offered an agreeable relief from the sultry heat and stifling lanes of Cairo. Here it was easy to fancy that you were entirely in the country."

The reign of Mohammad Ali must have been a wonderful time to visit Cairo. So much was changing, so much was new and the atmosphere was charged with vitality. Trade was flourishing. Cairo was the metropolis of Eastern and African trade. The wares one could buy were innumerable: rare fruit, miniature works of art, turquoises and emeralds, spices, and hippopotamus-hide whips. The caravans from Abyssinia and the Sudan brought gold dust, ivory, rhinoceros' horns, ostrich feathers, gums, and various drugs and medicines. The population, consisting of Arabs, Copts, Turks, Albanians, Greeks, Syrians, Armenians, Jews and "Barbarians from the country beyond the cataracts, in great estimation for their honest industry," numbered in all at the end of Mohammad Ali's reign over a quarter of a million. Never had they enjoyed such tranquility and order.

Most of the travelers were alive to the fact that Egypt was at a turning point in her history. They remarked on the introduction of the cotton plant, the building of a formidable navy, the training of an army of over 100,000 men, the work on the great dam near Cairo, at the beginning of the Delta, of which it was said, "this structure if it succeeds, as it is hoped it will, is likely to surpass almost any undertaking of the kind either ancient or modern." They saw the model school at Kasr el-Aini, a miniature city with modern educational facilities worthy of Cairo, once the seat of Eastern learning.

It is not to be wondered that even the most critical were forced to admit that "changes of unprecedented significance" were taking place before their eyes.

Below: The ceiling of a Nilometer on the Island of Roda built to measure the height of the Nile during flood time.
Right: A dam – one of many – built by Mohammad Ali.

One of the main landmarks of Cairo is the lofty mosque of Mohammad Ali, which is erected high at the southern side of the Citadel, commanding a bird's-eye view of the city equal only to that attained from the top of the Great Pyramid of Giza.

The mosque – known as the Alabaster Mosque for the extensive use of this delicate stone in covering its interior walls – has been described in detail by several architects and many travelers. Needless to say, none of these accounts is by itself complete. Yet gathered together, they all provide excellent material for the study of the elements that cause taste to change in time and space. In addition to this already extensive material is the following translation of an account of this mosque given by the Egyptian architect Ali Mubarak Pasha (1824–1893), who was one of the most brilliant of all Mohammad Ali's mission students. After graduating from the Faculty of Engineering (then called *al-Muhandiskhanab*) he was selected, among others, to complete his military studies in France at the Ecole de Metz. On his return to Egypt in 1849 he was appointed teacher at the Artillery School. In 1871 he became the Minister of Education. His contribution to the Egyptian renaissance is not confined to his great engineering, financial and administrative achievements only, but also to his many literary works for which the most interesting is his history of the Cairo of his time. This work – *al-Khutat al-Tawfikiyya* – written in 20 parts, is still considered one of the sources of Egypt's modern history for the second half of the 19th century. Its first edition, printed at Bulaq, is dated 1305 A.H. (1889–90 A.D.).

In his fifth volume, Ali Mubarak says:

"The mosque was built by the late Hajj (i.e. Pilgrim), Mohammad Ali Pasha, native of Kavala, founder of the Khedivial family in Egypt. He began its erection in the year of the Hejira, 1246 [1830–1831 A.D.], after he had set the affairs of Egypt in order, and completed those operations of vast utility to which we have referred in the introduction of this book. He selected for this mosque a site at the Citadel of Cairo, so that public worship might be enjoyed by the employees in the palace and public offices, since during his time all the ministries and most of the offices were at the Citadel. He prepared for its erection a wide area, around the remains of ruins that had been erected by former kings; he ordered the debris to be cleared away from the site till the solid rock was reached. There, he ordered the foundations of his mosque to be laid. He built a foundation of enormous stones, some three and a half meters in length; iron rods, welded with molten lead, connected each pair of stones. In this way, the foundations were laid till the surface of the ground was reached. The mosque was modeled on a mosque in Constantinople, called Lur

Osman, and on that of Sidi Sariyab in the Citadel. The building was continued in the style described. Four doors were made, two to the north, one admitting to the court, the other to the dome; two also were placed on the south side. The stone walls were completely faced with alabaster both on the inside and the outside. He who enters from the gate of the Citadel called Bab al-Daris finds a large court and the dome. The door leading into the court has an inscription in gilt on marble, a text from the Quran commending prayer. The threshold is of marble, the door of antique wood; the tympanum is of wood also. The height of the door is four meters, the wooden tympanum is one meter high. The wall is two meters thick. The court is 57 meters long by 55 wide, its surface being 3.135 square meters. It embraces five iwans, surmounted by 47 domes, mounted on marble pillars, eight meters high, exclusive of the base. The number of these pillars which surround the court and support the domes is 45. Each has a necking and torus of brass, and each column is connected with another by an iron bar making 94 bars in all. From each dome a brass chain is appended to which a lamp is attached. As one enters this door, one finds on the left the door of the minaret made of ordinary wood; 265 steps lead to the summit, exclusive of those which lead up to the iron obelisk which crowns it. On the left side in the middle, between the two iwans, is the door which leads from the court into the dome; it consists of folding doors of antique wood with a semi-circular tympanum; over it the date is written in Turkish. Some seven yards in front of the iwan next to the door of the dome is the door which leads to the second minaret, ascended by the same number of steps as the first; they both form winding staircases with bronze balustrades. On every door a text from Surat al-Fath is engraved. The height of each of these minarets is 84 meters from the ground to the iron summit, of which 25 and ²/₃ of which are from the floor to the roof of the mosque. On the left-hand side are the nine windows of the dome, heading each of which a text from the Surat al-Fath is engraved in marble and gilded. The door of the dome is decorated with a text promising Paradise to believers. In the middle of the court you find a wooden dome mounted on eight marble columns, seven meters high, and underneath there is a fountain with an alabaster cupola and 16 spouts, with a marble spout over each, decorated with texts from the Quran. In front of each spout there is a marble base. Between each pair of pillars there is an iron rod, holding a brass chain for a lamp, and over each is a crescent of bronze. Close by is the entrance to the cistern which is underneath the court; the coping is of alabaster and the lid of brass, and there is a pump for raising water.

"The gate of the southern court faces that of the northern, and both are alike. . . . In the iwans which surround the court there are 38 windows, two and a half meters in length and one and a half in breadth; the thickness of the wall is two meters. It also has one window in bronze. In front of the north door which gives on to the dome you find a gallery on 24 alabaster columns,

with bronze neckings and tori, each eight meters high, not including the base. The pillars are connected by 22 iron bars, and surmounted by 11 domes with bronze crescents. . . . Hence you proceed into the sanctuary, which is almost square, 46 meters by 45, exclusive of the iwan of the qibla, which is 17 meters by nine, covering an area of 135 meters. There you find a very lofty dome, some 61 meters above the floor of the mosque, mounted on four piers of hewn stone, faced with marble to a height of two meters. The dome has four semi-circles, one on each side, and four small domes. The whole of the great dome is elaborately painted and decorated with gold leaf. . . . There are circles painted round it, with some texts from the Quran inscribed in gold leaf. To the left of the sanctuary you find the mihrab, with a semi-circular roofing, while the niche itself is in marble with an inscription in colored glass. The niche is enclosed between two small marble columns with brass necking and torus. To the left, close to one of the piers that have been mentioned, is the reader's chair made of wood, with a carved balustrade. Five steps lead up to it and it is carpeted in red. To the right is the pulpit made of wood and decorated with gold leaf, reached by 25 steps, also carpeted in red and with folding doors. Above in a circle texts are also inscribed. Above the preacher's seat is an oblong dome on four wooden columns with a Quranic text written round it. At the bottom of the pulpit there is a wicket on each side, inscribed with texts; between them there is a sort of cupboard to which access is given by a door under the pulpit. Facing the mihrab is the door of the dome leading out of the court, surmounted by a dikka for the mu'azen, extending the whole breadth of the sanctuary, and mounted on eight marble pillars, eight meters high, surrounded by a bronze balustrade, which also surrounds the upper part of the sanctuary; this upper part has 31 windows with brass frames and white glass. At a distance of about 12 meters there is another balustrade, with 31 more windows, of stained glass. Between the two there are the 24 windows of the great dome, with brass balustrade, and bronze work with stained glass lights, and the balustrade at the top of the dome has in front of it 40 stained glass windows. Round each of the four domes mentioned above there are 10 windows with balustrades. The purpose of these balustrades is to support lamps. In the semi-circle of the mihrab there are windows, with a balustrade gallery, and round the wall low down there are 36 windows, two and a half meters long, with white glass lights, a portion of the poem 'Burdah' being written on each one. Access is given to the galleries from the two minarets and the roof of the mosque. The southern door of the dome, which faces the northern, has written on the outside: 'To God belong the places of worship.' In front is a spacious gallery, on 11 columns of alabaster, some eight meters high, with 22 iron bars connecting them; these are surmounted by 11 domes, similar to those in the gallery facing the first door.

"*The mosque was thus completed in the year 1261 A.H. [1845 A.D.].*"

Like all historical figures, Mohammad Ali has his antagonists and proponents. He is accused by the former of being a military dictator, which, for all intents and purposes, he was. The latter accede that he was a dictator, but a benevolent one who suddenly transformed Egypt from the Middle Ages to the modern world.

If we justly weigh the gains and losses during his reign, Mohammad Ali will be remembered as the initiator of the process that made Cairo what it is now, the mother of the world.

Dr. Morsi Saad El-Din

AL-KAHIRA

القاهرة

القاهرة